CW00730777

Journey on the
Manx Electric Railway

Written by Chris Pulling

Edited by David Umpleby
Designed by Jason Prescott

Published by Train Crazy Publishing
© 2015 Train Crazy Publishing

Published by:
Train Crazy Publishing, Videoscene, PO Box 243, Lytham St Annes. FY8 9DE
email: sales@videoscene.co.uk

Front Cover Cars 1 & 59 in a typical charming MER scene. *NM*

Contents

Chapter 4:   Laxey to Cornaa

Chapter 5:   Cornaa to Ramsey

Appendix A

Acknowledgements

I am grateful for the generous advice, information and help of the following, whom I am pleased to acknowledge with sincere thanks: John Clarkson of London; Alan Corlett, formerly of IoM Transport; Jason Cross, photographer, www.15c.co.uk; J. Maurice Faragher, retired MER Engineering Superintendent, for historical assistance; Mr. Alan Franklin, Manx Museum; the late Mike Goodwyn; the late David Haynes; the late David Huntley of Onchan; Ian J. Longworth, Director of Public Transport IoM; John Matthews, retired MER yardmaster; Nick Meskell, Videoscene and Trams Magazine; Paul Ogden, former Manager of Railways, Isle of Man Transport; Nick Pascoe of Baldrine Park; Andrew Scarffe of Laxey; David Umpleby, Videoscene and Trams Magazine; last, but definitely not least, the many staff of the MER, who have all contributed without exception.

The author would like to put on record a special 'Thank you' to David Umpleby. David is responsible for the excellent choice of photographs in this book and also for liaising with the contributors. He is the principal author of the detailed captions. I am grateful to him for researching the many questions which arose whilst overseeing this project. Without David's tenacity, the 1865 map of the island would not have come to light. In all these ways he has made my life easier and taken on far more than ever intended. Thank you!

Abbreviations

D&LCETCo . . . . Douglas & Laxey Coast Electric Tramway Company

GGR . . . . Groudle Glen Railway

IMR . . . . Isle of Man Railway

IOMT&EPCo . . . . Isle of Man Tramways and Electric Power Company

MER . . . . Manx Electric Railway

MERS . . . . Manx Electric Railway Society

MHK . . . . Member of the House of Keys (the Manx Parliament)

MNR . . . . Manx Northern Railway (Douglas - St. John's - Ramsey)

PW . . . . Permanent Way

SMR . . . . Snaefell Mountain Railway

N.B. I refer in the text to the Robert Newell Report. Newell was the Permanent Way Superintendent at the time of the formation of the MER Company. His report on the condition of the PW is dated 1903.

Photographers

RP . . . . Richard Pryke

NM . . . . Nick Meskell

DU . . . . David Umpleby

JC . . . . John Clarkson

IH . . . . Ian Hastie

CP . . . . Chris Pulling

Additional photographs supplied by:

Aaron Boyce

Peter Burke

Jim Copland

Alan Corlett

Jason Cross - Specialist art work

John Matthews

Jono Niblock

Vernon Linden

Foreword

The Manx Electric Railway is a remarkable survivor from the pioneering days of 1893 with such early forms of electric traction remaining in use today. Since that time, not only has the world around it changed beyond recognition but the purpose the railway serves has had to evolve as well. Starting as almost a technical novelty it allowed the tourist resort of Douglas to expand northwards accessing new land for development. As poor farming and barren lands opened up, property values rose just as other developers have subsequently copied the world over.

Constantly looking for new opportunities the Manx Electric Railway also invented new destinations for the tourist to travel to including Garwick, Dhoon and Ballaglass Glens. It diversified into the hospitality trade with catering and hotels established along the route. As well as the passenger business, it also carried goods and the Royal Mail; even diversifying into operating two quarries at Ballajora and Dhoon.

In the most successful period, traffic peaked with 500,000 passengers carried in the month of August alone. All the infrastructure and trams basically remain intact but the demand has shrunk as the Island economy has adjusted to the diminishing tourist numbers. The number taking holidays on the Island today is still actually greater than when the railway opened in 1893. But as these numbers decreased from the peak, they were to some extent replaced by increasing numbers of day trippers. By the mid 1970s around 150,000 day visitors continued to bring the volumes the Manx Electric Railway needed. These day tripper numbers fell away in the 1980s but some new markets have been found with a small number of visiting cruise ships and the Island's increasing resident population.

The detailed history of the Manx Electric Railway and its trams is well documented in numerous other books. This journey takes a refreshingly different approach allowing the traveller to connect the modern day scenery with its history. The numerous good quality historic photographs, many unseen before, also allow the traveller to see just where it all fits together. Modern houses and apartments, have in parts replaced the previous tourist infrastructure so you can appreciate the changing times. Then just around another corner, you are passing through country side and over cliff tops unchanged from the opening day.

During the journey you will start to appreciate how significantly The Manx Electric Railway and its owners have contributed to the Island, both culturally and economically. For all the remaining railways, the economic impact was last measured in 2011, with them all together making a total contribution of £11m to the GDP. The contribution has been recognised and much investment is being made to allow all the railways to continue to operate safely, thus enabling future generations to admire and enjoy the journey on the Manx Electric Railway.

Ian J Longworth
Director of Public Transport
December 2014

Chapter 1

Introduction

...how it all began

Part 1:

Introduction

Important Events From 1876 - 1893

Before our journey on the Manx Electric begins, I would like to acquaint readers with some of the important historical events and places which are intimately connected with the Manx Electric and its predecessor, the Isle of Man Tramways and Electric Power Company. The MER did not appear by chance; its origins and that of the Bay Tramway illustrate the pioneering, entrepreneurial spirit of that era.

The Douglas Bay Horse Tramway

The history of the Manx Electric Railway (MER) is inseparable from that of the Horse Tramway. The MER begins at Derby Castle, the far end of the promenade that curves round Douglas Bay, not far short of two miles away from Douglas Centre and the port. Logically, of course, it is the Electric that should begin at the Sea Terminal, to provide a through service from Douglas to Laxey, the North and Ramsey, and to provide direct access to Douglas for business and shopping, without the need to change modes of transport to or from horse-drawn cars or buses. The existing antiquated facilities belie the aspirations of those who dreamed of taking a line right through from the centre of Douglas to Ramsey, and opening up the East Coast of the Island, to provide a complete transport link and interchange with the various railways of the day.

The story begins with Thomas Lightfoot. He retired to the Isle of Man in his mid-fifties after building the first horse tramways in Sheffield, from the Wicker to Attercliffe, Carbrook and Brightside. His experience in this new mode of transport was extensive and he saw an ideal opportunity in the expansion of Douglas's promenade to provide a horse tramway. Work on the new sea wall began in 1874 and the attractive Loch Promenade was opened in 1875; Douglas was thriving and the building works had usefully been completed with space for a continuous sea-level tramway.

Lightfoot promoted an Act of Tynwald (the Manx Parliament) in June 1876; work had already commenced prior to the Royal Assent. By the end of July, the line was almost ready for operation between the Iron Pier at the bottom of Broadway and Burnt Mill Hill, which was renamed Summerhill around the turn of the 20th century. J Garrow, a highway surveyor, was appointed as inspector and passed the line on Monday 7th August and operation began the same day, with members of the Lightfoot family all involved, to the extent that Lightfoot's youngest son, 'JW', worked as a conductor. The cars were built by the Starbuck Car & Wagon Co. Ltd. of Birkenhead and were all double-deckers.

Extension of the line occurred simultaneously with a small expansion of the rolling stock, but Lightfoot's own involvement virtually ended with the sale of the undertaking to the Isle of Man Tramways Ltd. in 1882. There were four cars at the time and further expansion was necessary: the loops were inconvenient and limited the number of cars operating, their schedules and passenger volumes.

By the time that electric railed transport was in vogue (Blackpool's pioneering promenade conduit line opened in 1885), it was anticipated that the horse system would be absorbed into the modern wonders of new-fangled electricity. By 1890, the horse tracks had reached No.14, the south end of Strathallan Crescent, with the depot situated at the bottom of Burnt Mill Hill. The Derby Castle complex, with its pleasure grounds, theatre and ballroom occupied the land between Strathallan Lodge (the current Terminus Tavern) and the (later) electric tram depot. Derby Castle developed in a fairly piecemeal fashion as tourism increased, with the Dance Pavilion erected in 1877 and the Theatre in 1893, becoming a well-established all-day attraction during the last decade of Victoria's reign, and locals and holidaymakers alike flocked to enjoy its attractions, providing a raison d'être for the horse tramway to extend to that end of the bay.

The point should not be lost even now, that the 'quiet' end of the promenade featured attractions worth visiting. The former Summerland site is now on the market. It is a pity that the opportunity is not being taken to create a transport museum as an attraction at this historic location.

The Beginnings of the Douglas – Groudle line

Strathallan Lodge formed a part of the manor house of the Pollock family who owned Derby Castle. The lodge was converted into a public house and passed into the ownership of the 'Isle of Man Tramways and Electric Power Company' (IOMT&EPCo) in 1896. The north-east part of the building was converted into a waiting room with toilet facilities. The company was always keen to develop its property asset portfolio. In later years, as with the Station Inn at Laxey, the reality of post-nationalisation finances saw it sold off in 1957, including the waiting room, but not the toilets which survive today.

Various schemes had been aired in the 1880s to develop a steam link between Douglas and Laxey with the potential to carry on to Ramsey. For example, in 1882, the Douglas, Laxey & Ramsey Railway Co. Ltd. was formed, with the intention of branching off the IMR's Peel line at Quarterbridge in Douglas, and passing through Ballameanagh and Glen Gawne to Laxey; the route certainly had its merits however, the scheme failed to attract sufficient support. Two entrepreneurs took up the mantle of electric traction instead: Alexander Bruce, manager of the Island's Dumbell's Bank, and Frederick Saunderson, a civil engineer. The latter was born in 1841 in Ireland, and spent his

The National Library of Scotland turned up this fascinating map of the Isle of Man. Survey work was carried out from 1866-69, and the map was published in 1873, then revised and re-published in 1906. This map proved useful in solving the Ballastowell question (see later) and is reproduced here to show the route that the railway takes. The rural nature of the line - especially the northern section - and communities' dependence upon it - can readily be appreciated.
Reproduced by permission of the National Library of Scotland

early years up to 1865 in railway construction, but became wealthy through involvement with real estate promotion, particularly of the South Ramsey Estate in the late 1880s.

By the turn of the last decade of the 19th Century, plans were afoot to develop the Howstrake New Marine Road, which ran from the north end of the horse tramway towards Groudle. On 13th January 1892, the Derby Castle Company sold its 1888 foreshore rights to Saunderson. Alfred J Lusty, a wealthy London merchant, backed Saunderson financially and powers were obtained from Tynwald to develop part of the Howstrake Estate.

The farthest point of the estate was Banks Howe (an Old Norse word, Haugr, meaning 'Hill'), a 258ft summit, known to us as Howstrake, where the tram today curves inland for the descent to Groudle. Bruce and Saunderson arranged with John Travis, the Howstrake trustee, to buy part of the estate. The powers required to develop the area were realised in the Howstrake Estate Act of March 22nd 1892. Bruce and his colleagues formed themselves into the 'Douglas Bay Estate Limited' and registered in September 1892 with £50,000 capital.

The new roadway via Port Jack and Onchan as far as Groudle contained provision for the operation of electric tramcars. The promoters clearly envisaged Groudle as the first major attraction of the line. In spring 1893, work commenced on the first part of the line from Derby Castle to Groudle. With steam rejected on the grounds of excessive gradients and curves, Dr Edward Hopkinson of Mather & Platt Ltd. Electrical Engineers, took charge of the electrification of the line. Incidentally, the founder of the horse line, Thomas Lightfoot, died in January 1893.

Horse and Electric Developments in the 1890s and 1900s

Bruce's ambitions indicate that the single-line tramway to Groudle Glen served as a test bed for an extension to Laxey, some seven miles from Derby Castle. Before the Groudle section opened, Saunderson was already actively engaged on the project to carry the line forward to Baldromma-Beg, known more generally now as 'Halfway House'. Another company was created to construct the Laxey section and this was known as the 'Douglas & Laxey Coast Electric Tramway Company'. It was registered on 7th March 1893 with capital of £50,000. The two companies had the same signatories, although the D&LCETCo also boasted the addition of three Welshmen with legal, transportation and industrial skills, brought in by fellow Welshman Lusty.

A great deal of activity was underway to open up the North East of the Island to transport. The benefits were the obvious attraction of Groudle and a link between there and Derby Castle. The horse tramway was reaching the end of its natural life as tramway electrification developed rapidly 'across' in the UK and also further afield, for example in the USA. There could be no reason to think that the Derby Castle terminus was in the wrong place; it was surely only a matter of time before the systems were amalgamated and the new technology extended directly into the town centre.

Numbers 1 and 2 Strathallan Crescent (close to the current horse stables) had been bought in 1891 by the owners of the horse tramway, the go-ahead and influential Dr Richard Farrell being one of the five company directors. Farrell arrived from Ireland in 1881 and opened a private school, Victoria College. Farrell saw the potential of electric traction himself and considered it the best means of increasing the dividends payable on the Bay Tramway. The house, garden and stables of No.1 were put to use as offices, stabling and temporary storage for cars, and were referred to as 'The Brig'. No.2 was the Manager's residence. The buildings passed to the new MER Company in 1902 and remained owned by them until 1978. A memorial garden now occupies the area of No. 1's garden and stables, with the house becoming holiday flats.

Further property purchases saw numbers 13 and 14 Strathallan Crescent acquired in 1895 for staff purposes. Senior management occupied these houses; Frank Edmondson lived at No.14 before moving into the manager's residence and Mr. E. Barnes, in his time as Chief Assistant Engineer, lived at No.13, with Mr. Legg, the Hotels and Catering Manager, residing at No.14. Both properties were disposed of during World War II.

Calvary Glen

Captain Pollock bought a tract of land in 1830 from the Duke of Athol. This land included a wooded glen that extended to the high water mark, back up to the top of the brows and as far as Port-E-Vada Creek, where the electric railway depot was built on reclaimed land. Until the MER relinquished The Terminus Tavern, they retained ownership of the glen, which could be accessed via Summer Hill Road or the passageway down the west side of the horse tram depot. It was purchased by Father McGrath of St. Anthony's Church in 1957 for just £60. The name 'Calvary Glen' was coined when Father McGrath carried out renovation work and laid the glen pathway out as a 'Way of the Cross' similar to the one at Lourdes. Some magnificent statues made of cast iron enhanced the appearance and the crucifixion group was life size with a teak cross. The whole ensemble was floodlit at night, standing quite imposingly above Douglas Promenade until a bungalow was built on the cliff top in 1966. Father McGrath died in 1982 and the glen was closed, the statues eventually being removed to the back of St. Anthony's Church, where some remain today.

The Proposed Electrification of the Bay Tramway

It might have been expected that electrification right through to the Sea Terminal would have met with little objection, and so it seemed when Bruce purchased the entire undertaking for £38,000 in February 1894, the year of the extension from Groudle to Laxey.

Operation was handed over on 1st May. Bruce planned to double the remaining single-track sections of the Bay Tramway in preparation for electrification, providing that the Douglas Commissioners guaranteed they would not exercise their option to purchase the line. This was a possibility until 5th December 1897, a period of twenty-one years after Lightfoot commenced operation in 1876. The Commissioners duly agreed in principle.

In 1895, the IOMT&EPCo offered to build a new cable tramway in Douglas in return for Promenade electrification rights, as well as extending the electric line from the Bay Tramway terminus at the town end of the promenade to the IMR Station. In 1897, Bruce made generous proposals, including free electric street lighting for large parts of Douglas. Many of the Douglas Commissioners participated in a grand tour of European tramway systems, the upshot of which was their tentative agreement to electrify the horse tramway. Voluminous and vociferous grievances were voiced and written by hoteliers (many petitions were allegedly either in identical handwriting or with an 'X' mark for illiterate petitioners.). The decision was adjourned. The whole wrangle refused to die down through 1898. In 1899, such was the disagreement over the location of a power station, that no decision was taken.

Procrastination won the day and conjoined with the eventual collapse of Dumbell's Bank to crush any hope of modernising the Bay Tramway. The surprise failure of Dumbell's Bank on 3rd February 1900 resulted the IOMT&EPCo's share price plummeting from £1 7/- (£1.35) to just 1/- (5p) in six months; the company's liquidator sold the horse tramway and the Upper Douglas cable line for the knockdown price of £50,000 – and left the electrification of the horse car line to speculation of 'what might have been'. A new company - The Manx Electric Railway Company Limited - was incorporated on 12th November 1902; it has always been known simply as 'The MER'.

The New MER Company's Policy

The new MER Company's inheritance was the erstwhile pioneering technology of the 1890s. Their task was to set about re-equipping the trams and bringing the entire track from Douglas to Ramsey up to an acceptable standard within a very short time. Further trams were on order and were needed for the expansion of summer services as well as to make the operation more economical by trimming service times, which new technology would resolve.

Investment in new infrastructure and equipment came first, rather than resurrecting old arguments about extending the line into Douglas. The decision could reasonably be allowed to slide for a year or two without consequence, in view of the logic of electrification eventually winning the day. So, while Onchan and Port Jack enjoyed the soft, incandescent glow from their electric street lamps courtesy of the MER, Douglas remained dimly lit by feeble gas lamps with a low candlepower glow.

The existence of the unique horse tramway today illustrates the fruitless outcome of new electrification proposals by the MER in 1906 and 1908. Douglas Corporation proceeded in its quaint (but stubborn) way and found that their antique tramway had become something of a celebrity attraction in its own right.

The Horse Car Sheds

At some point before or after your journey, it is worth having a peep inside the horse tramway sheds, though do please ask for permission from Manager Peter Cannon. Many interesting horse cars are on display, but this is not a museum as some might be awaiting their next turn of duty. Some trams seem to slip out of use for several years, and then reappear. For example, in 2014 service cars included refurbished Car 42, which has been out of service in recent years. Restored double-decker 18 can be found here and operates some afternoons for one return journey. Ask staff for information.

The premises constructed over the horse shed in 1937 were rented by the Railways from the Corporation from 1978 until being vacated in 2000, when Railway office staff were moved to new, purpose-built offices at Banks Circus, adjacent to the IMR Railway Station.

1893 and All That...

Rails and sleepers arrived during May and June 1893. Construction of a Power House and car sheds was proceeding well on reclaimed land at Port-E-Vada Creek (an anglicised version of Purt-E-Vattey). The first three electric trams arrived by steamer in late July from G.F.Milnes & Co. of Birkenhead. The cars and their six trailers (it was originally assumed that each power car would haul two trailers) were prepared for service by 8th August, using the 'Hopkinson Bow', a form of overhead electric traction current collector. It operated inefficiently at first and delays were occasioned to the opening of the line. It was only on 26th August that a car finally reached Groudle. The new hotel there was designed by Mackay Hugh Baillie Scott (1864-1945), an artist of international repute and noted for his 'Art and Craft' style of architecture. Business looked good, as the glen itself was simultaneously being developed as a scenic attraction.

Opposite page A simplified version of the line's route illustrates the terminal points of Douglas, Laxey and Ramsey, Groudle Station and the main halts along the way, colour-coded for easy identification.

RAMSEY

Ballure
Belle Vue

Port E Vullen

Lewaigue

Dreemskerry

Ballajora

Port Mooar

Cornaa

Ballaglass
Glen

Glen Mona

Port Cornaa

Dhoon Quarry

Dhoon Glen

Bulgham Bay

Ballaragh

LAXEY   Minorca

South Cape

Fairy Cottage

Ballabeg

Garwick Glen

Baldrine

Halfway House

Groudle

Derby
Castle

DOUGLAS

Howstrake

Onchan
Head

Horse
Tramway

Douglas
Bay

Steam
Railway
Station

Douglas to Groudle - *Chapter 2 (page 29)*
Groudle to Laxey - *Chapter 3 (page 79)*
Laxey to Cornaa - *Chapter 4 (page 153)*
Cornaa to Ramsey - *Chapter 5 (page 223)*
Halts
Stations
Horse Tramway

N
W   E
S

Area covered by this map

The line was officially opened for traffic on 7th September, towards the end of the holiday season.

The tracks began almost at their present point, just slightly to the north of 14 Strathallan Crescent, a few feet from the horse car terminus in those days. A driveway was still in place between the landside track, which existed only to access the depot, and the seaside running line along Howstrake Drive. There was no delineation between road and rail. Only later was demarcation between the roadway and seaside tram tracks made by roughly-hewn stones, and in certain places between Derby Castle and Groudle this remains a feature of the line today. This remarkable survival can be seen towards Onchan Head and beyond.

By 1894, the horse tracks remained the same as previously, but the 'Electric' took advantage of modifications around Strathallan Lodge gardens and the entrance road to Derby Castle pleasure grounds, which included a new wall and a two-track terminal point, with a crossover parallel with the north end of Strathallan Lodge. These improvements clearly reflected the increased volume of cars once the line to Laxey opened on Saturday 28th July, mainly using the new 'Tunnel' cars, Nos. 4-9, pulling the lightweight trailers of 1893 and the ones dedicated to the 1894 cars. The landside track was removed in 1902-3, to create the present layout, with the traction pole formerly in the centre between the two tracks being repositioned.

A photograph exists of an unknown double-deck horse car standing at the end of the MER tracks in 1894, almost exactly next to where the present Booking Office stands. It was probably in use as a ticket office, though fortunately its top deck was closed off to prevent the inquisitive from touching the live overhead!

A Great Survivor: The Rustic Booking Office

The wooden, rustic-style MER booking office dates from 1897, and is neatly sandwiched between the terminal tracks and the lines of the horse tramway. It measures only 12' 6" by 8' and is notable for being the last survivor of an original IOMT&EPCo. structure in the region of Derby Castle. It possesses two window booking positions and accommodation for the Station Master. A cosy atmosphere

prevails in here, especially when the crew of the next scheduled car conceal themselves inside, though technically this is contrary to the rules, which are clearly stated on an ancient notice, reading: **Motormen & Conductors must not loiter in this office.**

Above On 7th July 1970, Horse Car 47 departs Derby Castle terminus on another journey along the promenade around the bay. The impressive canopy can be seen behind the array of advertising boards and leaflets attached to the MER booking office. All the signs were hand-painted by the MER's specialist signwriter. Of note is that both serving hatches are open, whereas today only the one on the right facing the single departure road is used. **RP**

Left This view from 10th April 1971 shows Winter Saloon 19 coupled to Van 14 in the Groudle Siding prior to working the 10.00 Douglas to Ramsey. The shunting of vans onto the siding for loading and unloading was a regular occurrence at this time, although no extra time was allowed on the timetable. The 'great canopy' looks in need of sprucing up, but still had several years of use before suddenly being deemed unsafe in 1980 and demolished. **RP**

The current and following week's duties are pinned up, with a variety of other fascinating pieces of information, relating to unusual workings on the line, single-line working or, in the MER tradition, the occasional satirical cartoon of a particular staff member. Lighting and heating are still provided from the traction supply.

In bygone days, the exterior was equipped with handbills and posters, but nowadays information is crudely conveyed on blackboards. A large clock face attached to the centre traction pole proclaims the next scheduled departure.

MER Paraphernalia at Derby Castle Terminus

A painted board details the route of the Manx Electric Railway. Many similar designs have publicised the MER during its history and this one is rather less extravagantly decorated than in the past, but does draw attention to several of the line's attractions. The stanchions that support the board are not original to the line.

Until 1999, only every fifth MER traction pole carried its number. All poles now carry their number with even numbers facing northbound cars and odd ones, southbound cars. Adjacent to

Below Car 19 and Trailer 41 in a traditional scene which has greeted visitors to Derby Castle for over 100 years: a Winter Saloon and a 40s type trailer waiting 'on the stop'. This is the 10.15 service to Ramsey on 25th May 1969, in the days when the Winter Saloons monopolised the scheduled (timetabled) services all year round. At this time, the 10.15 started its day at Laxey, running single motor to Douglas, where its trailer was usually waiting to be attached for a quick move into the station. The stationmaster is ready to shout the legendary words, 'Stand Clear!' as he keeps a watchful eye on 'his' railway. The impressive map of the island has survived and can be seen in the MER Museum. Weighing scales to the right are for public use; here and at Laxey, the plot was rented out by the MER for the season. **RP**

Top The track layout at Derby Castle evolved quickly after 1893. The landward track from 1893 ran directly into the depot yard, but the layout was improved in 1895-6 since when it has remained virtually unaltered. The starting point is the single track outside the booking office, or the 'Groudle Siding' to the right in this view, which in busier days was mainly used for short workings, including Onchan Head for White City, Howstrake, Groudle and Garwick. The frequent summer service required good planning on the part of the stationmaster. Winter Saloon 21 is ready for departure with the trolley turned and the crew finishing a quick break before commencing the journey north. The rather unimpressive bus-type shelter can be seen behind No. 21. 1893 Trailer 51 occupies the Groudle Siding. *NM*

Traction Pole 1 (the first of 903 to Ramsey, not including additional ones on curves and at Car Sheds) stands a huge girder set some eight foot into the ground, so that it can safely bear the weight of two sets of wires. Modern, home-made but comfortable benches, inscribed 'Manx Electric Railway', provide pleasant relaxation on sunny days and the octagonal flowerbeds brighten the area up.

The 'Great Canopy' and its successors

A huge ceiling was built in 1896 over the horse car tracks and sidings. The imposing structure of the 'Great Canopy', as it was

Left Van 12 of 1898-9 in the pleasing olive green livery with the great canopy in the background. This van was modified into a tower wagon in 1976-7. *RP*

popularly known, was originally erected by the IOMT&EPCo. Its measurements were 82' long, 18' high to the eaves, and 29' high to the apex of the roof, with a width of 35'. The canopy was a very fine ornate structure, with ornamental gables, fanlight windows and a 13' high clock tower in pride of place on the roof. Unfortunately, in 1902 it passed from the Liquidator to Douglas Corporation; it suffered progressive dismantling of the more extravagant features, although the deep eaves-board hoarding which was rented by the MER to advertise the "Laxey-Ramsey Electric Railway Station" managed to survive until 1974. It served the MER (and seasonal horse cars stored alfresco) until its surprising demolition in 1980, following a convenient decision by Douglas Corporation at a meeting on 20th February that it had become unsafe. The black-painted stanchions are the sole, savagely cut-down remains of the canopy.

Arrival of Cars at Derby Castle Terminus

It is an interesting experience to watch the gravity shunting operation of cars. Trains arrive at Derby Castle terminus either directly from the depot or after a service journey from Laxey or Ramsey. Occasionally a car set will be so arranged in the depot yard that it leaves trailer leading, so that it can run straight onto the terminal stub for service, though this is rare and undesirable. The power car customarily tows the trailer. If on service, passengers alight by the blue bollards, after which the coupling between motor car and trailer is released. The trailer is then parked by the end of the former Summerland car park wall with its hand brake firmly set, as the motor car moves onto the terminal stub and reverses, as if returning to depot on the landside track. After clearing the crossover's trailing points, the motor car's trolley is turned and the tram is driven carefully back over the crossover to be coupled to the trailer's Ramsey end. The car set is driven into the station, the conductor standing at the Douglas end of the trailer, giving appropriate signals to the driver of the motor behind.

Gravity shunting manoeuvres are employed on the Manx Electric at Derby Castle and Ramsey (though not for much longer at the northern terminus); any shunting of a trailer elsewhere, such as at Groudle, has to be carried out with more manpower involved as the station lies on the level. Overhead wiring of the crossovers

Top A general view looking towards the car sheds on 25th July 2012, including 1906 Motor 33 and Van 4 in its unauthentic red livery. *DU*

Bottom Weather has always been a problem for the Manx Electric Railway. Whilst the sun might be cracking the pavements at Derby Castle, the weather can take a distinct turn an hour's ride away at the top of Bulgham Bay. Experiencing the four seasons in one day has often precluded the use of the popular open cars, although passengers can be sheltered with the shutters pulled down. However this is no consolation to the brave motorman battling on the front. With this in mind several contraptions have been tried. This example on Car 25 looks the most home made... is it an old door? These devices were often referred to as 'dodgers' due to their purpose of dodging the weather! *JC*

with frogs means that cars leaving the depot and traversing to the seaside line no longer have to have their trolleys manually lowered by the conductor, as happened previously, although the practice can sometimes still be observed to avoid dewirement. Peter Price of Bradford, an expert in overhead wiring, designed and installed the wiring from the station to the depot, as well as other places on the system, such as Dumbell's Row at Laxey.

Reaction to the Line in 1894

A journey on the MER is memorable for numerous reasons, but let's go back to see how early passengers remarked upon the line in 1894:

> *The Douglas Station is close to the entrance to Derby Castle, at the northern end of the bay ... and here we have one of the most agreeable differences between travelling by steam and travelling by electricity brought prominently under our notice. There is none of that shrieking of steam whistles, and none of that belching of great clouds of mingled smoke and steam – without noise, and without disturbance or annoyance of any kind, we set out on our journey.*

Derby Castle Station to Summerland

Leaving the historic terminus, we notice the newness of track, pointwork and overhead, all the result of frenetic work in late April and early May 2006. When the Summerland Complex was demolished by contractors JCT Ltd over the winter of 2005-6, access to the site was only possible across the MER tracks. Consequently, the overhead was removed from the terminus to the sheds and the track turned over to the demolition company. Trams were denied access to the running line. Demolition ran almost to schedule, leaving a fortnight to relay the track and overhead for the advertised service to re-commence on Monday 15th May. The new track between Derby Castle and the sheds came with prefabricated pointwork and the rails were laid on traditional wooden sleepers using Pandol clips instead of traditional "dog spikes". The new ballast is grey.

When it has to, the MER can pull out the stops; the final Sunday, May 14th, saw almost forty staff working on the site, with then

Engineering Superintendent George Lawson busily engaged on reconnecting the overhead and checking that the frogs worked. The service duly recommenced with the 09.40 departure to Ramsey being performed by Car 22, after the longest break in service in MER history, some thirty-two weeks. It is believed the 2006 Easter was the first when no MER service operated.

Top Unique Locomotive 23, in its post-1925 guise, temporarily borrowed the trucks from either Ratchet 17 or Car 33. Here it is on Brill trucks pushing the delightful diminutive 1896 Trailer 60 towards the terminus. *IH*

Bottom An outstanding image of 1898 Ratchet Car 14 in the morning line-up of cars waiting to take eager holidaymakers to Laxey and Ramsey. This tram has been out of use since 1982 but has recently been evaluated for potential resurrection as part of the running fleet. *JC*

25

The Derby Castle Complex and Summerland

The whole aspect of the area between the terminus and sheds has changed immeasurably; not since the demolition of the original Derby Castle in the 1960s has the area looked so desolate, though a section is now in use as an MER PW store. Standing at the station, we can see cars being prepared and emerging from the depot for service.

The demolition of Summerland proved incomplete: parts of the swimming pool's deep end remain visible and generally there is uncertainty whether the section of the complex built into the cliff is the stabilising factor or vice versa. The decision was taken to leave things as they are there, creating some unusual, not necessarily attractive, photographic opportunities.

This site has an interesting history. Douglas Corporation bought out the Derby Castle entertainment complex in 1963 and immediately proposed to erect a new swimming pool and solarium on the site. Unfortunately an attack was simultaneously launched on the alleged incongruity of MER cars passing on service or to the depot. Suggestions were even made that the MER relocate its depot to Onchan Head and the (perhaps apocryphal) tale circulated that surveyors were found lurking in the MER depot yard without permission and duly frog-marched off the premises. At one stage, a tunnel for the trams was included in the design, but the final plans published in August 1964 reflected a more sensible re-evaluation of both development and existing requirements.

Right Seen in numerical order on 16th April 1995 are all four Winter Saloons, 19, 20, 21 and 22. The only slight livery difference is on Car 22 which has the simpler title 'Manx Electric Railway' without 'The … (and) Co. Ltd'. The sight of all four Saloons in the same place is possibly the hardest image to obtain on the railway. With their constant use and three sheds on the line, they are normally either in service, under repair or stabled far from Derby Castle overnight. This especially posed shot shows their tidy uniform appearance.
John Matthews

Demolition of the Derby Castle Theatre and Ballroom was completed in 1965, but the subsequent withdrawal of the Manchester firm of developers occasioned further delays in the Corporation's plans. Construction finally began in 1967, with the Aquadrome opening at the end of July 1969, as work progressed on the adjoining solarium and leisure centre. 'Summerland' finally opened on 9th July 1971 and was ironically proclaimed 'fire proof', although the Island's fire chief insisted on an extra emergency escape from the upper terraces in the form of a bridge well away from the acrylic Oroglas cladding of the exterior walls. This additional structure contributed to the unusual finished appearance of the complex with part of the building cantilevered over the MER tracks, and a now-demolished footbridge crossing over to the seaside pavement.

The rest is tragic history: the worst peacetime fire disaster in the British Isles since 1929 saw fifty people choked or burnt to death on the evening of 2nd August 1973. Thirty more suffered severe burns. The fire started accidentally at 7.50pm and was caused by three boys playing with matches in a kiosk outside on a terrace. Failing to extinguish the flames, they knocked the kiosk over and it fell onto the outer skin of Summerland, where a fire started in a hidden and combustible cavity wall. A 'flash over' saw flames

Above Taken from the long-demolished overbridge at Summerland is a composition including original Cars 1 & 2. Car 1 is seen on the right in the Groudle siding, and behind Car 1 can be seen Lisbon 360. This tram was purchased at a rumoured cost of £23k for the purpose of operating evening and winter services on the MER. Its only useful role was as a waiting shelter before being removed from the railway. Car 2 is seen in the foreground. The picture shows the closeness of the Horse Car Sheds on the right next to the Terminus Tavern, a favourite of tram enthusiasts! *NM*

Above Trailer 62 glides gently down to Derby Castle in the 'Millennium of Tynwald' year 1979, painted to match its motor 32 in celebration of the Nationalisation livery. *JC*

burst furiously into Summerland itself where there were 3,000 customers and 200 staff. Emergency doors had been locked earlier in the day. The fire brigade only heard of the fire at 8.05pm, some time after it had begun to engulf the complex.

The main findings of the Enquiry into the disaster were that there were "No Villains", only numerous inadequacies and failings. Repairs were carried out as quickly as feasible during the course of the enquiry and swimming resumed in June 1974, though it was the end of 1976 before the new Summerland was beginning to move towards completion. The basic structure was ready in September 1977, but additional fire protection regulations delayed the opening of "The Cave" basement discotheque until February 1978, with the sports and leisure area opening at lunchtime the same day. An official opening took place on 22nd June, when Governor Sir John Paul unveiled a commemorative plaque. He described the building as, "A memorial to the past and an act of faith in the future."

Chapter 2

Douglas to Groudle

...our journey begins

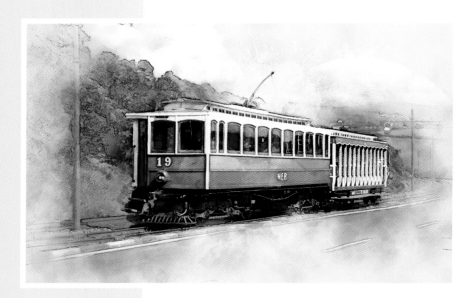

Chapter 2:

Douglas to Groudle

Our Journey Begins

… with ceremony! Once a car set has taken up its position in the station and the trolley turned, the main concern is to get passengers on board quickly and safely. If the weather is fine, most will opt for the open trailer, but beware … those much-vaunted health-giving breezes can chill to the marrow and once departed, there is little opportunity to change cars! The driver will assist in loading as the conductor ensures that all the seated trailer passengers are in possession of tickets, which is done prior to departure. Conductors are no longer allowed for Health & Safety reasons to check tickets whilst standing on the trailer footboard as the cars are moving. Once the crew is ready, the stationmaster will check for late arrivals and then shout the legendary 'Stand Clear!' The bell is rung twice and the hissing air being let off the brakes causes a small cloud of dust to rise from beneath the two bogies of the motorcar. Power is applied through the controller simultaneously with brake release and a couple of toots of the horn. Our train moves off slowly on its seven-mile journey northwards to Laxey or perhaps on a further

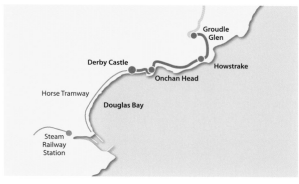

Above A view from the MER's own glen shows the site of the demolished ill-fated Summerland complex, Derby Castle terminus, the Horse Car Sheds, the Terminus Tavern (a former MER property) and in the distance the Horse Stables at the bottom of Summerhill. It is also possible to see how the area we term Derby Castle is land reclaimed from Port-e-Vada Creek. **NM**

Left The map shows the first section of the line opened in 1893. Already noticeable is the disconnect between Douglas Town and the remote terminus of the MER at Derby Castle at the far end of the bay.

eleven-mile trip beyond Laxey over the Northern Line to Ramsey. The great adventure has begun.

The Derby Castle Car Sheds

Car sets proceed past the blitzed Summerland site and approach the MER depot on a maximum of five 'points' of series power. Each tramway system had its own 'glossary' of operating terms. On the MER, 'points' refers to the controller's 'notches' in other systems' parlance, which provide a graded power supply, five being connected in series and four in parallel running. The cars' controllers have no electric braking (rheostatic) facility as such.

The Manx Electric depot was one of the most fascinating railway depots anywhere until reconstruction that commenced in 1997. The new structure's design is functional if not exactly sympathetic to the line's vintage status. The one-off opportunity to improve the system of simply stacking trams one behind the other on parallel lines was lost. Its failing leads to the operational drawback of mainly using cars positioned at the front because of easiest access. Perhaps a 'Roundhouse' system would have proven more efficient. The wooden doors that you see today have replaced original metal ones which proved ineffective.

Above The Depot, redolent of MER history: trespassers will be prosecuted! Blue signs advise a penalty of £3k while red signs in other places only state £1k! *NM*

The principal issue immediately after erection was where best to set the approach roads so that cars could enter and exit the various sections of the shed in safety. A serious failing occurred when the former single entry point from the running line was replaced by two sets of facing points in 2000, which on more than one occasion saw service trams take an unannounced diversion from their journey to Laxey to show unsuspecting passengers the delights of the depot yard. Fortunately, during the next spring, the track fan and access were ripped up and a revised plan effected a re-lay with sensible curves and a single point

Right The inside of the running sheds is glimpsed on 29th August 1971 almost at the end of the MER's short season. On the left can be seen several ratchet cars, perhaps waiting for their last duties that summer, Cars 17 and 30 being visible. In the middle are the 'lightweight' trailers with 49 on the left and 36 to the right. It would appear that all the enclosed motors were on service, as was normally the case at that time. An interesting aspect of this photo is that the trams seen are reaching their last service years. Car 17 was placed into store two years later in 1973, as was trailer 36. In 1970, Car 28 had already become the first tram to be officially withdrawn. Car 49 was to become a car of special interest when it was chosen for a historic repaint in 1978/79, but it is now stored, languishing with wheel defects. The roof lights are a vain attempt at improving the cramped and dark conditions. *RP*

access from the running line once more. The current fanwork was carried out by contractors Trackwork of Doncaster and this successful design is not dissimilar from the pre-1997 layout, which leaves the historically accurate situation of two main sections at right angles.

It is still the case that not all cars can use any road. Poor design stage work replicated the same problem with the old piecemeal construction of the old sheds. Various safety improvements have been made, however, including the use of point tumblers with neat levers and removable, safer handles.

Left A sight no longer seen at Derby Castle works: Snaefell cars here for refurbishment, in this case Car 5. This work is now carried out in the new SMR depot at Laxey. Car 27 sits patiently at the back of the depot, already dried out and prepared for another busy summer. *JC*

The 'Electric Railway' sign proudly stands on the rough hillside, surrounded by thorns and gorse. Originally placed as a superb piece of free advertising in 1923, it was illuminated by bulbs until recently when a simpler method was employed, by placing individual floodlights on the hillside. Less maintenance when bulbs blow also means less likelihood of damage to the health and welfare of staff attempting the rough climb up!

Going back to the beginning of the line's history, by May 1893, much work had already been completed on the car shed. Saunderson had selected the site of the erstwhile floor of Port E Vada Creek. Dr Richard Farrell described it thus: 'There is now no such creek. There was, two years ago. In yonder cave, boys undressed to bathe in this charming little creek. The creek was in the way of modern progress, and modern progress, like necessity, knew no law…'

Above Tunnel Car 5 rests on trestles while work is carried out on its trucks on 30th January 2006. The teddy bear leaning out of the window is keeping a sharp eye on progress! *NM*

Right Rebuilds are nothing new on the MER. Over the years many trams have been completely rebuilt. Here we see the skills of master coachbuilder Jimmy Yewdall gradually bringing Car 5 back to life. *Alan Corlett/MER*

The yardmaster's office at the top of the yard is an original 1924 structure. It is pleasing to note that instead of scrapping this structure when asbestos was recently discovered, it was rendered safe and retained. Keeping to the left on entry to the yard, the first road leads to the former loading dock. At the very back of the buildings on the left side stands the former engine house, since 1904 the Machine Shop, with new state-of-the-art sub-station equipment in the northwest corner; the old equipment is preserved. The section between the Machine Shop and the loading dock has served as the New Paintshop since 1988. This building used to be the Boiler House until 1904, then the Goods Shed from 1908 until 1966; it served as a store until its last conversion in 1988-89.

No.1 Car Shed of 1893 is now widely referred to as the 'Hospital Roads'. Both major restoration and refurbishment work is carried out here, as well as day-to-day running repairs when a car is signed off by a driver as defective. Pits are provided in the two south side roads. The Smithy (enlarged and rebuilt in 1992) lies at the back of this shed. A wondrous array of paraphernalia related to the running of the MER can be found here.

Above Rebuilding and refurbishing ancient tramcars is a highly skilled art. Here we see the 'new' Tunnel Car 7 taking shape. The tram was in a reasonably advanced state when the decision was taken to build an entirely new body. **DU**

The rest of this building is given over to Stores. Smaller stores to the rear used to contain spares from the Aachen cars, the electrical equipment of which was placed into the SMR cars in the late 1970s. This area is still nicknamed the 'Aachen Store'.

Atop the shed is affixed the wooden weather vane and mascot of the MER: Tommy Milner. Legend has it that the MER would close if Tom were to be removed. Quite what Tom's origins are and why that name is lost to history, but suggestions include a reference to 'Milnes', the builder of the early tramcars and also a former staff member by the surname of Milner, again from the early days.

A new messroom was built in 1988 between the Stores and the former Bonner wagon siding, next to which the main depot buildings stand. And now we come to the new Derby Castle shed, which has attracted much negative comment. Perhaps the least controversial and most objective view that can be taken is to say that the original, largely wooden sheds were appallingly dangerous. They presented a serious fire hazard as well as offering very scant opportunity for staff to work there in reasonable conditions that would conform to modern Health & Safety requirements; for example, the floor was nothing more than a century-old amalgam of dirt and grime, held together by lashings of oil, reminiscent of one of Orwell's dark satanic mills.

Above A scene of the day-to-day work undertaken in the 'Hospital Roads' at Derby Castle. Works Car 27 is in the centre of this view, whilst Winter Saloon 22 is undergoing a truck overhaul and is seen on trestles. For the majority of their lives the Winter Saloons have not had a 'float' set of trucks and therefore when a truck overhaul is needed, the tram has to wait to be reunited with its own overhauled bogies. This problem will be eradicated with the use of Trailer 55's trucks, which are to be motorised, meaning less 'down time' for the Winter Saloons. **NM**

Right The local fire service carry out a practice in the event of an emergency taking place at Derby Castle or a similar location such as the IMR. **Alan Corlett/MER**

Incidentally, Robert Newell was concerned about cars coming from the shed on to the main landside running line. *It would be well if some sort of signal and lock were connected with the facing points to the shed and Derby Castle Station as at present there is no particular system, merely a man at the yard gate on a busy day…I believe several instances are on record where a car has started with passengers from the bottom, while an empty motor and trailer was on its way down to the station.* Plus ça change…

Top Tunnel Car 6 is caught on camera in May 2005 during its protracted overhaul, which took from winter 2004 to summer 2006 to complete. Car 6 is one of the most original Tunnel cars with many features retained including the longitudinal wooden seats. *NM*

Left February 2005 sees 1930 English Electric Trailer 40 receiving the final touches after a repaint. At this time repaints took place in the former rather cramped goods shed at Derby Castle, which is now part of the MER Museum. *NM*

Bottom Royal Saloon 59 nears the end of its overhaul in November 2004. This diminutive 18-seater tram has required very little workshop attention due to its minimal use. *NM*

Top 1893 Car 2 and 1894 Trailer 37 return to the depot on 16th May 2005. The facing point off the mainline can be seen, whilst Steve Hislop's statue looks down from the memorial gardens. *NM*

Right Car 33 is seen leaving the lower car sheds on 31st July 2010. With most service cars stored in the upper car sheds, this is a view not often seen. The gradient and curve of the track requires careful driving by the motorman to ensure safety and avoid the wheels 'locking' *CP*

Bottom All of the trams are still washed by hand in the traditional method. Unfortunately the job is being done less thoroughly than it once was, as can be seen by the accumulated grime on Trailer 47 in July 2010. Dirt flying off the trolley head, especially in wet weather, contributes to a never-ending task! The trams are also washed at Ramsey in the station, but not at Laxey. *NM*

Above Routine maintenance is vital to the safe operation of such a historic and vintage fleet . The 'yardman' is responsible for the oiling of trams scheduled for service and for accurately marking oiled trams on the relevant board. Trailers have their oil topped up regularly and periodically changed. This procedure has resulted in a reduction in wear to the bearings and 'out-of-service' time. As well as the axle box bearings, the older motors also have 'plain' bearings on the motor armatures, which are being replaced by 'roller' bearings as the trucks come up for overhaul. *DU*

Above With various depots on the 18-mile system, it can be tricky to know a tram's location! The correct use of the 'Cars in Traffic' and 'Car Location' boards is vital to the smooth operation of the railway. The top left section refers to the particular route diagram a car is working on that day and the right side the tram's location in the depot. *DU*

Above A rack holds all the coupling bars. These are cranked differently for each motor, as surprisingly there are height differences even between cars delivered in the same year. This can cause problems when unusual combinations are used, as there isn't always a corresponding bar. *DU*

Above Ancient equipment from the dawn of the line is still used in the workshops. During 2014 considerable work has taken place to bring the workshops up to scratch. As part of this process, it has been decided to keep the traditional belt driven workshop machinery in use, as it still fulfils its role! *DU*

Above 3 images A motor undergoing attention and trucks in various stages of refurbishment. *DU*

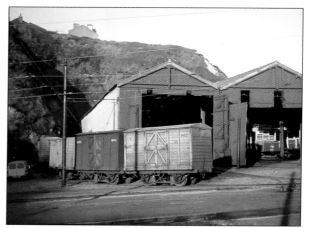

Above Standing proudly atop the hospital roads shed in 2009 is the MER mascot, Tommy Milner. It is said that if Tommy Milner were to fall then the MER would close! Therefore maintenance is always done promptly. It's good to see that Tommy has been brought up to date with Health & Safety regulations and sports an orange hi-viz jacket! *DU*

Top A selection of vans from the days when the MER still used this typical railway stock. The differing styles are evident in this photo. *RP*

Right A rather tall looking Car 16 alongside a tired looking Winter Saloon 19 with a pronounced lean. The fire alarm can be seen attached to the car shed, a must for a wooden shed filled with century-old wooden rolling stock. *IH*

Bottom Pristine Ratchet Car 29 being trolleyed into the sheds by Maurice Faragher, whose favourite tram this was. This must have been a special occasion as Ratchet Car 14 and Trailer 60 can be glimpsed in the background ready to go. *JC*

Top Trailer 60 stands on the historic Bonner siding with ex-Aachen 1010 alongside. The desk is believed to have come from the Onchan Head Inspector's office. *JC*

Left 'Ghost tram' Car 15 emerges from the gloomy depths of the original Derby Castle Car sheds. The motley collection of wooden sheds was expanded in piecemeal fashion, as and when new trams were delivered over several stages, hence their dissimilarity. Van 13 is visible to the left. Car 15 carries advertising boards for the MER: it was driven down to the Groudle Siding and displayed as an advertising hoarding for the last two years of its life, being withdrawn in 1973. This dates the photo to either 1972 or 1973. *Jim Copland (Photobus)*

Bottom The remains of the dilapidated Derby Castle buildings were demolished in the 1990s to make way for a much-needed new depot. This scene shows well the doors at the back of the depot and the various additions. *Alan Corlett/MER*

A set of views as the visitor and tram passenger sees Derby Castle, with trams awaiting their next turn of duty or on display courtesy of the yardman. The legend 'Electric Railway' is set into the cliff side. A refurbishment of the sign is planned so it can shine once again in the evenings.

Top July 2001. A rare scene of all the surviving Tunnel Cars in numerical order: 5, 6, 7 & 9. It might be imagined that this apparently simple line-up would have been recorded many times. This is, however, the only known photograph. The similarities and differences between members of the class all constructed simultaneously in 1893-4 are surprising, but can be explained by their great age. The depot was almost new at the time and the Tarmac is a work in progress after various realignments of the trackwork proved necessary. **NM**

Right 1893 Car 2 was painted for a short time in an unusual livery which incorporated something akin to the perceived original blue scheme of these cars. As it was only a partial repaint, it looked odd and was soon replaced. The venerable Car 5 - 'The Shrine' - stands alongside in May 2004. **NM**

Bottom Car 19 adorned by the basic and plain version of the 1950s 'austerity livery' with Winter Trailer 57 in tow - a full winter set. Trailer 43 is quite elusive nowadays as its heaviness makes it unpopular with crews. It is seen on the left on the depot fan. It features regularly in the scenes that follow throughout this book, which shows that at one time it was in regular use as much as the other 40s trailers. **NM**

Above Winter Saloons 21 and 22 are joined by Car 2 masquerading as long lost Car 3. This is a typical scene that the reader may see during a visit to the car shed, as trams are prepared for service - albeit with Car 2 carrying its correct number! *DU*

Left Especially extracted from the darkest depths of the depot, withdrawn Ratchet 18 and 1894 lightweight trailer 37 remind us of riding these cars comparatively recently. Car 18 is unlikely to see service again, but there are hopes for an early return to frontline service for 37. *DU*

Bottom The highlight of the final view in this section is undoubtedly Car 3. The original open vestibule tram of 1893 was destroyed in the Laxey fire in 1930, but on several occasions a temporary renumbering enabled Car 2 to work in the guise of Car 3 for photographic purposes. To the right of Car 3 can be seen Royal Trailer 59 with Car 1, green liveried Car 16 and in the shed Tunnel Car 9. A great selection of tramcars for the Winter Photography event in 2013. *CP*

Above A newly overhauled set of trailer trucks is offloaded at Derby Castle on 9th April 2009. These were overhauled at Ramsey Shipyards and included new wheels and axles. *DU*

Right The wheels and axles crisis which caused the withdrawal of so many trams in 2008 was a turning point in the history of the MER fleet. Here we see a selection of wheels which have been cut from their axles. The poor condition of the wheels is clear in this view. Many of the lesser used cars had their wheel sets built up with weld before turning once again for another season's work, especially in the MER's long history of 'make do and mend'. This situation has largely been rectified with many trams fitted with new wheels and axles along with overhauled trucks. *DU*

Bottom The sad remains of Winter Saloon Car 22 following the fire in 1990. Thankfully, in 1992 No. 22 took to the rails again with a completely new body and several improvements. *Alan Corlett/MER*

The MER Museum

Opened on Mad Sunday, 1st June 2014, this new museum features a comprehensive selection of artefacts that illustrate the history of the MER, going back to the very earliest company days in 1893. Visitor numbers in 2014 now demand opening every Sunday in summer months. The museum is found in one of the most historic parts of the sheds, which has served as part of the power station, a goods shed, a store and paint shop over the last 120 years! A knowledgeable guide is always present to answer questions. The museum is enthusiastically supported by the line's management, including Workshop Supervisor Steve Hall. It is signposted from the main road, but please be aware that there is no disabled access yet and parking facilities are only available on the main road.

Above A new venture for the MER is the museum located in the former paint shop. A sectioned Snaefell truck with an original motor forms part of a miscellany of fascinating artefacts both outside and inside. Volunteer guide Norman Dowd is on hand to answer visitors' questions. A vehicle of special interest is usually positioned on the adjacent track to attract passers-by and visitors can look around the tram and take photographs, which all makes for a welcoming and informative experience. **DU**

Derby Castle Car Sheds – Port Jack

As our wooden-bodied land-galleon sails its sedate way past a flotilla of sister vessels resting in the shed, we hear the motors noticeably higher pitched and louder as the motorman moves the controller into 'parallel points', producing a traditional strident tramcar sound. Alongside the Derby Castle Depot wall is a series of colour advertising boards, recreating slogans from the past about 'health giving breezes' and exhorting tourists to visit Ramsey's Mooragh Park, naturally travelling by the MER. A

hand painted Isle of Man Transport logo incorporating the Three Legs of Man symbol and the Latin legend, 'Quocunque jeceris stabit', which translates as, 'Wherever you throw (it), it will stand'. This motto is thought to have first appeared in Manx coinage from 1688. Note the bomb-shape stencils on poles 10 and 11, which are meant to give the instruction to whistle. Our car quickens towards Port Jack, where the gradient officially peaks at 1:23½, but in fact it is slightly steeper by the road crossing, making it more severe than sections of the long climb from Laxey to Ballaragh. A sign just after the Car Sheds tells us we are entering Onchan.

Above Seen from the Steve Hislop Memorial, freshly-repainted Car 6 hauls a grimy 40s trailer up the steep 1:23.5 climb to Port Jack at the beginning of the 18-mile journey to Ramsey. It is noticeable again in this picture how Derby Castle shed and the road carriageway are on reclaimed land. *NM*

Port Jack — Narrow Creek - was famous in the past for its sea bathing. MER passengers could catch sight of bathers enjoying the 'bracing reparative powers of the bright clear water.' Nowadays, Port Jack is probably most famous for its Chippy and restaurant. Fortunately, the exterior design of the buildings here has not drastically altered, so photographers can recreate shots of the past as the trams pass Port Jack. The stop here is southbound only.

Behind Port Jack, the grandly named Imperial Terrace runs through to Nobles Park. Mornington Place luxury apartments dominate the local architecture and possess a fine view over Douglas Bay. The former Park Hotel and many others in this area have undergone conversion to flats.

An interesting walk starts at the Steve Hislop Memorial Garden on Imperial Terrace and passes along a reasonably secure but narrow pathway down through the MER's own glen; if you follow it through from the road, it is a relatively easy downhill path leading to the area behind, then to the side of the MER depot. This is a good location for photography of trams in the depot yard from your vantage point overlooking the MER as far as the terminal point.

Port Jack – Douglas Bay Hotel / Skandia House

As a safety measure, tramcars are required to whistle as they approach King Edward Road and their wheel flanges squeal rebelliously across the ungated level crossing, frequently the scene of near-miss, and occasionally, actual accidents.

When Lisbon 360 arrived, it was intended to be a source of spare parts or, more realistically, to operate on the line. Works Trailer 52 was rigged up with a mock Lisbon 360 end to test clearances, but legend has it that the car failed to pass the Ladies' Toilets at Port Jack without the fragile mock-up structure hitting the masonry, a matter of some inconvenience and embarrassment considering expenditure rumoured to be in the region of £23k. Realisation of the fiasco involving 360 dawned: the MER had a fine tramcar in its possession, but one that could only ever operate on the line after significant modifications beyond the scope of the MER workshops. We all know the sad end of the story: a de-trucked 360 once used as the Derby Castle waiting room, then secreted amongst the other unwanted 'fixtures and fittings' of Homefield Road Garage, only to end up in a back yard at Ballasalla near to the office of Tours Coaches, and in 2014 languishing in the back garden of a cottage at Ballasalla.

A red painted sign perched in the grassy bank adjacent to the toilets threatens a £1000 fine for 'trespassing on the railway'; in fact a similar sign is affixed to the wall that runs alongside the sheds, only that is accompanied by a blue sign threatening £3000! If you are a keen photographer of the MER, try using the steps that ascend from Port Jack to the Skandia building. The curve's overhead here repays a look, as it reveals how the MER is finally adapting to modern state-of-the-art equipment out of simple necessity. New overhead was erected here in the winter of 2004-5 and poles were repositioned. Grooved wire here – and now near to Eskadale and on the curve at Dumbell's Row in Laxey – produces a slightly different sound from the hiss that round wire generates.

The Douglas Bay Hotel once stood on the site now occupied by 'Skandia House'. The former hotel's lineside white walls largely remain on the curves, clearly visible as the car advances towards Onchan Head. Sadly this hotel, built by Samuel Horatio Marsden in 1894 on land owned by him, fell victim to the Manx curse of fire in 1989. Photographs of it in the Victorian and Edwardian

Right & above A feature of the many enthusiasts' events during the 1990s was parallel running between Douglas and Groudle. Seen here passing Port Jack Chippy / Diner returning to Derby Castle are the two newest motors, Cars 32 and 33 of 1906, driven by greatly respected motormen sadly no longer in the MER's employment: pipe-smoker Tony Gillett on No. 32 and coachbuilder and chargehand Jimmy Yewdall on No. 33. **IH**

eras show it standing proudly on the bluff overlooking the bay and its sea-view rooms surely gave some of the finest views in Douglas. The sharp curves here were referred to by longstanding staff as 'Marsden's', just as Newell did. A long-disused postal box was set into a section of the wall but was destroyed during the construction of Skandia House. It is conceivable that the postal box at this location had featured in the GPO - MER arrangements of the pre-1908 era. The cast lettering read 'Private Letter Box – Douglas Bay Hotel'. Skandia House belongs to a Swedish Financial Company. The use of modern construction techniques and styling, along with large glass sections, has created a very appealing and individualistic example of modern architecture, which serves as a fine modern backdrop to pictures of the MER's antique vehicles.

GPO Postal Arrangements with the MER

Perhaps this would be a suitable point for a small digression about MER postal services. The conveyance of mail on the line began to Onchan and Lonan parishes almost immediately after the 1894 opening to Laxey. Postmen were carried between Douglas and Baldrine. Sealed mailbags were transferred between the horse cars and the IOMT&EPCo cars at Derby Castle. At one time, a spur was mooted from the Bay Tramway down Regent Street to the main Post Office, but it failed to materialise. The Manx Northern Railway also provided a mail facility serving Ramsey and the North, but the IOMT&EPCo line to Ramsey offered a much quicker service, and was far more reliable than the financially precarious MNR. However, the collapse of the company's fortunes in 1900 meant that a deal was not reached until late July 1903, although this perhaps formalised already existing arrangements.

MER conductors became auxiliary postmen and were sworn in under the same oath as conventional postmen, signing a Statutory Declaration not to, 'Open, delay or impede, destroy or mutilate or endanger the Mail, and to expedite His Majesty's Royal Mail with all despatch'. They were not given any additional pay for performing these responsibilities, nor did they wear a formal badge. No additional time was given to motormen on mail-collection duties.

Lineside boxes were moved to be closer to the line and sometimes placed on the company's land. By 1908, the value of the agreement was an annual £225 to the MER. A regular postman was carried once or twice daily as far as Baldrine (depending on the season) and he assisted Mrs. Cannell, whose duty was to meet the designated car to collect the Baldrine area mail. An express single-motor passenger and mail service commenced in the 1920s, with scheduled stops only at Baldrine, Laxey and Ramsey and was timed to run in just under an hour – an incredibly fast run on what must have been well-maintained track. The car left Derby Castle at 3.30pm and was also known as a 'Boat Car'. This service ceased in 1937. An accompanying poster from the period ran as follows:

MANX ELECTRIC RAILWAY **Boat passengers are** **notified that the** *MANX ELECTRIC RAILWAY* *PASSENGER AND MAIL EXPRESS* **(stopping at** **Baldrine, Laxey and Ramsey only) and due in Ramsey** **within one hour from time of departure from Douglas** **will not leave Derby Castle Station before 3.30pm. This** **is the quickest passenger service in operation between** **Douglas and Ramsey.**

The contract increased in value to £540 p.a. by 1934 and mail was carried on cars leaving Derby Castle at 7am, 3pm, 8pm in summer; 3.30pm and 9pm in winter; from Ramsey at 7am, 1.30pm and 4.30pm in summer; 7am and 2.15pm in winter.

The mailboxes were of various kinds, divided mainly into free-standing and wall-box types, both kinds having different sizes. The system operated very well, with only a few hitches or complications, including frequent infestation by wasps at Groudle and Belle Vue boxes. The Hotel Majestic box used to stick and was once 'opened' (in other words, fractured and destroyed) by excessive use of Car 22's coupler bar! It is reported that a conductor fell foul of the regulations when he carried a single letter from a box to the tramcar, as GPO regulations required the bag to be taken to the box and the letter inserted into the bag.

After Nationalisation, the contract was renegotiated and the 1959 charge was £637. In 1967, mail was taken through 'The Gap' at the site of the Northern Line Bulgham landslip by road vehicles and Isle of Man Road Services buses. The end was in sight in 1972, when winter services were drastically pruned as the MER's fortunes waned again and the boxes at Laxey, Baldrine, Halfway House, Groudle and Onchan Harbour (Majestic) were abandoned after 9th September that year. The ones at Belle Vue, Ballajora and Glen Mona survived until 30th September 1975, when mail was collected and carried for the very last time, as the line between Laxey and Ramsey was closed.

An excellent photograph of the last emptying of a post box - at Glen Mona on 30th September 1975 – featuring Conductor David Hodgson exists in Robert Hendry's 'Manx Electric Album' of 1978. David returned as a motorman in the early 2000s. The boxes at Belle Vue and Glen Mona closed for good that day and were later removed by the GPO.

Skandia House – White City – Onchan Head

And now back to the main line. Originally the single track was laid on the alignment of the current seaside track, with traction poles located in their intended central position for when the tracks were doubled; initially single bracket arms held the overhead. Note the jagged line of stones that in places is the only demarcation between the highway and reserved tracks after the new section of highway. Our car now climbs King Edward Road towards Onchan Head Station at a gradient of 1:141. The first high-level spectacular views over the Irish Sea and Douglas Bay are seen from here.

Left An earlier view of Port Jack shows Winter Saloon 19 and Trailer 41 on the 11.00 to Ramsey on 25th May 1969. Note the 'Outside Service' at the Chippy, the Coke adverts and the traditional hotels overlooking the bay, a scene that has changed as can be seen in the following picture. **RP**

In years gone by, a glance towards the sea from the tram would have revealed a huge sign for 'White City', which was essentially the Island's theme park in miniature. Bare bulbs picked out the letters on the wooden frame after dusk. This area has undergone many changes over the last thirty years, not least affecting the MER's fortunes. Sea Cliff Road runs almost parallel to the MER and emerges into King Edward Road, facing Harbour Road. The old Blair's Guide (1902) had it that the coastline from Port Jack to Onchan is 'declivitous, rifted and torn into bleak, wild, and dangerous rocks all the way to Onchan Bay'.

White City possessed a proper roller-coaster and smaller rides, so that there was something for all the family. By the late 1960s, the 'Figure Eight' Big Dipper's structure was held together by a selection of steel scaffolding tubes for reinforcement, but an atmosphere of decay and closure was in the air already. The MER ran a useful summer service to Onchan Head, mainly operated by the 'Ratchet' hand-braked cars running as single motors – Car 17 seems to have been a favourite. Late 1960s' records show that White City business generated approximately 100,000 customers for the MER annually, and indeed so busy was it that the station was once the proud owner of an automatic ticket dispenser and had its own station master.

Above Running wrong line and single motor at the end of the 2014 season appropriately is the 'new' Winter Saloon 22, showing a different backdrop from the previous photograph. Neither the environs nor the MER are quite as 'timeless' as people might claim! **CP**

The leisure park had been owned by the Myers family since the 1920s, but had been leased for some years prior to closure. Several parts had actually closed for safety reasons earlier, including the theatre which was lost through fire, and the 'Figure Eight' ride closed simply because it was falling apart. Perhaps the final nail in the coffin came with the opening of several modern 'amusement arcade' types of entertainment in the town centre and on the promenades. A lack of investment and an eye to profitable building land sealed White City's fate.

Right Rounding the curve at Port Jack and nearing home on a damp foggy Monday morning are Car 6 and Trailer 44 on D1 in July 2012. The overgrown bushes conceal remains of the original Douglas Bay Hotel wall. **NM**

Various plans to build a new White City, with a central race track in Noble's Park, came to nothing and on 16th September 1985, the park and its cluster of wooden buildings and stalls with their sideshows and fun fair games, fell victim to closure. The Ghost Train, the giant slide, dodgems and Go-Kart track were demolished during the following winter and housing development began soon after. It is fascinating to note that winter work in 2008 on the old site revealed a dumping ground of buried MER tram wheels!

The abandonment of White City meant that the tram station, which had seen intensive local traffic for so many years, became redundant. It now looks quite scruffy and needs a tidy up. The sight of an inspector on daily duty there, dispatching cars back to Derby Castle, disappeared earlier when the 1899 shelter and booking office were demolished, and the site cleared, in 1978.

Beyond Marsden's curves to Onchan Station, trams have several hazards to negotiate, including fast cars emerging at speed from Skandia House and the obstacle course of wheelie bins perched outside lineside houses. On the use of the word 'station', it is worth remembering that the IOMT&EPCo and MER always

Below Skandia House replaced the razed Douglas Bay Hotel. Captured on camera towards the end of the 2013 season is the unusual combination of Cars 20 and the charming 1896 Trailer 60 ready for the next part of the climb to Onchan Head. The support for the side wall of the house 'above' Car 20's Ramsey end stands on the site of the former 'Parnassus House'. *CP*

referred to the main stopping places, such as Derby Castle, Onchan Head and so on as stations and not stops. The smaller stopping places are either referred to as stops or halts and shelters are properly 'waiting rooms'. Platforms are non-existent and passengers board all cars from ground level. Robert Newell comments about platforms 'instead of being blinded by sand, they are only made of soil, which makes it very sloppy in wet weather'.

Onchan Sidings

In the line's early single-track period, a passing loop was situated just after Harbour Road, roughly where Howe Road begins today - 'Howe' comes from the Old Norse meaning a hill overlooking the sea. Of interest is precisely where the Onchan siding was situated. Most records from those early pioneering days have not survived, but opinion traditionally has it that the single track possessed a tiny spur located just to the south of Harbour Road (formerly Onchan Lane) on the landside of the main line, but further in than what became the inside track. The area has altered because of housing development. The siding's use was limited after the doubling of the track in 1894 and it seems to have disappeared in the early years of the MER Company, possibly as part of the radical improvements introduced after Robert Newell's survey of the Permanent way in 1903.

Below Car 1 with 'heavy' Trailer 43 passes White City on a journey from Laxey. Unusual livery combinations frequently appeared when motors were painted in the post-1957 Nationalisation livery of green and white, but lacked a matching trailer. Car 1 of 1893 vintage was usually returned to service in the peak summer each year, being allocated to P-Way duties again from the end of August. *Jim Copland (Photobus)*

Above Busy days at Onchan Head in the past demanded the presence of an inspector. Happy in his work, this inspector supervises traffic including a rare outing for 1895 Royal Saloon 59 and a single motor 'Ratchet' car travelling south. Much of the White City funfair still survived and brought huge custom to the MER, business now sadly missed. *Jim Copland (Photobus)*

Left A bright and sunny Saturday 2nd November 2014 featured a variety of special 'Winter Photography' opportunities organised by Dave Martin and friends of manxelectricrailway.co.uk, including a parallel run from Onchan Head performed by Tunnel Cars 5 and 7. What a great way to end the season! *DU*

Onchan

It is quite a pleasant walk up Harbour Road to Onchan, which is an ancient parish extending right to the mountains near Beinn y Phott, and containing the former small village of Kiondroghad. The village expanded rapidly after 1945, acting as a dormitory for neighbouring Douglas. The village had its own commissioners after 1894 and acted very much as a separate entity though it was reunited with the parish in 1986. The present church is well worth a visit; known properly as 'Kirk Conchan', the name derives from Saint Connaghyn, as mentioned in the

Above Green liveried Winter Saloon 20 is married with a Winter Trailer. The set is seen passing The Café Royale which has survived in various forms, and is currently a Chinese restaurant. An intending passenger can be glimpsed standing by the seaside track towards Douglas. *Jim Copland (Photobus)*

early part of the Traditional Ballad, which claims to be a history of the Island in verse and dates back to the 16th Century. The church was built in 1833; the ancient remains of the previous church stood at the bottom of the old graveyard. In 1781, Captain William Bligh of The Bounty fame married Miss Elizabeth Betham in the old church.

Onchan Head – Howstrake

The MER crosses Harbour Road and passes the Majestic Chinese Restaurant, which is the latest reincarnation for a venue known variously as Churchill's, Woodford's, Boncompte's, The Sizzler, Café Royal and others. It opened in 1924 as the Café Royale and remained until requisitioned in WWII as a convalescent home. The views onto King Edward Road and the sea are spectacular on sunny summer evenings. The tram stop used to be at Harbour Road but is now in a safer position by the north end of the restaurant.

A stop exists by poles 50-51, serving the housing development and formerly the Majestic Hotel. The Majestic - known as 'Mansion House' to the MER in the past - was once one of the Island's finest hotels, but sadly its demise in the early part of the 1990s only illustrates the difficulties the Manx tourism industry

Above In more recent times, the Café Royale metamorphosed into The Water Margin, the first Chinese restaurant here. The plinth was in fact made of resin but is no longer in situ. Wearing the 'Raad Yiarn Lectragh Vannin' livery - Manx for MER - Tunnel Car 5 and Trailer 47 hurry south back to Derby Castle at the end of the day's duty, the motorman already having prepared his bag by the saloon door for a quick getaway home. *NM*

faces during ever-shrinking holiday seasons. Originally built by Baillie Scott, the hotel also saw use in WWII as a military hospital.

As we ride this part of the line, we become very aware that the opening of the road and the tramway, and the construction of beautifully apportioned villas, was really a single project, the parts of which nurtured each other simultaneously. The road itself was originally a toll-road. The bushes that run alongside the track at this point have a neatly-trimmed gap in them immediately next to Pole 54. This is an unofficial MER stop, unsurprisingly called 'The Hole in the Hedge'. Some regular MER passengers use it. Photographs of Car No 3 on trials with an unknown trailer in August 1893 were taken at the point known as Braeside, by Pole 57. Braeside House was half of a well-proportioned villa on the seaward side of the line. The crossing with the bus/tram shelter was referred to by long-serving MER staff as 'Williamson's'.

Sustained climbing continues on a gradient of 1:29, easing to 1:47.5 at Far End (Pole 66) named after the house on the seaward side, which was the last house to be built overlooking Douglas Bay, hence the name. Douglas's sprawling housing is now behind us. The crossover located at Lag Birragh was removed in the winter of 2013-14, being deemed unnecessary or perhaps simply

Top Car 1 has successfully completed a test run to Laxey on 2nd August 2010. Electrician and motorman Nick Pascoe had replaced one of Car 1's motors with one taken from stored Car 26 to keep the aged veteran on the road. The famous 'Hole in the Hedge' unofficial stop by traction pole 54 is clearly visible - part of the hidden MER. *CP*

Bottom A beautiful 2005 shot of a hazy Douglas Bay with 1893 matching set Car 2 and Trailer 51 at Lag Birragh. *NM*

too expensive to justify replacement. On the section beyond the residential development, it is easy to imagine the line's appearance a century or more ago as even today it is set against a barren, rocky and heather-clad background up to Howstrake.

A rather incongruous sign showing a 40 mph speed limit is placed on the landside by Pole 75. Near to Pole 92, some of the early spiked fencing survives, as it does at Howstrake curve and beyond. Now concealed in the thorns, this replaced the original basic wire fencing, the maintenance of which was a constant cause of dispute between Douglas Corporation and the company. The Lag Birragh curve appears to have caused Robert Newell some vexation: 'It t would be quite possible to get rid of the Laghbirra (sic) curves by acquiring a bit of land on the west side of these and fetching the road in a gradual sweep…' Taking a look today, we can't help feel that a partial job was done as the line definitely has a half-finished appearance after all this time.

The plant known to the Manx as 'cushag' and to visitors as 'ragwort' takes quite a hold on this section of track. Interestingly, Manx law dictates that all cushag is to be removed island wide before 1st August each year, otherwise strict penalties can be enforced and indeed MER PW crews have been spotted periodically removing it.

Below Parked up specially to pose for photographers at Lag Birragh on a special working is the usual combination of Car 32 and matching Trailer 62. The crew sport the brown dust jackets associated with the MER through the 1970s until the end of the Jackson era in 1987. The trams display the hideous yellow plastic stick-on 'Isle of Man Railways' letters, too. Traction poles are newly repainted. *JC*

Right The Douglas side of the Lag Birragh crossover is the location for 'Paddlebox' 25 and Trailer 37. The motor showcases the end of the Jackson era house livery, with brown footboards, grey painted trucks and plastic lettering. Trailer 37 carries an unauthentic livery with maroon trucks and kickerboard. The landside curve in the picture was 'eased' by Robert Newell after 1903 but would have benefited from more of the rock being cut away. *IH*

We know we are at Howstrake, when the motorman 'switches' off power at the 258ft summit and the tram swings sharply inland. We catch sight of the gaunt remains of Howstrake Park's former entrance gates. A makeshift tarmac crossing to assist tipper wagons reminds us of the former land fill area, fortunately out of passengers' view. The King Edward Bay Golf Links are situated behind here. This section of track is one of the most uneven on the line, but is scheduled for renewal.

Below Looking towards Howstrake, typical road vehicles of the early 1990s enhance a view of 'original' Tunnel Car 7, Trailer 41 and Van 11 in a consist that typifies MER practice, but has been lost to history for some years... until perhaps Van 16 is authorised to run after its current restoration. *IH*

The arched portico stone shelter has survived, with the wording Howstrake Holiday Camp still discernible; on the rear of the shelter the painted 'Howstrake' remains visible. The shelter was built and maintained by the former Howstrake Holiday Camp,

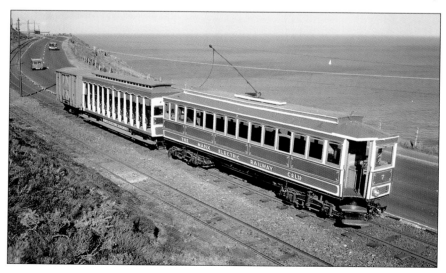

not the MER, which perhaps explains why it was built in an inconvenient spot on the curve. Recognition that this is still a stop was made when a tram stop sign was put up in the 2000-01 winter. The shelter is now fenced off due to a body-width hole in the masonry, which leads directly down to the sea!

As you travel on the MER, the variety of traction poles becomes noticeable; it is a subject worthy of a treatise in itself. Original poles on the Douglas to Laxey section were tapered. On curves, much stronger but still tapered poles were found. Finials were routinely fitted and in stations such as Laxey, stepped shoulder poles were used too. The abandonment of the Douglas Head Marine Drive route (it closed for business just after the outbreak of war in 1939 and never re-opened) yielded a supply of strong poles which are dotted around the MER all the way to Ramsey. These can usually be distinguished by the two collars on each pole; however, closer examination of some poles reveals a few similar in design to the ex Marine Drive ones yet slightly different (see Pole 95); these represent the very early years of the company.

Above On 5th June 2007 Car 19 is on the descent towards a sunny Douglas at 08.20, working the TT Commuter Special from Ramsey. Seen at Lag Birragh crossover, sister car 20 is running solo northbound on the 08.10 to Ramsey. The commuter services were not deemed a success (only one passenger was aboard Car 19!) and have not operated since. **DU**

Howstrake Holiday Camp

The chronicles of the MER too often seem to be an account of the ravages of both fire and the decline of Manx tourism. It is sad that Howstrake Camp, on the bluff overlooking Groudle Bay and enjoying unrivalled views, closed. 'Men' and 'Women' used to be visible on the decaying roofs of the buildings, hinting at elements of the puritanical history of the place. A set of steps and a pathway - now blocked off - runs down from the roadside to the former camp, a couple of buildings being the last tangible remains of development begun in the 1890s.

Right Approaching Howstrake in the capable hands of popular Transport Planning Manager, Les Cannon, is Car 16 with trailer 59 on an extra service to Laxey on 31st July 2010. The tram stop has been removed but the bus one survives! *NM*

A camp was founded in 1887 by Joseph Cunningham, a Liverpool Scot who came to live on the Island in 1884. He had been visiting the Island annually with a group of young men from his Presbyterian Church in Liverpool and he resolved to find a permanent site where young people could enjoy a cheap but invigorating holiday. He also intended to exercise discreet supervision, which would find approval with their parents. Howstrake was acquired and the all-male holidaymakers lived under canvas every summer until 1901 when Cunningham needed a larger site. He acquired land at Victoria Road, which became known as Cunningham's Camp, later the Douglas Holiday Camp, and Isle of Man Holiday Centre, which became a famous Island institution.

Meanwhile this site continued to be used and in 1910, the Howstrake Holiday Camp Limited was formed by another Liverpudlian, Mr. T Carrick, who recognised the benefit of the

Left Threatening skies add another dimension to the unusual operation of the MER's illuminated car, unusually on overhead wire duty through the winter months. Car 9 is seen without a number on the dash panel and no headlight, with a bag placed over the hole for protection whilst working on the overhead at Howstrake. **NM**

adjacent railway. It was another all male camp until 1937, when women were admitted, though strictly segregated from the menfolk, even if they happened to be married! The Royal Marines took over this idyllic location for the duration of the war, but the famous Manx Indian summers from 1946-51 ensured great success for the camp. Major renovations were implemented in 1969 as part of a period of modernisation, including a new room for 500 visitors, with very modern facilities.

It was a shock when the 28-acre site closed at the end of the 1973 season for reasons that remain unknown, save to say that the company went into voluntary liquidation but succeeded in paying off its debts in full. Various schemes were put forward by the Tourist Board, but it seems that the required injection of private capital, as well as restrictive planning orders, curbed the interests of a German syndicate in 1975 and, quite possibly, those of Sir Fred Pontin in 1977.

Right A phoenix arises... rebuilt Winter Car 22 is seen after Howstrake curve on its maiden journey in 1992 after being destroyed in a fire at Derby Castle in 1990. *IH*

Below The legendary loadings of the 2007 Centenary TT are exemplified in this photograph of Car 1 and Trailer 41 squealing round the Howstrake curve, overlooking Groudle Bay. Both cars are stuffed to the gunnels, with a standing load on Car 1 - including a seated extra by the driver - and four passengers squeezed tightly on to each of the trailer bench seats. The MER doing what it does best! *DU*

The main block of buildings, including the concert room, kitchen and recreation areas caught fire on Monday 24th July 1980 at about midday. At its height the blaze shot flames over 50 feet into the air above the buildings and the road had to be closed as firemen from Douglas, Peel and Castletown tried to extinguish the flames, which were fed by a store of 500 Dunlopillo mattresses in the recreation room. Although the wind direction spared the accommodation buildings, the heart of the place was reduced to twisted girders and ashes, until very little remains to remind us of this once thriving site of happy holidays remembered by many young people from the North of England.

The MER used to own the Groudle Road and impose restrictions against competition. Hence, many thousands of 'captive' holidaymakers used the railway, bringing in considerable revenue; indeed, the short-working timetabled evening journeys on the timetable were effectively dedicated Howstrake trips. In its day, the camp was another non-MER property which drew its electricity from the MER 550V DC supply; others included the Douglas Bay and Majestic hotels, which shows to what extent the MER displayed its entrepreneurial spirit in harnessing its assets to maximise revenue.

Howstrake – Groudle

Besides its many claims to fame as a railway or tramway, the MER provides its passengers with some of the finest views anywhere in the world. Opening out before our eyes is a most magnificent view of the rocky coast north of Groudle Bay to Clay Head, so-called after the deposit of clay with which Laxey miners affixed candles on their hard hats. The restoration of Groudle Glen Railway means that on summer Wednesday evenings and Sunday

Below Amid a multiplicity of road and house-for-sale signs, Motorman Harry Christian in charge of Car 32 operating single motor halts at Groudle Old Road on 30th July 2009. **DU**

afternoons, passengers on the MER have this charming vista enhanced by the delicate wisps of smoke curling skywards from the tiny locomotives, as the train with its two or three coach rake, looks like a toy-town fantasy chugging its way to the headland. The line is clearly etched into the hillside and the café building at Sea Lion Rocks is easily discernable. All this means that today's passenger of the technological age can delight in the same sights and sounds that our Victorian ancestors revelled in: the new tramway to Groudle, a walk through the glen, then a train ride uphill to the sea where special entertainments were laid on.

Above Winter Car 20 and Trailer 46 working the 14.00 to Ramsey on 27th May 1969 on the approach to Groudle Old Road. The fencing on the seaside of the road is original IOMT&EPCo work and much survives intact including a gate by Groudle Old Road. *RP*

Our MER car now coasts gently down towards Groudle Old Road on an almost constant gradient of 1:24, with rural and wooded views rather than simply coastal. Groudle Old Road is a regular stop for visitors using the cottages down the lane. Our car now rolls round the corner, descends past 'Solheim', the house in permanent shade tucked neatly away from the landward line by Pole 112, and glides into Groudle, the terminus of the original 1893 line, with the name 'Groudle' picked out in cream lettering on concrete set into the grass just before the station.

Worthy of note is the attractive Art-Deco design 'Glenholme' just south of the entrance to the glen, adding attraction to the style of housing in the area. This building dates from the 1930s and once functioned as a high-quality café in the era when tourists flocked here. A small cutting in the bank is still discernible opposite Glenholme. It is from this point that many of the famous photographs in the 1890s were taken, which show the smart hotel and the equally smart tramcars which served it.

The outside (seaward) track from Groudle towards Groudle Old Lane was renewed in 2012 and is the first on the line to trial concrete sleepers and sliding extension points; these proved successful in the hot summer of 2013.

Groudle Station

The well-maintained 1894 shelter still survives, complete with booking office; it was another erected on land not originally owned by the MER. Groudle is spruced up annually and exudes an air of Edwardian gentility. New signs were erected in 2009 at both ends of the station, advising passengers to 'Change here for the GGR' – the Groudle Glen Railway. Posters adorn the waiting room's back wall with those typical breezy seaside exhortations and bad puns, reminding us that Snaefell is the high point of one's holiday. Just beyond the shelter are a functioning post box and the plaque unveiled on 7th September 1993 by His Excellency the Lieutenant Governor, Air Marshal Sir Laurence Jones, to celebrate the line's centenary. The plaque becomes encrusted with a soft salt deposit. Local enthusiasts remove this with suitable tools and regularly polish the plaque.

Opposite page, bottom The two 1906 trailers 61 and 62, although technically identical, are clearly far from being so. Although the liveries exaggerate the differences, 62 is actually higher and the Ramsey ends of both cars look quite different as a result of bodywork attention through a century of operation. The trailers are seen during a run round at Groudle as part of a parallel run with their matching motors (33 and 32 respectively) to celebrate their centenary in 2006. *NM*

Left Groudle was the first terminus on the way north in 1893 and the plaque here commemorates the opening, the centenary and a century of often precarious operation. *CP*

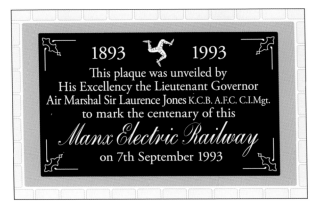

1893 1993

This plaque was unveiled by
His Excellency the Lieutenant Governor
Air Marshal Sir Laurence Jones K.C.B. A.F.C. C.I.Mgt.
to mark the centenary of this

Manx Electric Railway

on 7th September 1993

Top The summer of 1974... sweetly singing 'Seasons in the Sun' by Terry Jacks, the MER station painter informs us of a 'Special Service of Electric Cars' on the MER. The shelter boasts many original features including the inspector's office (still extant), at the side of which stands a wooden pole, only one of which now survives on the MER. Car 6 has the grey trucks of the period and has been fitted with shock absorbers of debatable usefulness. A classic MER view. *RP*

Bottom A mid 1980s view of Car 1 and Trailer 43 at Groudle Station still in its 1960s' paint scheme. It was regrettable that even Car 1 had to carry the unfortunate IoM Railways lettering, which marred its pleasing but less than authentic livery carried after refurbishment in 1979. *RP*

Top Sometimes during enthusiast events, novelty but highly photogenic and enjoyable attractions are staged, such as this one on 2nd August 2009. Car 16 was paired with Van 4, to operate between Laxey and Groudle all day without returning to Derby Castle apart from the final journey. A special plaque 'Laxey - Groudle SHUTTLE' was affixed as shown on the day and has now passed into preservation. *DU*

Bottom White-walled tyres and a very smart livery show off Car 5's lines to perfection as it comes into Groudle Station, pulling Trailer 46. *DU*

The Arrival of the Line at Groudle in 1893

Life today makes it difficult to conceive the miracle of electric traction to Groudle in September 1893. The Isle of Man Examiner of 2nd September 1893 wrote about it in the measured terms of the age, but the achievement is clear:

'Operations in connection with the electric railway along the new road from Strathallan to Groudle were successfully concluded on Saturday. The experiments were superintended by Dr Hopkinson … and were witnessed by a large number of persons. One of the electric trams was dispatched (believed to be Car 3) … and traversed the line into Groudle in a highly satisfactory manner. A few carriages were run over the line on Monday. The carriages run with remarkable smoothness, and did the distance in good time though high speed was not aimed at. The carriages were crowded, and a considerable number of would be passengers were disappointed, as only four or five trams were run … by way of an experiment, with an every way successful result. The passengers on reaching the Groudle terminus visited the beautiful glen. Dinner and tea were provided in Groudle Glen Hotel, of which not a few of the tram excursionists availed themselves. There is every prospect that, owing to its proximity to the town, the ride to Groudle Glen by the electric tramway will be a favourite one with Douglas visitors.'

Groudle and its exquisite narrow river flowing through a glen of magical delight, was an undoubted attraction for late Victorian and Edwardian holidaymakers, as well as Manx visitors; indeed even into the 1960s, extra cars were run just to Groudle, a haunt of the Ratchet cars. Exploitation was undertaken by the lessee of the glen, R M Broadbent, who had assisted progress as far as Groudle by ensuring land was added to the Douglas Bay Estate to extend the road and tramway to a terminus immediately opposite his intended new Groudle Hotel. Broadbent also owned Bibaloe Farm to the north of Groudle and we will see later how the extension beyond Groudle benefited from this.

It seems that Alexander Bruce and his colleagues had always intended the tramway to reach Laxey and probably Ramsey in two or more stages. Saunderson had already planned the route through to Baldromma Beg (Halfway House, near to the present Liverpool Arms) by early 1893. The complete plans for a double-track tramway exist in the Manx Museum.

Left Genuinely meriting the word 'iconic', Baillie Scott's Groudle Hotel is a feature associated with the line since its inception. It has functioned variously as a hotel, pub and upmarket restaurant until comparatively recent times. A few years ago, rumours circulated that it had been classed as structurally unsafe, although at the time of writing it has surprisingly been put on the market for sale. The entrance to the Groudle Glen Railway is to the right and the 'Art Deco' corner of 'Glenholme' forms an unusual contrast with the hotel. **CP**

The Manx press announced the arrival of rails weighing 56 lbs per yard on 15th May 1893. We can readily imagine the sheer volume of activity being undertaken along the line's length at this time, with a power station, car sheds and the new roadway all under construction. It is regrettable that some aspects of the construction were distinctly under par: although good quality Scots fir and larch sleepers were used, they were only 6ft long by 7ins and 3½ inches thick. Worse still was laying them on earth ballast, which was a penny-pinching mistake, given the Island's climate and the expectations of the small company at this stage.

The Groudle Hotel received its licence on 4th July, being opened for business the next day, though the road metalling was unfinished. A contemporary writer wrote thus: 'Immediately adjoining the Groudle Station is the Groudle Hotel. A picturesque, red-tiled building, with a broad covered veranda extending along its front, under which a number of tête-à-tête tables are placed for the convenience of those who affect an al fresco life when touring.'

The hotel is another fine example of Baillie Scott's work. It has been the victim of tourism's vicissitudes; its most recent incarnation as La Casa Restaurant quickly faltered, although a pleasing aspect was the restoration of much of the building's ornate frontage to a period style more in keeping with its original appearance. The premises were 'for sale' in summer 2014, despite notification of demolition due to subsidence in 2012! It would be a pity if one of the key buildings associated with the MER since the dawn of the line disappeared.

A memorable occasion was the re-commissioning of Car 22 on 13th April 1992, when a celebratory lunch was held at the hotel. A fire broke out under the floor of Car 22 on 30th September 1990 whilst the car was out of service at Derby Castle. A picture in this book shows its badly gutted body. A decision was taken to rebuild the car broadly to the original design, but construction drawings could not be found, so the first task was to produce a design that the builders could work to. The construction of the body was put out to tender and the department's own workshops completed the interior fitting out and mechanical and electrical installations. The main contractor was McArd Ltd. of Port Erin, and the project co-ordinator was Eric Cleator. Several modifications were incorporated in the rebuilding of 22, such as a strengthening of the roof structure to support the trolley, use of modern adhesives and sealants and a public address system. The timber used was carefully chosen to follow the original and includes English oak, pitch pine, teak and western red cedar. The crew for the celebratory occasion was Yardmaster John Matthews and Gordon Clague.

Groudle Glen

The glen is situated on the boundary between Onchan and Lonan. It consists of a valley about 400 yards in width, enclosed by weatherworn slate cliffs, and extends for a distance of one mile from the sea. A branch of the glen is known as Lhen Coan ('The Quiet Glen'), as is the Groudle Glen Railway's station. Visitors were greeted by rustic paths and bridges through the glen and an advertisement appeared on 5th August 1893 for Groudle's opening with the statement, 'approached by and at the terminus of the New Electric Tramway'. The trams had yet to commence operation, the delay caused by current collection problems, specifically Dr Edward Hopkinson's patented fixed bow collectors. These were very similar to the existing collectors on the Snaefell Mountain Railway cars. Direct wiring suspended at the cross arms drooped between poles but often lost contact entirely with the bows.

The first car, No.3, reached Groudle on Saturday 26th August and several more test runs and dress rehearsals (which provided some of the well-known photographs with passengers receiving a free ride) took place on the following Monday and Tuesday. Passenger carrying service commenced on Thursday 7th September, but only 19 days of operation took place until 28th September, as Sunday running was forbidden. On 30th

Below The Groudle Viaduct is a glorious example of the work of Mark Carine. It carries the MER over the Groudle River and is best appreciated by walking into the glen on a fine afternoon. *DU*

September, the Manx press complained about the season's early closure, although over 20,000 delighted passengers had paid the 3d minimum fare (1¼ pence in today's money). The three power cars had run 1,689 miles in service, with excellent revenue of 35.4d (just under 15p) per mile. The line's potential revenue earning ability was already clear after a short period of just three weeks' operation.

Groudle Glen and its Railway

Groudle Glen's development continued apace during the 1895-96 period to attract even greater numbers of visitors. Broadbent established a small zoo at the mouth of the glen by Groudle Bay, where he exhibited sea lions and two polar bears. A flimsy-looking bridge enabled those who paid their 6d (2½p) to view the two separate enclosures. An elegant café was built and a picnic area created near to the rocks, with an exhilarating view over the breezy bay. The whole area took the eponymous name of 'Sea Lion Rocks' and the culmination of Broadbent's achievements was the opening of the Groudle Glen Steam Railway in 1896, its aim to transport visitors 'uphill' through the glen to the zoo.

One of the most amazing things in our high-tech age is that we can still catch one of the original tramcars to Groudle and enjoy a walk through the glen, which is illuminated with strings of pretty coloured lights during operating evenings. We can ride the GGR to Sea Lion Cove Station, which is still commonly known as Sea Lion Rocks; we can even partake of Victorian teas there. The only thing missing - and I am sure most visitors do not regret that - is the animals. Their story is somewhat shrouded in the mists of the glen, but Manx folklore has it that the animals, which were provided by Belle Vue Zoo in Manchester, were disposed of at the beginning of the First World War. The polar bears were apparently shot and stuffed, the sea lions being liberated or returned to the zoo, as different versions claim.

The railway opened to the public on 23rd May 1896 using the locomotive Sea Lion and carried over 30,000 visitors annually. Improvements in 1904-5 saw a longer shed constructed at Lhen Coan Station and a run-round loop at Headland, so that trains could pass once the new locomotive, Polar Bear, arrived. The railway closed in August 1914 once war had broken out and the visitors departed, but it reopened again after the war.

The cost of running the steam locos rose sharply in the early 1920s, so they ended up in store, replaced by conspicuously unsuccessful battery electric locos. They had a propensity to derail, which caused one to come to a final halt at the bottom of the glen following an accident. The electric locos survived for only six years, when the two original steam ones were overhauled and recommissioned. The railway continued until a second closure for the duration of WWII from 1939 and beyond, until 1950, when a reinvigorated Island boasted tourist booms again. The railway operated from this time until closure in 1962, but only as far as the Headland after a major rockfall between there and the terminus.

The well-known story of Manx tourism's decline was a contributory factor in the death of this little railway, whose spasmodic service seemed doomed by the early 1960s. Like other glens, such as Dhoon and Ballaglass, people wanted more 'attractive' venues – or at least some with modern attractions – and the traditional popularity of glens seemed passé. The end arrived abruptly after considerable repair work had been undertaken in the winter of 1962-63. Vain attempts had been made to replace the failed Polar Bear, which had soldiered on heroically alone for some time. The line simply never reopened and by 1965, when the Groudle Glen Railway Preservation Society was formed, the atmosphere had changed: the new owners ordered that all railway equipment should be removed in the course of 1967. The Manx Press of 1970 carried various reports about the process of finally demolishing the engine shed and station, noting with regret that the few remains were those of carriages wrecked by vandals.

It is strange how often the matter of the Island's declining tourism crops up in the media. It was none other than Sir Hall Caine, the famous Manx author, who raised the issue as far back as July 1929 whilst receiving the honorary freedom of Douglas. In his address, the well-travelled author warned that the Island would very soon face serious competition from continental resorts, as more and more people were heading for the Riviera, because it was 'cheaper to go there' than the Isle of Man. Not much had changed by 1954, when 'H & C Running Water' was a strong attraction for visitors choosing their hotel and weekly use of the cruet cost 2/6 (12½p), whereas Mediterranean resorts were already offering guests far more value for their money. What a pity Island tourism was so slow to wake up to its own imminent decline. There are those critics today who aver it has never fully woken up to the situation.

The Groudle Glen Railway 1962 - Date

The GGR then entered an amazing chapter in its life. The track was ripped up, Polar Bear shipped 'across' and Sea Lion survived at Kirk Michael - but required complete restoration. It looked as though any hope of seeing the tiny trains run again had disappeared. However, an association was formed to rescue Sea Lion in 1981 and the next year the Isle of Man Steam Railway Supporters gained the support of the Manx Government and the new owners of the glen to commence reconstruction of the line. The entire Dodington Narrow Gauge Railway was purchased in 1983 and at the same time work began in earnest. A great moment was the running of Santa trains to a grotto at the Headland in December 1983. Work continued quickly; the few original rails were deliberately left in situ and the line moved further inland for safety reasons. Sea Lion's restoration work proceeded on the Island until she was moved to the BNFL Apprentice Training Centre at Sellafield, Cumbria, where remaining work was carried out. Sea Lion returned to the Island in October 1987. The Railway Inspector passed the line fit in November 1985 and regular services began after the official opening of the line on 25th May 1986, when Diesel loco Dolphin was used.

1990 was a significant year when land was purchased to enable the GGR to run to its original location at Sea Lion Rocks. Track laying advanced during 1991-2 and safety fences were erected at the cliff edges at the Rocks. Permission to operate services was given on 29th March 1992, and regular services began on Easter Sunday 19th April; the extension was officially opened by Mr. James Cain, Speaker of the House of Keys, on 23rd May 1992, bringing Sea Lion and steam operation back to that point after an absence of 53 years. Trackwork is constantly upgraded and Sea

Lion is now supplemented by the replica Bagnall 0-4-2T Annie and occasional visiting steam locomotives, especially Polar Bear which has found its way back from Amberley Chalk Pits Museum in West Sussex to celebrate the second flourishing of the GGR.

The only intermediate stop at 'Lime Kiln Halt' is named after the kiln which is visible on the left-hand side of the line. The remains of the erstwhile Headland Café can be seen here and a brief but invigorating walk can be taken to the beach. At 'Sea Lion Rocks Terminus', the remains of the polar bear house can easily be picked out high up on the rocks above sea lion pool and the other remains.

The GGR bears eloquent testimony to the dedication of committed individuals, who have resurrected the charms of this little Victorian line. It is a great debt we owe them and there are perhaps few more pleasurable ways in our modern age of spending a transport-themed evening than riding the MER to Groudle, strolling through the glen and riding on the GGR for a complete vintage transport experience. Nostalgia regained!

Below 'Sea Lion' and 'Polar Bear' are seen at beautifully preserved Lhen Coan (Lonely Valley) Station at Groudle Glen. The MER uses the name Lhen Coan too for the stretch from Groudle curves northwards to Eskadale. Built in 1896 by Bagnall of Stafford, 'Sea Lion' is one of the line's two original locomotives. Battery operated 'Polar Bear' is a replica of the 1920's unsuccessful models, which unfortunately did not survive. It was constructed by Alan Keef in 2003. **DU**

Nowadays the only cars using Groudle as a short-working turn-back operate in connection with the GGR's Wednesday evening services. In 2014, this consisted of one timetabled journey from Douglas at 20.10 and return at 20.25, although other timetabled journeys which operate to Laxey that same evening also serve Groudle.

Some of the original buildings in the vicinity have now disappeared; the Battery House which latterly supplied supplementary power at the height of the season, was demolished in the early 1930s and the 1893 thatched Toll House was demolished in 1988 after 62 years in private ownership; it was situated by the landside track coming out of the first curve. The substation survives, of course, and in 1988 had a new transformer installed, supplied by the Manx Electricity Authority at a line voltage of 11kv, which is stepped down to 6.6kv.

The entrance to the glen formerly incorporated the entrance to the Douglas Iron Pier. Such were the grand days of Groudle Glen.

Chapter 3

Groudle to Laxey

Chapter 3:

Groudle to Laxey

The First Winter 1893-94

The D&LCETCo underwent rapid development during the harsh 1893-4 winter. Bruce paid great attention to the electrical infrastructure: at Douglas, an additional boiler, engine, generator and switchgear improved the 1893 equipment. An eight-car shed was built at Derby Castle and staffing levels improved the spread of the workload. In early days, the smith, fitters and carpenters, and general hands, were trained as conductors and motormen, so that they could crew trams when seasonal loads demanded – a tradition maintained today. A further power plant was erected at Laxey quite near to the line itself but lower down from the Laxey Car Shed, on the south bank of the confluence of the Laxey and Glen Roy rivers.

Construction work on the extension to Laxey began from Groudle in earnest in late February 1894. It is surprising that no effort was made to ease the turning of cars at Groudle especially as the station lay beyond a blind curve itself on an incline into the station, which made shunting on a busy day difficult and dangerous. In fact, Newell wanted a loop to handle the 'Groudle only' summer traffic, which would solve the problem of manual shunting holding up traffic on both roads, but his recommendation was never acted upon.

The first task facing the hundreds of casual workers was to double the entire Derby Castle to Groudle section, using the existing seaside track as a construction line and adding the northbound landward track. Significant improvements to the track bed were made at this time, with improved drainage in many places, which stood the newer track in much better stead than the original, a point later noted in Newell's 1903 report.

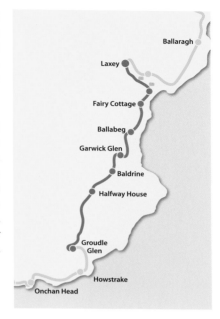

Above The map illustrates the second section of the route from Groudle to Laxey, opened in 1894.

Groudle – Eskadale - Halfway House (Baldromma Beg)

Many new poles were planted at Groudle in the quiet winter of 2005-6; others were repainted. The overhead was completely renewed. Poles have kept their original numbers but additional ones on the Groudle curves incorporate a letter for reference. All poles received new plastic number tags in 2014. Most are white against a blue background, but every twentieth pole has white on green, feeder poles carry a red background.

Leaving Groudle, the car rounds two sharp 90-degree horseshoe curves accompanied by protesting flange squeals – even on the new rails, which have been very expertly laid. It is planned to fit automatic greasers here; some are already in place at Port Jack, Howstrake and the Garwick curves. Unfortunately, the tall trees hide the beauty of the masonry viaduct that carries the tramway at this point, but a brief descent into the glen reveals the magnificent structure executed by contractor Mark Carine in 1894 to make possible the line's onward extension to Laxey. The three 20ft spans and culvert over Lhen Coan are very pretty, especially if silhouetted in the late afternoon sun during summer.

Above Gary Moore drives 'Big Open' 33 and Winter Trailer 57 carefully around the first of Groudle's tight curves in a reverse pattern of coupling motors and trailers, which was a favourite of former Transport Supremo, David Howard. This pairing only became possible after the air cocks and air brakes had been removed from the heavy trailers 57 & 58. *NM*

As the tram rounds the first curve, we can see Groudle substation housed in the stone building on private land. Back in 1894, the line did not open for Easter, as work was proceeding apace towards a deadline opening date of Whitsuntide, 12th May. The line was carrying upwards of 80,000 passengers a week by early July, utilising the first three cars, some of the new 'Tunnel' cars (Numbers 4 – 9) and their trailers, which must have had an incredibly quick turnaround time. Two trailers were towed early in the morning, or on the first quieter trip, so that a spare could be left at Groudle. The new cars arrived from May onwards and were essentially enclosed versions of the first cars, with identical equipment. Cars 5-7 and 9 survive to this day, the others, 4 and 8, being victims of fire at Laxey Car Sheds in 1930. The single line to Baldromma-Beg (Halfway House) ran on a 19ft reservation adjoining a 21ft roadway and was duly completed one day ahead of the 1st May deadline. Between May and July, it was used as a construction line for the push northwards to Laxey.

After Groudle curves, the wooded run on the level for a short stretch along Lhen Coan contrasts with earlier marine views. Cars accelerate quickly until the more sinuous track on a gradient of 1:29 towards Eskadale at pole 147, passing an easily missed bridge by pole 143 where the feeder box is located. These boxes

Top Car 7 spent a long period as P-Way Car, gradually falling into a shocking state of decrepitude, which necessitated its complete rebuild. Here it is seen passing through Lhen Coan in the company of P-Way flat ex-trailer 45. **NM**

are no longer in use, of course, but remain as a part of the ancient infrastructure of the line. Cars virtually stop at the blind exit from the narrow lane called 'Bibaloe Beg' where we note the exquisite example of peacock topiary in the adjacent garden of the house that was owned by Broadbent. There are two interpretations of the name Eskadale: the first is that it refers to the birthplace of a long-forgotten resident, one 'Eskdale', as the name appears in early Company accounts, or it might descend from the Old Norse Eschadala, meaning 'ash tree valley'.

Bibaloe Beg is an outstandingly beautiful lane, which continues past an ancient burial tumulus, the Clypse Reservoir and Ennemona Plantation towards the Creg-ny-Baa Hotel (the name means 'Rock of the Cows'), on the Mountain TT Course. It is an invigorating walk and the Creg is a good location for a lunch break. The history of the TT Races can be seen in the photographs carried on the walls of the hotel.

Bottom Car 5 accompanied by Vans 4 and Wagon 10 glides down from Eskadale. Van 10 was restored by members of the Laxey and Lonan Heritage Trust and is now authorised to run on the MER, a fitting tribute to the many hours of work spent on its restoration. **DU**

Right A remarkable photograph of 'Paddlebox' 26 at Eskadale, towing the restored IMR steam crane actually in steam for an event at Laxey Station. The Chief Engineer at the time, George Lawson, is at the handles, having admired the exquisite topiary in the garden to his left. *IH*

An excellent walk continues from Eskadale into Laxey along the Creg-ny-Baa back road. It is a somewhat tortuous route but passes through some beautiful scenery, via Shonest and Ballaskerroo, Ballacogeen and Pooil Villa, towards Laxey. It can be followed easily by using the 1:25,000 scale Public Rights of Way map.

Beyond Eskadale, our tram accelerates at full power to climb at an average gradient of 1:26 to Halfway House, or Baldromma-Beg. On 21st October 2002, freak storms caused significant damage to the track by traction pole 154. The stream rose and took to the track bed, washing it away and leaving a section of the inside track suspended in mid-air. Work was undertaken immediately to rebuild the section and create a concrete retaining wall. This was one of the very rare occasions when the damage here and elsewhere, including landslips and debris strewn across the tracks at Skinscoe on the Northern Line, caused operation to cease for several days until 25th October.

Below Much more typical of attractive MER liveries is this example carried by Car 19 with a 40s series trailer and van on 2nd July 1968 photographed at 13.05 on the descent towards Groudle. *RP*

The line soon adjoins the main Douglas - Laxey Road, sweeping in from the left, where we can also see the Liverpool Arms. The building's fresh paint always makes it stand out as the image most of us have of a classic, vintage public house. A local resident owns a beautifully restored London Transport RF single-deck bus. You might just catch sight of the rear part of the RF snuggled in its parking space. We are now at the end of the former Howstrake Estate and are about to join the Douglas and Laxey Coast line proper.

Some doubt exists about the MER's use or ownership of the trackbed as far as Halfway House. The acknowledged expert, Mike Goodwyn, believed that the MER only has use of the trackbed as it actually belongs to Howstrake Estates (whose own current legal existence or otherwise is unclear). If the railway ever closes, ownership reverts.

The road crossing at Baldromma Road (with the sign for a public footpath to Ballameanagh) at the top of Baldromma straight adjacent to the station was usually referred to as 'Kelly's Top Crossing'. Many of these names have drifted into obscurity by now. They reflected the early years of the line when points of reference were mainly farms, muddy lanes or cottages and owners' names. Until recently the Kelly family had at least two farms in this area and the crossings would lead to their fields.

Left Rolling down from Halfway (Baldromma) towards Eskadale are Car 21 and Trailer 45 in a mis-matched combination of liveries. The historic livery on Car 21 was an improvement on the Bill Jackson 'house style' but is spoilt by the maroon paint on the underframe. The car still carries its oil lamp holder and strangely the number is slightly obscured by the awkward positioning of the headlamp. Trailer 45 sports the varnished teak pillars. The ensemble looks garish and odd! *IH*

Baldromma possessed its own shelter as far back as 1900, only to assume a nomadic role, ending up at Minorca, where it stands to this day. Halfway House is still home to a Victorian letterbox of the wall type. The shelter carries 'Bus Vannin' and MER stops, a point which illustrates that the MER is not simply a vintage or a tourist line; it is both – but also very much part of the transport provision, if only seasonally.

Halfway House (Baldromma Beg) – Ballameanagh - Baldrine

There are three sets of 'wig wag' crossing signals on the system: here, Ballabeg and at Ballure, just outside Ramsey. The ones here are new LED lights, put in as part of the rolling maintenance programme for the railway under the auspices of the Department of Infrastructure. The tram-priority traffic crossing is operated by a treadle device, easily discernible to passengers sitting in the front seaside seats of the motor car. The treadle sits at track level just after the bus/tram shelter so that the off side wheels trigger the system. The black poles with a white button at either side of the road crossing enable the motorman to reset the traffic signals in the event of the trackside device failing. They are also required, of course, if the service is operating single line with cars travelling on the wrong line. The tram traverses the road and an identical device on the curve resets the signals. Experienced motormen always look back to check that the lights changed correctly.

As the tramcar re-enters its private right-of-way separated from the roadside by an earthen bank (a good perch for the photographer), you can see the local Lonan Parish Commissioners' Notice Board: the Parish of Lonan is home to several historical sites.

The car maintains acceleration down Scarffe's Straight, until the section feeder by the crossover, which was put in during 1904, as part of the improvements requested by Permanent Way Supervisor Robert Newell. He complained about excessive wasted mileage. Previously the two nearest crossovers were

Right At the same location a generation previously is the paired set of Car 32 and Trailer 62, which almost invariably operated together until recent years: 62 is currently awaiting new wheels before coming back into service and 32 operates as the Wire Car outbased at Laxey, where it can be extracted for passenger service if required. *Jim Copland (Photobus)*

Above Seen at Halfway House - Baldromma - with a Victorian postbox and request stop (but no place name!) on the seaside, Car 1 is matched with 'umbrella' trailer 51 on a private charter. Motorman Harry Christian is at the controls, assisted by well-known Laxey historian Andrew Scarffe. **DU**

Garwick and Groudle: 'We lose a lot of time by running dead miles to shunt and get on to our proper road with the loco'. The farm crossing by pole 193 is known as 'Scarffe's', after the owner of the farm at the time of the line's inception; the present owners are the Gellings, whose green hut is well stocked with fresh eggs for sale on a trust and honesty basis.

The name of 'Scarffe' was closely associated with one of the first plans for a tramway. The Mona's Herald of November 9th 1892 referred to a meeting held in the Infant School, Laxey Glen, when Mr Williamson MHK referred to the 'making of an electric tramway from Derby Castle to a point known as Scarffe's House, a few hundred yards on the Laxey side of the Halfway House.'

The track here was originally laid on a bog and has always required the close attention of the PW gang. During periods of heavy rain, the water tends to gather in the field by the track and, as well as providing a temporary home for local ducks, tends to overflow onto the MER. Newell wanted a willow fence planting here as that would prove more resilient to the wet than the thorns.

Passengers are rewarded at this broad inland plateau by glorious views of the inland hills of Mullagh Ouyr, Claugh Ouyr and of

Top Happy passengers and a bemused driver in the traditional MER dustcoat of the time, smile for the cameraman on a packed Car 33 and Trailer 61, as the trams cross the main A2 road at Halfway House on an extra journey to Laxey. *JC*

course Snaefell. Beyond Scarffe's Crossing, our tramcar glides sedately down to Ballameanagh, 'Road of the Middle Farm'. The stop is found between Poles 197-8, a convenient stop to alight for Old Lonan Church. A visit is recommended. The church is dedicated to St. Adamnan, or Onan. St. Adamnan's personal reputation as an important figure in the Celtic Church rests upon his biography of his famous ancestor Colomcille (Columba). He enacted a measure later called 'Adamnan's Law', which aimed to guarantee the protection of women and children in wartime. Ancient customs connected with this church include a long blast on a cow's horn to announce to the parish that a wedding has taken place. At funerals, the corpse was carried three times around the Lonan Cross before entering the church. One of the Island's oldest churches, its walls date back to the 12th century. The nearby cross house contains a number of interesting crosses, but by far the most interesting is the Lonan Wheelcross of the

Bottom Here we see Car 20 on a test run having suffered from a hot axle box a few days previously, sporting the 'austerity' livery, having just passed the re-set treadle for the Halfway road lights. *DU*

fifth century, located in the graveyard in its original position. Services are regularly held at the church.

A duck pond, bedecked with reeds and irises, is found by Pole 208 as the tram coasts with a gentle hum down to Baldrine. Taking its name from the Celtic Balla-drine, 'Place of the Blackthorns', this is a pleasant little community, which boasts a traditional Methodist Chapel and Millennium clock. This location has various different colours of track ballast. The soft yellow ballast is described as 'golden brown igneous rock', and was extracted from the Department of Transport's 'Stoney Mountain' quarry.

Baldrine

Baldrine's shelter dates from 1907 and even featured in the Isle of Man Times of the day, which further noted that Baldrine 'is rapidly becoming a desirable residential area. That popular Laxey builder, R Corlett, has built a number of houses in the locality'. The shelter was renovated in 1991-2 and repaired in 2012 when a section of the north end was damaged by a lorry. The 1903 vintage GPO letterbox formerly cleared by MER staff stands in situ.

This is a fairly typical MER shelter, of wooden construction with corrugated metal cladding. The ladies of the local Women's

Institute voluntarily maintain the flower beds and generally ensure the area is tidy. The policy of adopting shelters, or working with local people to help maintain them, is proving successful, with Ballabeg, Fairy Cottage and South Cape on the Douglas – Laxey section returning to their former glory. A plaque inside the shelter reads as follows: 'Adrian John Pilgrim (1948-2013). For many years Adrian Pilgrim lived opposite this Shelter. He was a remarkable man: a scholar, poet, musician and pioneer of the Manx language revival. He loved the trams and all the railways of this Island. The Baldrine Tram Shelter, built in 1899, was restored in his memory by the MER in 2014, at the request of his friends. S'maynrey eh ta troailt gys niau! How happy is the Pilgrim's lot!' A very fitting tribute.

Right Unusual combination Car 19 and Trailer 51 pass Baldrine Park a little less than halfway between Laxey and Douglas. Ballameanagh is the next halt. **NM**

The lineside shelters are often charming features of this line and remind us of bygone days. The drab, run-down feel of boarded-up waiting rooms in the late 1970s and 1980s has given way to attractions in their own right. All of this enhances the aspect of a heritage railway and local participation is invaluable. Shelters were not actually built simultaneously with the line. The IoM Times of February 22nd 1896 reported complaints from waiting passengers and that the company had 'made arrangements … for waiting rooms along the route.' Baldrine stop is regularly used by some of the MER faithful to this day. In fact, Baldrine boasts two stations: this one at the southern edge and Garwick at the north, the line moving right away from the road to maintain the higher ground between the two stations.

Top Baldrine Station on 23rd June 1968 appears dilapidated and reflects the period quite accurately. 'Paddlebox' 26 is married up with its regular trailer 56 long before the latter was rebuilt into the trailer for the disabled. Shutters down and a well wrapped up but gloveless motorman indicate an inclement Manx summer day. *RP*

The house adjacent to the landside track at Baldrine is known as 'Broadclyst' after the village in Devon. Thorns and bushes were cut away here to facilitate easier visibility of trams and cars, after a serious accident occurred late in the 2003 season. Car 20, which had only returned to service after refurbishment a few weeks previously, collided with a milk tanker. Serious damage was caused to the tram's Ramsey end bodywork and underframe.

Construction of the line beyond Baldromma to Baldrine was quick and enabled the company to seek professional civil engineering and electrical inspectors through the auspices of the mainland Board of Trade by early May 1894. Two were appointed: Colonel Rich for the engineering side and Major Cardew for the electrical infrastructure. Rich had once served as senior inspector of railways for the Board of Trade.

Bottom Baldrine Station with Car 6 unsuccessfully masquerading as 1895 Car 10, and Trailer 59 and Van 4 in tow. The new, safer and even surface can be seen extending to the landside, as well as the refurbished shelter and new traction pole 215A. A much older pole carries the Howard era stop sign. *DU*

Above 16th May 2005 and motorman Andy Marshall poses Car 1 and Trailer 59 - both recently repainted - on the southbound curve immediately before Baldrine Station, showing these trams to perfection. Also noticeable is the roadside mirror for motorists and the red board on the traction pole looking down towards Sunnycot, to signify an area of restricted vision. **NM**

Right In an earlier era, Car 20 typifies the much denigrated green livery, which is quite a different shade from that carried currently by Car 16 and Trailer 60. Perhaps it would be interesting to recreate this livery on a winter saloon as in retrospect it looks not unattractive. **Jim Copland (Photobus)**

Bottom The plaque in Baldrine shelter is dedicated to local resident Adrian John Pilgrim: a fitting tribute. **CP**

Adrian John Pilgrim (1948-2013)

For many years Adrian Pilgrim lived opposite this Shelter. He was a remarkable man a scholar, poet, musician and pioneer of the Manx language revival. He loved the trams and all the railways of this Island. The Baldrine Tram Shelter, built in 1899, was restored in his memory by the MER in 2014, at the request of his friends.

S'maynrey eh ta troailt gys niau!
How happy is the Pilgrim's lot!

Baldrine – Sunnycot(t) - Garwick

The speed of the line's construction was reduced somewhat by the complicated course of the line from Baldrine. The tracks twist and turn, approaching Garwick by reverse curves. Our tramcar has a couple of points of power applied at Baldrine just to ease its coasting into the line's first main section of private right-of-way from the road alignment. The motorman applies a 'nibble' of air from the tanks to ensure safe brake control as the car approaches Sunnycot at Pole 220. This is no longer an official stop and indeed it only ever was a winter season request stop.

Above Car 26 with Trailer 56 on an extra to Laxey on 27th May 1969 at a very open looking Sunnycot. This picture could not be taken nowadays on account of the tree growth, the withdrawal of Motor 26 and rebuilding of the trailer. The first of Garwick's two stations was located just to the north of this point and its disadvantages on a curved gradient are immediately apparent. *RP*

The first temporary Garwick Station was situated just after Sunnycot (sometimes spelt with a double 't') immediately past the old Packhorse Lane. It was clearly badly located on the gradient, and too close to Baldrine. New track was laid in 2006 from here all the way to the entrance curve to Garwick Station; the track bed, ballasting and railwork are superb. Close to the last curve before the present station, heavy traction poles have been planted on both sides of the running lines. At the same time, the overhead has been replaced with modern fittings. In order to keep the same pole numbers as before, the overall increase in the number of poles required produced a number system that retains the original numerical pole numbering, accompanied by 'S' on the seaside and 'A' on the landside. This differs from the Groudle numbering system, apparently at the request of the Railway Inspector.

The curves after Sunnycot have been the scene of a couple of accidents concerning staff attempting to retrieve a de-wired trolley. The Isle of Man Examiner of 27th August 1991, for example, wrote about an incident involving the seasonal, but very experienced, conductor of Car set 9 and 41. The train had departed Laxey at 3.50pm for Douglas. Car 9's trolley pole de-wired in the region of Pole 226 on the climb to Sunnycot. The conductor attempted to retrieve the trolley, which is usually done by signalling to the driver to stop immediately, seizing the trolley rope and pulling the trolley arm downwards, to avoid it colliding with any part of the overhead infrastructure. The conductor lost his footing and was dragged, as he hung on to the rope, into a position between Car 9 and trailer 41. He lost his balance, let go of the rope and somehow his right foot went under the second wheel of the landside front (Douglas end) bogie of 41. Unfortunately, the conductor's right leg sustained appalling injury.

Ironically, the same conductor had been involved in an incident one month earlier, when, through absolutely no fault of his own, a passenger simply walked off moving motor Car 21 just after Port Jack toilets, as the tram was working the 16.00 service to Ramsey. By walking off in the direction opposite to that of the tram, he immediately hit the wall, 'bounced' off and went under trailer 40. His injuries necessitated amputation of his legs. We note that the safety record of the MER is excellent; no system can be perfect, but the MER's is outstanding and those rare accidents that have occurred have usually been avoidable. Additional safety measures were introduced after the conductor's experience above.

Our tramcar glides down the average gradient of 1:27, winding its way between Baldrine's well-kept gardens. Until recently, a white gate stood hidden in the undergrowth on the seaside by Pole 238; in winter it was partially visible. It is said that the old trailing-connected Garwick siding, which served the second, permanent, Garwick Station a little further down the line, was located opposite this gate. MER records are not complete by any means and the general belief is that the siding was removed early on (by 1910?), because the stationmaster could handle the numbers of returning visitors by an occasional Ratchet and Bulkhead trailer set sent through to Garwick only, which would be shunted just as at Groudle, despite the gradient. Evidence also shows that space for Garwick passengers was deliberately left on cars departing Laxey as specials to Douglas. Seats were also needed for the high numbers boarding at South Cape in the late afternoon.

The line descends through a glorious sylvan setting until Garwick main curve. In early days, the track here was relaid several times. In 1961-2 MER Board Member Mr. T W Kneale, a retired engineer from the North Western Railway of India, supervised a relay which lasted until 2006, which shows that with careful driving and proper maintenance, even curves on the MER can last for two generations. The acutely curved embankment demands driving skill; it should be approached slowly, of course, but should be driven out of, and the car's motors can be heard moving onto full 'series' power, or even 'parallel' points, as the car emerges into the straight.

Garwick Station and Garwick Glen

Garwick itself comes from the Norse Gjar-vik meaning 'cave, creek'. The great attraction of Garwick Glen and caves generated considerable revenue for the MER. All the glens along the route were heavily promoted from 1893 onwards and the successor company maintained that policy. A fine station was constructed here in 1895 on land not actually owned by the company. The 1902 Blair's Guide, 'Holidays in Manxland', described Garwick in poetic terms:

'A halt should be made here, for the Glen is very picturesque. The whole place is full of wild flowers, and the sparkling little stream chattering over its pebbly bed on its way down the glen, forms deep pools, from which a good-sized trout or two may be captured'.

Advertising and ticketing made breaks of journey desirable. A traditional MER style rustic kiosk, or 'gablet' (demolished in 1968) was put up and the traffic even demanded a stationmaster, whose duties included supervision of extra cars. The station building was clearly modelled on the one at Groudle. A few

Below Illustrating the magnificent reverse curves near to Garwick, this photograph highlights the new traction poles at both sides of the tracks and modern wiring, as well as Car 32 and Motorman Harry Christian. *DU*

stones remain to show where the station stood prior to demolition in 1979, thus effectively ending the years when hundreds of thousands of visitors swelled MER passenger numbers and still enjoyed the simple pleasures of strolling in beautiful glens.

The Glen itself passed into private ownership during the late 1960s and has seen a succession of owners, very few of whom have been Manx. One owner, a Mrs. Nikimaa, did allow residents to access the glen, but that lasted for only one year (1969) until she divorced. She married a Mr. Bibby, and after her untimely death in Spain, he appears to have terminated access. Interestingly the issue of a public right of way along the old packhorse road was confirmed by Tynwald in 1978, which reflects general concern that the glen was regrettably removed from Manx government ownership. Garwick has been opened on very spasmodic occasions since.

Access to Garwick beach is still possible: from the station area, a leafy, overgrown but quite wide path leads to the main road; following this route, you need to turn off the main road, down to 'Raad Ny Foillan', the walkers' long-distance footpath around the Island. This is clearly marked on maps and leads right down to Garwick Bay. The peaceful cove and beach are worth a visit and it is easy to picture smugglers in the past storing contraband in the caves.

Garwick is famous for its Cloven Stones (see O.S. 4281). These are also known as the 'Giant's Grave' after one of the stones which is split from top to bottom. The Mona's Herald of July 1st 1885 described this place as 'The most picturesque of all the picturesque places in Mona's Isle (which) will be opened on Monday next. Admission 3d.' The stones are now surrounded by housing. An 1865 survey showed that it was then an almost semi-circular barrow with a two-compartment gallery grave. Tradition has it that they mark the position of a Welsh prince slain during an invasion of the Island.

Garwick might have returned to solitude over the last generation, but its fame and glory lies in its former status as a great but genteel Manx pleasure beach. Features included an ornamental lake, a maze and a public house. It even has a Shakespearian connection! In the Bard's Act 2 of King Henry VI, we see reference made to Dame Eleanor Cobham: 'Live in your country here in banishment / With Sir John Stanley in the Isle of Man…' These remarkable verses refer to the banishment to Peel Castle of the Duke of Gloucester's wife, Duchess Eleanor Cobham, after she and her husband were accused of high treason in 1447. Sir John Stanley, then Lord of Mann, was appointed her jailer but she escaped and supposedly concealed herself at Garwick. Unfortunately, that is where the history books - and Manx legends - run out on Duchess Eleanor!

In their publicity materials, the MER freely used Garwick's connection with Sir Walter Scott, understandably considering the Victorians' familiarity with his name and literary works. One of the Garwick caves was named after Dirk Hatteraick, the hero of Scott's novel Guy Mannering. The character was based on the real-life Captain Hawkins, famous for his smuggling between Scotland and the Island.

If you have a romantic streak in your character, spend an hour on Garwick Beach as dusk falls and let your imagination run freely!

Garwick Station – Ballagawne - Ballabeg

The MER's lineside bushes and trees periodically receive a blitzkrieg clean up; Garwick is less claustrophobic since it was recently tidied. Quality fencing was erected all the way from the heights above the entrance curve through to the exit curve near to Ballagawne.

Garwick possesses a rarely used crossover, which our car rumbles over before it enters the sharp left curve to Ballagawne, followed by prolonged hearty whistling as it crosses a car-width lane that also leads to Creg-ny-Baa. This is a danger spot and demands the ability of motormen to have control over their trams to effect an almost instant emergency stop, as car drivers do not anticipate the trams. A shelter here serves buses and trams; the stop at the roadside is unique in that it serves southbound trams and northbound buses.

A famous local resident was Willie White, who lived at the now demolished 'Canny Hill Bungalow' at the Douglas end of

Right Garwick as rarely seen: 27th May 1969 and the station has closed but the inevitable dereliction has yet to appear, so that we can imagine the queues, the gablet kiosk selling souvenirs of happy Manx holidays, MER postcards and a busy service of MER cars, such as Tunnel Car 6 and Trailer 43. The livery on Car 6 is attractive and yet simple, though not austere, with plain lining out. By this time No. 6 already has the modified windscreen. *RP*

Below A blaze of hi-viz jackets and photographers clearly indicates that this is a group of enthusiasts enjoying the rare experience of crossing over at Garwick in more modern times. Motorman Christian stands at the controls of Car 16. *DU*

Ballagawne straight, almost opposite the stop described above. Willie was in charge of the rowing boats at Garwick Beach for five decades; he also constructed his own deckchairs and lobster pots. Lobsters were regularly transported by tram to Douglas to sell to the hotels there! On occasions in summer, local fishermen would sleep under his boats down on the beach. The former beach boathouse was purchased and renovated by Willie's grandson, Michael, in 1986.

The Ballagawne straight is a long, steady 1:30 haul towards Ballabeg on a high shelf above the road. This section once boasted experimental elastic spikes and rubber sole-pads, made by the Clyde Rubber Works Co. of Renfrew, inserted between rails and sleepers. It is puzzling why no further use was made of the pads, as this was the best section of track as far as Laxey until the almost full-length relay of the MER in 2008-9. The track forms a long curve inland to cross the main A2 Douglas to Laxey road, with tram priority again operated by a treadle system. The line's development resulted in an ancient graveyard called 'Kist Vaens' being cut through to form the continuation towards Ballabeg station. A cross erected in 1896 alongside the MER embankment, with a public notice, and white painted stones, has long since disappeared. As you pass the station building, the wall by the outside track represents the boundary line of the original graveyard. Perhaps there should be a plaque here to mark the site as we pass through 'God's Acre' as the IoM Examiner called it at the time.

At the time of construction, the press was concerned with this ancient burial place, which was just behind the old Parochial School; the schoolhouse survives to this day standing on the eastern side of the main road at Ballabeg, just before the tram lines and easily seen from the MER. It later became the Ballabeg

Above Car 32 and Trailer 56 have negotiated the Ballabeg Crossing and begin the descent to Ballagawne. This unusual photo was taken from the front platform of Car 33 on 25th July 2005. **NM**

Top In the class of 'scenes never to be repeated' features this shot of a typical Ratchet set: Car 29 and lightweight Trailer 50 hurrying down the Ballagawne straight towards Garwick. A new shelter now stands where the redundant post is in the picture; the road leads up to the Creg-ny-Baa on the Mountain Road TT course. *Jim Copland (Photobus)*

Reading Room. The Manx Sun of January 20th 1894 reveals that many bones had been found, some perfectly preserved and that 'Mr Ward, the intelligent foreman of the section… measured a skeleton at 6 feet 9 inches'. The paper commented that, 'It is to be hoped that due respect will be shown towards those fragments of humanity and they will all be reverently buried again'. The

Bottom A spotless Car 21 at Ballagawne on test driven by senior fitter 'Little' Willie Gelling, 14th May 2007. *NM*

Left A rather bare looking Ballabeg Crossing on 23rd June 1968 with the 'old' 22 as a Mini politely waits for the tram to pass, in a time of minimalist road markings. *RP*

reason why so many graves had been found was surmised as 'centuries of ploughing have considerably lowered the hill on which the burial ground is situated.'

Old maps had marked the place as 'Killkellan' meaning 'The Church of the Bell', as parishioners had been summoned to services by the bell ringing. Further work in February 1894 reached an even older Pagan burial ground, with cinerary urns and other items discovered, which suggests that the initial highway construction had cut through the older cemetery, just as the workmen on the tramway cut through the later one; the pagans had therefore been unwittingly divided from the Christians.

The IoM Examiner of June 10th 1899 reported an accident on the crossing here. Mr Kinrade of the Bridge Inn at Laxey was returning there in a waggonette driven by Joseph Senogles. As the last car from Laxey was approaching, the crossing keeper, Mr Quinn, warned Senogles but he carried on driving and a collision occurred, with the whole party being thrown from the waggonette. No serious injuries were sustained; the horse was uninjured but the trap was smashed. Echoes of modern times as road vehicles attempt to be beat the crossing lights!

Ballabeg, meaning 'little place', is a small hamlet, a couple of miles by road south of Laxey. The tram swings round away from the road and approaches the Ballabeg station building, one of

Above John Mason is seen at the helm of the 'new' Car 7. At this time the station name board for Ballabeg was removed for re-painting. *CP*

Right A tribute to the local people of Ballabeg who care for and maintain their local halt and have made it one of the most pleasant locations to stop on the MER. This is also a place of considerable historical interest: the building to the rear is the old Ballabeg schoolroom and the line itself was cut through an ancient burial site at this location. *CP*

Bottom On the seaside at Ballabeg is 'Paddlebox' 27 with a 40s trailer on a Laxey - Douglas journey. Car 27 is in pristine condition sporting the traditional MER crest as well as the IoM Railways crest from the time when Bill Jackson was chief executive. *JC*

the best-maintained shelters on the whole line. It was the subject of renovation in 1992 and dates from 1905. This is one of the prettiest locations on the line, thanks to Robbie and Margaret Gill and other locals, who have adopted the shelter. It always looks charming thanks to the hanging baskets, bowls of summer bedding plants and other features such as wind chimes in the garden. There is even a small pond complete with garden gnomes. Inside the waiting room passengers find an accurate clock, beautifully prepared information leaflets about local bird and wildlife, as well as useful heritage brochures and timetables. The traction pole and former feeder box have been skilfully painted with the ornate IOMT&EPCo highlighted in cream. The Heritage Railways department of Isle of Man Transport is to be congratulated for supporting this project and supplying materials, as well as the signwriting on the nameboard (now curiously removed). This spot is well worth a visit and a photo – as well as our admiration for the way that local pride in the MER has enhanced their station and our journey.

Ballabeg again featured in the IoM examiner of April 28th 1894, which described the use of two traction engines 'constantly engaged drawing sleepers and rails from the (Laxey) quay and depositing them at various portions of the line, and rail-laying has commenced at Ballabeg.' Rails are still often stored on the grassed area just by the A2.

The excessively wet autumn of 2012 caused the culvert above Strooan ny Carlane (Stream of Callan), just before Ballabeg Station, to collapse. The culvert here had a very old grill on it and had been known for becoming easily blocked. The tram service had to be split: a bus connection was provided to cover the section from Baldrine to Laxey, where passengers resumed their journey by MER to Ramsey. Immediate reactive repairs were carried out, with Burroughs Stewart Associates as project managers and JCK (IoM) the contractors. The MER took responsibility for the track and overhead, as expected. This triumvirate ensured that repair works took only two weeks, an achievement that indicates the current management's positive attitude to keeping trams and services running; in the past, the service would have been suspended throughout the line for the remainder of the season.

Above The combination of Winter Saloon 21 and Trailer 45 is illustrated here on the outward leg of a 'private hire' - we saw the return journey south of Halfway - driven by Jimmy Yewdall. The set has climbed and crossed Ballabeg and now coasts gently down towards Lamb's Crossing and onwards to Laxey. Laxey Bay is already in view to passengers, a sight sadly almost closed off now, because of excessive and unrestricted tree growth. *IH*

Ballabeg – Lamb's Crossing

The sustained run down from Ballabeg is surely one of the most magnificent anywhere on the line, the Island or any other tramway. Blair's 1902 Guide noted: 'The view of Laxey breaks on you with all its outstretched loveliness. Anything more pleasing in the way of scenery cannot be found in the British Isles'.

The first panoramic view of Laxey Harbour and Head appears and the line beyond to Ramsey can be picked out on the hillside by the elegant scarecrow traction poles and bracket arms. Laxey's pristine white and cream-painted houses add to the charming scenery.

A profusion of plants adorns the line, their origins dating back to the time of the line's construction. Several types of bush or thorn were planted by the company, including hawthorn, fuchsia, honeysuckle, brambles and gorse, all along the route to Ramsey; ferns and garden perennials are commonly found. Spasmodic trimming and clearing take place. Discussion is currently taking place with interested parties about controlling the growth and number of trees, which already partially obscure this and other famous historical views.

The cliff-top descent often proceeds at speeds in excess of the line's original limit of 18mph. The car slows down for various crossings, however, the first being 'Lamb's Crossing' at poles 304-5. The bank by the inside track has been reinforced here with gabions of stone, banked by two short sections of girders with reinforcing sleepers.

The Railway's management appear unsure of the status of Lamb's Crossing, which used to be designated a winter stop only, probably due to the potential danger of an accident on the curve if cars follow in close succession, although that risk is minimal given today's operating scenario. Lamb's no longer appears on the MER's official list of stops. The lack of a winter service means that effectively the stop has been discontinued, although all drivers, when asked in 2014, confirmed they would stop here. Similar ambiguity exists throughout the line to Ramsey.

The Lamb's Crossing Accident of 1928

The area approaching Lamb's Crossing was the unfortunate scene of the line's worst accident back on Wednesday 8th August 1928. The Island was incredibly busy with a record 35,000 visitors having arrived the previous Bank Holiday Saturday, 4th August. The frequency of trams was such that they departed Derby Castle every few minutes. Car 1 coupled with Trailer 39 departed Derby Castle for Laxey at 3.30pm and made stops along the way, so that the following set, comprised of Crossbench 16 and Trailer 56 were close behind - instead of five minutes as the minimum stipulated, they encroached on Cars 1 and 39 and by Garwick were only a minute or so behind, as 1 & 39 stopped at all the main halts.

Motormen have to negotiate the approach to Lamb's Crossing very carefully. The run down from Ballabeg can be fast, but as soon as the cars reach the feeder box, they enter a blind curve. It was just past the curve immediately before Lamb's Crossing that motorman John Cannell halted Car 1 after being hailed by two members of the 'Poles and Wires' gang, who had just finished some bracket repair work and wanted to 'hitch' a lift down to Laxey. This was common practice. The rear of Trailer 39 was apparently about thirty yards beyond the feeder box in the Laxey direction. The conductor of Car 1, Fielden Leaver, did not alight from the car and go back along the line with a red flag, as he should have, but that was probably because the tram had stopped for what was envisaged would only be a few seconds. The

Above The MER Rule Book is a fascinating piece of literature, which covers all the conventional and potentially unusual operating circumstances a crew could ever expect to deal with, including the skills of shepherding sheep and herding cows away from the line! Copies of the rule book have been made available over the years, however this is an original rule book.

Next page A comprehensive new rule (in red) was glued into existing rule books after the 1928 accident at Lamb's Crossing. Page 106 covers normal operating practice in a single-line section, whereas Page 107 describes the introduction of a measure to eliminate the danger of rear-end collisions, incorporating the new red and white coloured board system in restricted areas. This practice remains in force today.

When passing Snaefell Sub-Station and the Signal Post situate near the Summit, Motormen must, on the Up Journey, give THREE DISTINCT RINGS of the bell, in order that the Brakesman may know everything is in order in the front compartment. Should a Brakesman not receive the signals at the proper times, he must with all speed proceed through the Car to the Motorman's compartment, and ascertain the reason, taking whatever steps may be necessary for the safety of the Car, this is, the opening of switches and applying the brakes.

The Brakesman must immediately report to the Superintendent of the Section any occasion on which a Motorman fails to give the requisite signal in compliance with this regulation, and any failure to make such report will result in the Brakesman's instant dismissal from the Service.

CAR MUST NOT BE LEFT UNATTENDED.

UNDER NO CIRCUMSTANCE WHATEVER MAY A CAR BE LEFT UNATTENDED ON THE RUNNING LINE by both the Motorman and Brakesman. Either one or the other must always be in his proper position ON BOARD THE CAR. Any breach of this Regulation will result in instant dismissal from the Service.

SINGLE LINE SECTION.

When it becomes necessary to prevent a Car from entering the Single Line Section, the Crossing-keeper will exhibit a RED FLAG, and the Motormen of Down Cars must keep a careful lookout for this. When the "block" on the Single Line Section has been cleared, the re-start signal will be given by the Crossing-keeper exhibiting a WHITE FLAG.

BELL SIGNALS TO BE OBSERVED

BRAKESMAN TO DRIVER —
TWO RINGS .... START.
ONE RING .... STOP.

DRIVER TO BRAKESMAN (when Car is Running)—
ONE RING................ Apply Centre Rail Gripper Brake.
SINGLE RINGS (continued) .... Harder Application Required.

TWO SHARP RINGS ..... Release Centre Rail Gripper Brake.

DRIVER TO BRAKESMAN (when Car is in Station)—

ONE RING .... Release Ordinary Wheel Brake.

After the first Car has left the Car Shed, no further Cars must be allowed to occupy the Down Line UNTIL THE FLAG-MAN HAS TAKEN UP HIS STATION AT LEAST 50 YARDS DISTANT FROM THE DEPOT SWITCH.

No Cars must be returned to the Depôt until a similar precaution has been taken, and in each case the Section Super-intendent must personally see that this regulation is strictly observed.

SPECIAL RULE RESPECTING DANGEROUS SECTIONS OF THE LINE.

As a special precaution against rear-end collision at any points on the line where the motorman's view is restricted, warning boards have been erected. These consist of a red board at the entrance and a white board at the outlet of the dangerous section.

All motormen are forbidden to stop their cars for any purpose in these sections, and in the event of an unavoidable stop IMMEDIATE precautions must be taken to warn a following car.

Special Rule respecting men working on the Line

Motormen must approach men working on the Line with caution, sound the gong, and must STOP if necessary to avoid passing a workman in the seven foot at the same time as a Car proceeding in the opposite direction.

workmen attached their ladder to the stepboard of trailer 39, but in the meantime, motorman Thomas Kelly in charge of 16 & 56, was descending the hill from Ballabeg.

The crew of the second car set could not see the parked set in front. Unfortunately, Cars 16 & 56, also very heavily laden by this time, came round the blind curve, apparently coasting at normal speed (probably 18-20 mph), to be confronted by trailer 39 some thirty yards in front. The driver applied the emergency stop procedure and just managed to throw himself off the car before it careered into the parked trailer, the rear part of which was 'reduced to matchwood', according to the department's own report. Several rows of seats on the trailer were ruined or pushed forward; the side struts supporting the roof broke off on impact. The Ramsey (front) end of 39 caused serious damage by careering into the back platform of Car 1. The roof of Car 16 rode over the rear section of 39's roof and 16's Ramsey platform was badly damaged. Indeed after repairs the platform length has always been visibly shorter than sister cars. The Douglas end of Car 16 was severely crushed by trailer 56. Someone had the foresight to run back towards Ballabeg to prevent a third tram compounding the accident.

At least thirty people were injured in the accident, four of them seriously, and a Douglas-bound MER car and passing Manxland motorbus took the injured on board. The worst injuries were sustained by 22-year-old Lillian Stillard of Birmingham, who suffered leg injuries and had her right foot amputated. Other injuries included compound fractures as a result of passengers making a headlong jump onto the lineside in the seconds before the collision.

The MER conducted its own enquiry. Car 16 was repaired extremely quickly – in fact (somewhat suspiciously) before the official enquiry. Signs of burns on the brakes showed that 16's motorman had tried desperately to stop the tram; he also stated that he had applied the electric brake, which is effected by reversing the controller key and forcing the motors to reverse polarity. It is a drastic measure that can cause serious damage to the car's motors. There was, however, no evidence of sand having been dropped onto the track by the motorman, which is normally part of the emergency procedure as it provides extra adhesion.

An official enquiry was held under the Regulation of Railways Act of 1896, opening in Douglas on September 13th 1928, under the chairmanship of Mr. W Blaker. The MER's manager, Frank Edmondson, stated that 60 million passengers had been carried on the line without any incident and that measures had been immediately implemented to ensure nothing like this could ever happen again.

General Manager Frank Edmondson put the blame squarely on Motorman Kelly, who might have avoided the accident either with greater vigilance, by dropping sand and using the electric brake; Kelly had stated that he had used the electric brake. Readers will have to make their own judgement. I think that when we ride this section of track, the most likely explanation of why 16 failed to stop is the 'human' one: Cars 16 & 56 were travelling too quickly and the driver did not imagine he would come upon another train parked at that location. Inspector Blaker's report supports that view with a verdict that blamed, 'the transient relaxation of habitual vigilance in observing the rules ...'

Measures to ensure no further accident like this would ever mar the MER's fortunes, included the erection of red and white 'Curve Boards' at the entry and exit to each blind curve. Cars are not permitted to come to a halt between these boards, or if forced to do so, the conductor must at once be sent back to the entry board armed with a red flag to stop any following car.

Ad addendum to the 1926 'Staff Rules and Regulations' is worth quoting in full. It was stuck into all books on Page 51 and was printed in red:

SPECIAL RULE RESPECTING DANGEROUS SECTIONS OF THE LINE.

As a general precaution against rear-end collision at any points on the line where the motorman's view is restricted, warning boards have been erected. These consist of a red board at the entrance and a white board at the outlet of the dangerous section. All motormen are forbidden to stop their cars for any purpose in these sections, and in the event of an unavoidable stop IMMEDIATE precautions must be taken to warn a following car.

An Accident 'Black Spot'

Two other accidents have occurred more recently in the general region of this 'MER Black Spot', one in 1991 just north of South Cape (see below) and another in the area of Fairy Cottage in 2007.

On 18th September 2007, Car 5 was running as a special to Laxey. It ran into the hedgecutter on the long curve at Lamb's Crossing just south of Fairy Cottage, sustaining some Ramsey-end cab damage, including broken front steps, damage to the coupler and bogie pins, and a broken headlight. Fortunately there were no injuries to staff or passengers in either of these two more recent accidents. The procedure whereby by the Derby Castle stationmaster advises motormen of the location of work taking place on the line on any given day appears to have failed in 2007. The driver of the hedgecutter is also obliged to display a sign to warn oncoming trams.

In terms of the Rule Book in respect of men working on the line, a supplementary regulation, again printed in red, was affixed to Page 27:

> **Special Rule respecting men working on the Line.** Motormen must approach men working on the Line with caution, sound the gong, and must STOP if necessary to avoid passing a workman in the seven foot at the same time as a Car proceeding in the opposite direction.

One of the earliest recorded accidents, however, was reported by the Ramsey Courier on April 5th 1895. A certain 'George Crellin, who was travelling from Laxey to Douglas, went to the rear platform (to smoke)... when he lost his balance and fell onto the line. The empty luggage car, which was following, passed over his right arm ... it is feared that amputation of the arm will be necessary.' We can see again that the tramway has always been inherently safe, whereas individuals' actions are unpredictable and dangerous.

Lamb's Crossing - Fairy Cottage – South Cape - Laxey Car Shed

Fairy Cottage Station comes into sight as soon as we have rounded Lamb's Crossing. The name 'Fairy', as seen in 'Fairy Cottage', appears frequently in Manx names. There is no proper word in Gaelic for 'fairy', being known as Ny mooinjer veggey – 'The Little Kindred' or simply 'Themselves'. The term includes many varieties of supernatural beings and they are usually regarded as malevolent. As the car drifts past Fairy Cottage, the

Above Car 27 in better days before it was allocated to the P-Way Dept. on the climb between Fairy Cottage and Lamb's Crossing. On the southbound journey the line climbs all the way from Laxey Car Sheds to Ballabeg, a long stretch of parallel 'points' running, apart from when the tram either stops to pick up passengers or slows for a crossing. *Jim Copland (Photobus)*

Left Car 16 now carries a version of the green livery but here at Fairy Cottage on 26th May 1977, it was in traditional red and white, pulling Trailer 48. This was the year when services to Ramsey were reintroduced, but parts of the line still appeared careworn and down at heel, including the shelter here. *RP*

proximity of the line to the houses on both sides is noticeable, reminding us of the same phenomenon between Cleveleys and Fleetwood. The Fleetwood Tramroad was constructed and operated in many ways similar to the Douglas - Laxey - Ramsey line, even down to manpower, many of their crews being Manx. The legendary former manager of the Manx Northern Railway, John Cameron, ran the operation until 1920, with trams that resembled the IOMT&EPCo ones.

The descent continues towards Laxey, passing through 'Preston's Crossing' at Old Laxey Hill, where the steeply inclined roadway leads to Old Laxey, the shore and the harbour. It seems likely that the name Preston refers to a well-known headmaster of South Cape School, who was also the Member of the House of Keys for Garff.

The line moves a little inland now and over an unnamed crossing (the one with yellow painted 'No Stopping' signs). Former staff unofficially referred to this as 'Olive's Turn', presumably after a one-time local regular. A new flower garden, made from old sleepers given a new lease of life, has appeared just before South Cape. This is the next stop, where the traditionally painted sign advised passengers to 'Keep their seats for Laxey, but alight for Laxey Beach', always presuming that only northbound passengers took any notice. This sign has been renewed and no mention is made now of 'keeping seats'.

Above One of the 'timeless' shots from the days when a ratchet set would complete seven Derby Castle - Laxey journeys in a day. The photographer is looking towards Laxey from Preston's Crossing, with Ratchet 14 and lightweight 1893 Trailer 53 on one of those many extra trips back to Douglas with a happy complement of passengers. The dustcoated conductor takes fares as he steadies himself on the footboard … these are sights that have passed into MER history. *Jim Copland (Photobus)*

Left The success of Car 16 and Van 4 running between Laxey and Groudle prompted a repeat in 2010, this time utilising Car 33 and 'matching' Van 4. *DU*

The Newell Report makes a point about the South Cape waiting room: 'The waiting rooms in this section, with the exception of the Cape, are not used badly by the public.' The result of the MER's opprobrium was that this waiting room was made more open and lacked the same protection from the elements that others had. Some of the graffiti carved on the wooden panels inside is quite revealing!

South Cape was one of the first areas of Laxey to cash in on the arrival of the tramway. On December 2nd 1896, the Mona's Herald reported that 'Mr Orr has put up a couple of semi-

Top A scene still to be seen fortunately is that of Car 6 entering South Cape; this one dates back to 23rd June 1968. The Cape shelter was always open fronted on account of the unruly nature and practices of the locals, according to Robert Newell! *RP*

Right A more recent photograph from July 2010 shows Tunnel Car 5 and Trailer 47 at the Cape, which has been much improved by Tarmac walkways and a spruced up, but still open, shelter. 'Dracula's Castle' (Glamorgan House) is now painted white, a great improvement on its appearance in the previous image. The house cost only £1000 to build and is supposedly named after Glamorgan in Australia. *DU*

Bottom Car 27 is seen pushing a tower wagon whilst on 'wires' duties. The screen added to the front dash panel (sometimes referred to locally as a dodger) was for 27s all year round use, obviously something its designers never had in mind. This tram is now stored and faces an uncertain future with a return to use looking very unlikely. The road crossing here is treated with respect by an experienced MER motorman as the angle and steepness mean that a road vehicle can enter the crossing very quickly without being seen. *NM*

detached houses overlooking the Bay, near to the large boarding house erected by him two years ago. Mr Killip has commenced with a large house on a plot adjoining the Electric Tramway, and Mr Clague is putting up similar properties.' Leaving South Cape, we pass 'Dracula's Castle' (Glamorgan House) by the seaside tracks and enter the Laxey valley; we might just catch a glimpse of another car set on the Northern Line climbing beyond Minorca towards Ramsey.

The 1991 Accident

One of the accidents referred to above occurred on July 9th 1991, at a point just north of South Cape station, when Car 6 was in collision with the hedgecutter. The tram, which was operating on Douglas - Laxey specials, collided with the front-mounted bucket of the hedgecutter, which caused considerable damage to the Ramsey bulkhead and one side of Car 6 was more or less ripped out. The Ramsey end controller, air and hand brake controls, and its unique speedometer, were destroyed. Car 6 was quickly rebuilt and back in service the next summer.

Onward to Laxey through the Valley

Once past Miller's (the lane up to the A2), our MER car gathers speed as it rushes deeper into the valley on its approach to Laxey. The lineside is now surrounded by huge trees, which were saplings on the first photographs of the cars in the 1890s, when this was a favourite spot to pose for the camera. A contemporary account described the ride: 'We run down the rapid descent into Laxey Village … in front, the famous Laxey Glen, shut in by high mountains, the huge bulk of Snaefell itself at its upper end.'

In fact, the company experienced difficulty obtaining this stretch of land for the tramway to Laxey. Constituting an ancient part of 'Clague's Field', it had been bought by local philanthropist Henry Bloom Noble for property development. In 1893, Mr. Ring, the company's legal representative, made overtures to buy the land or a part of it – some 850ft that was in Noble's ownership. In early 1894, Noble suggested the company pay £120 strictly for the land required for the railway only, having in the meantime drawn up plans for a row of cottages running from South Cape Hill as far as the Queen's Hotel. He was perturbed by the regulations

Above Beyond South Cape and Miller's Crossing, Laxey Valley is nowadays sadly obscured by excessive tree growth, but back in 1985 this was the view of Car 1 with Laxey Football Club clearly visible. *RP*

involving gates, retaining walls and other building works to safeguard the permanent way - if built - along his property, but was essentially in favour of the tramway.

By March 1894, the company's position was difficult, especially as Frederick Saunderson had to apologise for their contractors going onto Noble's land without permission. An involved relationship existed here: Noble had bought the land from William Henry Rowe, administrator of the estate of his brother, Mines Captain Richard Rowe. William Rowe was married to Saunderson's sister, Saunderson being one of the original two entrepreneurs (along with Bruce) who had initiated the railway. Richard Rowe had been a party to early schemes to build a railway to Laxey and had acquired the land for that purpose. Business and family politics: a dangerous concoction!

The matter dragged on until April when the legal arrangements remained unsatisfactory; the company then offered to buy the whole field for £500, but the cost rose to compensate for loss of potential building to £620 (Victorian inflation of 24%!). Further problems involved a local tenant called Watterson who was owed compensation for loss of his crops; Saunderson offered to resolve that privately. As late as July 1894, Noble was exchanging letters with his nephew John Chadwick in London, who eventually urged his uncle in a letter dated July 22nd 1894 to settle for a deal worth £620 – bear in mind that the tramway as far as Lower Rencell opened on July 28th and the season was well underway at that stage, so the company must have been desperate to get the line open and earning revenue! Mr. Nuttall, who also owned land affected in the area, sold his section directly to the company. Land not required for the tramway was subsequently acquired by the Department of Agriculture, Fisheries and Forestry. And so D-Day, July 28th, was achieved; it was no mean feat.

Left During the summer of 2014, the old South Cape water tower area was cleared by volunteers, offering the opportunity for trams to be photographed next to this formerly overgrown feature during enthusiast events. This odd and often overlooked piece of early infrastructure was part of the former Laxey Power Station, used as a source of clean water for the batteries at the power station below on the Glen Road. The concrete top is a hollowed out water tank which still holds water!
CP

Between traction poles 335-336, the Water Tower of 1895, which is the only extant remains of the distillation house for the supply of distilled water to barrels for the line's Battery Houses, especially the Laxey one, has recently been uncovered and stripped of ivy by local enthusiasts. The new Laxey Car Shed, built in the style of the former depot, looms up beyond. Its appearance is pleasing, because it preserves the feel of the shed we knew, itself in fact the second on the site. Access is by wooden doors at the Douglas end of the shed. Inside everything is spotlessly clean, sterile and functional; the three roads provide sufficient tramcar accommodation. There is no track on the site of the former shed's fourth road on the Rencell Hill side; the reason given is to facilitate vehicular storage (no such use has been made so far). Track 3 emerges from the rear of the depot towards the old substation to enable transfer of MER stock to road vehicles. Interestingly, if the opportunity to explore the new shed arises, note how the framework of the new shed is bolted on to the cut-down frame of the old shed at ground level. The new facility is the same size as, and a modernised copy of, the old in potential capacity and appearance and is in keeping.

The Great Car Shed Fire of 1930

The original 1894 Car Shed was 240ft long and 36ft wide. It was a mainly wooden structure which was entirely destroyed by fire during the night of Saturday April 5th 1930. In those days, on Saturday the only timetabled duty prior to the season was the first car at 7.30am to Ramsey. The car then worked on main line service for the day. Another crew took a car to operate a 'short' to Dhoon Quarry to collect the workmen and bring them back to Laxey at mid-day. The sheds were locked at 12.30pm. It is claimed that smouldering dust from a cigarette end turned the sheds into a huge conflagration by 10.30pm. The fire must have started some considerable time before the flames were first noticed. A maroon signal was fired to summon local firemen. The captain of the Laxey Brigade realised on arrival at 10.40pm that this major incident was well beyond the capacity of his Laxey crew and equipment, so Douglas brigade was summoned, in the hope that their new tender would be quickly on hand. In the meantime, a Laxey Commissioner, Mr. J P Grime, was struggling alongside the other Laxey men in a desperate attempt against time to unseal the nearest fire hydrant in the main road that roughly runs parallel with the line. Unfortunately, the Highways Board - quite incredibly - had covered the hydrant with tarmac.

The shed mainly contained seasonal rolling stock which was still hibernating until the annual 'drying out' and tidying up process began, so it came as no surprise that the power cars included Car 3 and open 'Paddlebox' toastracks, in company with some of the less intensively used older trailers, such as 34-39 and 49-54. 1894 'Tunnel' Cars 4 and 8 were also present.

The local hydrant's pressure was poor and had little success against the rampant flames now fanned by opening the shed doors. Laxey MER employees and other locals rushed to the scene to assist, but sadly little could be saved: 1896 trailer car 60 (nowadays painted in 'Nationalised' green livery to match Car 16) was rescued by being manhandled while ablaze; 1893 trailer 50 was scorched. By 11.30pm, when the Douglas brigade arrived on the scene with their Leyland appliance, it was too late to save 1893 power car 3, 'Tunnel' Cars 4 and 8, 'Paddlebox' 24, 1894 lightweight trailers 34, 35, 38 and 39, and 1903 Trailers 40, 41 and 44. Various freight cars and wagons perished, including all three tower wagons and a mail van.

The whole episode was a disaster: the mains water supply proved inadequate and the Douglas men had to dam the Glen Roy River below the shed to pump up water, but flames had long since engulfed the place. The overhead supply was switched off, of course. Even the three jets in use from the Leyland were ineffective, because the cars' timberwork construction only fuelled the inferno. The shed's galvanised iron sheeting glowed white hot, the heat shattering the glass rooflights and offering the residents of Laxey a bonfire with flames shooting 55ft skywards.

Such was the danger to local residents and their properties that they were evacuated and firemen abandoned the car shed to douse the flames that danced around timberwork on windows and eaves that had ignited from the radiated heat. 3am came and the water jets were still pumping. The Douglas men only left at 6am. Their assistance was charged to the Laxey Commissioners at £20 1s 0d (£20.05). Four Laxey firemen were left on watch until the MER's breakdown gang arrived from Douglas at 9.30am to find a twisted mass of metal and smoking embers, and to count the losses: four power cars, seven trailers and works equipment, amounting to a value of £10,000. It was by far the worst experience of fire the line suffered and unfortunately insurance payments of just over £6,000 only covered the replacement of the shed and the three bigger trailers 40 41 and 44, which were rebuilt in heavier style on their own frames by English Electric in 1930.

One last thought: which tram was the guilty party – if it was a tram? The journey to the Dhoon to bring Laxey quarrymen back to the village was not a timetabled journey. As Cars 4 and 8 were both based at Laxey, it would probably have been one of them, but the more likely candidate was Car 4. This tram had always retained the 1898 Milnes trucks that it received from Car 16, which in turn gained Car 4's ancient 1894 technology until 1903, when it was given new Brush trucks. Hence, of all the 'Tunnel' Cars, Car 4 was the odd man out, and is rumoured to have been utilised very much as a second choice car. Car 8, equipped with Brush trucks, would have always been first choice for passenger service, but Car 4 would be a likely regular for workmen's journeys, including that fateful day. However, whether a tab end from a cigarette would really have been the cause of a fire several hours later is, I believe, somewhat doubtful.

Above Tunnel Car 7, with a tower wagon in tow, leaves the old Laxey Car shed in a scene where time seemingly stood still. The condition of Car 7, the car shed and track are clear to see. Glimpsed in the car shed are some of the historic tramcars seldom seen by the public. *NM*

The new 1930 Laxey Car Shed and the 'Reserve' Fleet

The shed you see before you today is a replica of the 1930 shed, whose last years became a graveyard for long-disused MER cars. Many had quietly slept there since the 1970s, forming a 'Reserve' fleet, MER heirlooms or perhaps hopelessly faded causes, depending on readers' subjective views. Handbraked 'Ratchet' power cars and lightweight trailers found themselves redundant in the late 1960s and early '70s, as tourism diminished or their equipment failed, and were sentenced to long-term residency here … until spring 2002, when most were removed to Homefield

Right It's the 1st June 1969 and Car 20 is working the 10.15 Laxey to Douglas, seen coasting past the 1930 Laxey Car Shed. The red oxide painted doors and green Car Shed were a feature at the time. *RP*

Top By 2008, when this photograph was taken, Laxey Car Shed was life expired. The open roof provides no protection from the elements for 'Big Open' Car 32 on Wire Car duties or for 'Bertie', the loco used by RMS Locotech on trackwork. *DU*

Bottom The new Laxey Car Shed is home to Car 20 in July 2009. The tram sits on Milnes accommodation bogies, giving an interesting impression of what it looked like after delivery in 1899 when it ran on similar primitive trucks until swapping with those from Car 28 in 1904. *DU*

Top Inside Laxey Car Shed on 2nd August 2014, 'Paddleboxes' 26 and 27 on either side of Ratchet Car 28. Although Car 26 could potentially be returned easily to service, the other two trams will not be so lucky and present a problem rarely raised: what should the current management do with all their withdrawn and no longer needed cars? Was the new shed built simply to function as a more modern graveyard than the previous version? **DU**

Bottom Loco 23 is not owned by the MER. It is seen here at Laxey sitting on sleepers and very unlikely to grace the rails in the near future, despite previous refurbishments in the 1980s and '90s which enabled it to operate successfully for enthusiasts' events. **DU**

Road, the former bus depot and maintenance facility in Douglas. This left the old car shed in a state of progressive deterioration and home to Poles and Wires Tunnel Car 7. The current choice for Poles and Wires car is 1906 Crossbench 32, but that may change in2015 as Car 34 is scheduled to be fitted with a 'cod's mouth' - a brand new pair of Hughes patent couplers - which will enable it to assume a proper role on the railway, and then Crossbench 32 can be returned to the running fleet.

The new shed stables a car set overnight for the first working to Douglas at 09.55 in summer. Other cars have now gravitated here: currently stored are all three Paddlebox Cars 25-27 (41-43 when delivered as trailers in 1898). Of these, 25 was the subject of a half-hearted refurbishment in 1997-8, when a new dash plate and a lick of paint was about as far as it got. The car 'donated' its trucks to the 'new' Works Car 34, itself a rare bird, being the reincarnation of the SMR's No. 7 'Maria', an attraction resurrected for the Snaefell Centenary in 1995. Car 26 is a relative newcomer to Laxey. It yielded its Brush trucks for refurbishment and these now sit under Car 7; its canopy switch is also in that car. Despite this, there is a (perhaps forlorn) expectation that 26 will eventually return to service. Car 27 will surely not see service again. Once a fine passenger car, its years as a Works Car took it to the graveyard that is Laxey.

Above MER staff have to have a sense of humour... with the climate and often harsh working conditions, it's a must! Seen behind Laxey Car Shed is this rather happy looking broken sleeper! Sporting a red hairstyle and contented smile, it is not known if it was ever named or what its fate was! **DU**

The Poles and Wires department's trailer 52, now modified and fitted with a scissors lift for overhead work, resides here, as does Ratchet Car 28. If there ever is a project to restore a ratchet car, this would be an ideal candidate, as any ratchet refurbishment would have to include everything from the underframe up. The pleasing aspect of bright paintwork on Car 18 at Derby Castle, and Car 31 here at Laxey belies their true condition.

Locomotive 23, the amazing 'Kruger', the electric locomotive of 1900 vintage, as rebuilt in 1925, rests here on sleepers. Purchased in the 1970s by a preservation society, the car was occasionally restored for use in the early 1980s and again in 1993, but sadly this unique piece of equipment requires considerable work for operation.

The plans for a new transport interchange at Ramsey involve the demolition of life-expired Ramsey Car Shed. At the end of the 2014 season, the last tram to Ramsey, Winter Saloon 22, was the

Right 1894 Milnes built Trailer 36 is seen in the headshunt at the rear of Laxey Car Sheds in May 2002. Withdrawn around 1973, Trailer 36 has remained stored ever since, although it appears to be in remarkably good condition as can be seen here. It is often thought that after a good clean 36 could be serviceable again, although this is probably wishful thinking! This headshunt was an unusual feature of Laxey Car Shed, so constructed because of the closeness of the rock face at the front of the depot which restricted access to the fourth road, hence the ingenious idea of gaining access to that road by running the trams through the depot before using a point at the rear. Trams had to be manually manoeuvred there, of course, which resulted in the least frequently used trams being stabled here, usually the lightweight trailers. *NM*

final service car to stay over at Ramsey on Sunday 2nd November. The following morning, it was out assisting with the removal of stock from Ramsey, which included Ratchet Cars 14 and 30, Trailer 50 and Freight wagon 26 (formerly 1895 motor No. 10). Over a couple of days, these trams were put on a low-loader owned by Captain Carter of Laxey and taken to Laxey, where each was moved into Laxey Car Shed. The result is that all MER trams are now on site at either Derby Castle or Laxey, but that once again Laxey is a store for mainly withdrawn and unserviceable trams. The lack of storage at Ramsey for the 2015 season will inevitably result in the first service from Ramsey at 1010 having to be operated from Douglas or Laxey, the latter being more probable; the 09.55 from Laxey will also stable overnight at Laxey, meaning that two of the peak five service cars will be Laxey based, the first time for many years.

It is true that the MER's present level of patronage sadly makes many cars redundant, and it seems unlikely that tourism could ever again prosper to the extent that stored cars and trailers at Derby Castle and Laxey will be required again. Nonetheless, we should also remember that these cars represent Manx history and heritage: they should not be lightly discarded and their continued survival does mean that they could at some stage be rebuilt or utilised in some way. In that sense, perhaps they form a 'Reserve' fleet. On the other hand … one wonders how the department's management views Laxey Car Shed: is it a running shed or a weatherproof graveyard? I do not advocate dispensing with stock but was the new shed erected by the previous management with a clear objective in mind or is its usage determined by the law of ad hoc activity?

Access to the Village of Laxey

An official crossing point for pedestrians to link Laxey's main street with Lower Laxey and the former power house, down past the MER lines, has been in popular use for generations. It is located just to the north of the car shed. The proximity of the Queens Hotel makes this a well-patronised stop. The section of the path between the tracks and rails was levelled to rail height and covered with tarmac in 2001, to make it safe to cross. A fenced-off waiting area is a much-needed improvement. The request stop used to declare 'Laxey Car Shed, for Queen's Hotel, New Inn (now closed unfortunately) & Shops', but that sign now sits in the car shed.

The IOMT&EPCo. Power Station (1894)

Laxey Power Station was located on the south bank of the Laxey River and opened in 1894, providing power until 1934 when power generation was abandoned in favour of taking current from the Isle of Man Electricity Board, to be rectified through the several substations. Local stone was used for the boiler house (65ft by 27ft, and 19ft high) and engine room (58ft by 24ft and 25ft high), with a corrugated-iron roof and a 60ft high chimney, some 5ft in diameter, which became a great Laxey landmark. The size of the plant clearly permitted expansion of the railway, another indicator that Bruce and the team did not intend stopping at Laxey. Feeders ran to locations part way up the gradient from the car shed towards Miller's Crossing and to Fairy Cottage. At this time, Derby Castle supplied current via underground feeders with intermediate section boxes as far as Halfway House. Groudle Battery House was designed to obviate problems with two cars simultaneously starting uphill, which could have 'blown' the Douglas supply.

The buildings (except the demolished chimney) remain and it is interesting to see how sections were added on piecemeal until the 1920s. The location was handy for the transfer of coal from Laxey Harbour. Of considerable interest are dual gauge tracks of 12" and 36" still in situ on the bridge from the power station to the Glen Road. At the time this bridge was constructed in 1923, the Great Laxey Mines and the Glen Tramway were still open. It is just conceivable that a plan was drawn up to transfer coal by that method. Perhaps we will never know!

The First Laxey Station

The first Laxey Station was a 65ft 6ins by 15ft building located opposite, and slightly to the north of, the present car shed, but south of Rencell Lane. The Mona's Herald of June 23rd 1894 commented about the eyesore of ancient thatched cottages that stood in this area and that 'no-one grieved that the cottages must come down to make way for the tramway station… soon this old relic of past generations will be swept away.' The cottages actually stood on the site of the present-day depot. On June 23rd, the IoM Examiner was clearly excited by the station being 'in close proximity to the business part of Laxey, viz the New Road.' It is easy to forget that this was not just a tourist tramway but a very tangible economic boon for Laxey. Again, 'scarcely any visitors are to be seen' on the sailings of The Fairy Queen steamboat from Douglas would soon be a thing of the past. The opening of the tramway was earnestly anticipated to bring in flocks of previously absent tourists, touting their holiday savings.

A much-publicised photograph of Car 2 standing on the crossover in front of the station and about to return to Douglas, hangs in Laxey Café to this day. It is of interest also because it shows the mark two version of Dr Edward Hopkinson's bow collector, as well as the pleasant waiting area for passengers. Palisade fencing was all that indicated the line's terminal point (it quickly became ruinous according to Newell).

The former Laxey substation was erected in 1934. The original roof of the substation was corrugated asbestos sheeting; this was removed and the building re-roofed in 2004 with modern PVC based material. Until 2013, current was rectified from DC to AC by 1930s' Hewittic Mercury Arc Rectifiers. It was an amazing sight to see the bubbling and sparking mercury, as well as the exposed live copper switches from an even earlier era! The new functional substation beyond Rencell Hill uses solid state technology and is controlled by the Laxey stationmaster. Apparently the old building is to be emptied, with the other-worldly rectifiers going on display in the former Goods Shed in the station, and given over to the Laxey-based Poles & Wires Department.

The first Laxey tramcar shed was constructed quickly and necessitated a move for the station. At this time - 1894 -the prospect of the proposed Snaefell line spurred Bruce's syndicate

Opposite page The mysterious and eerie light of the mercury arc rectifiers formerly used in the Laxey substation always fascinated visitors! These have been replaced by state-of-the-art equipment in the new substation on the site of the former Shanty, though there may be some possibility of them eventually being put on display for visitors. *DU*

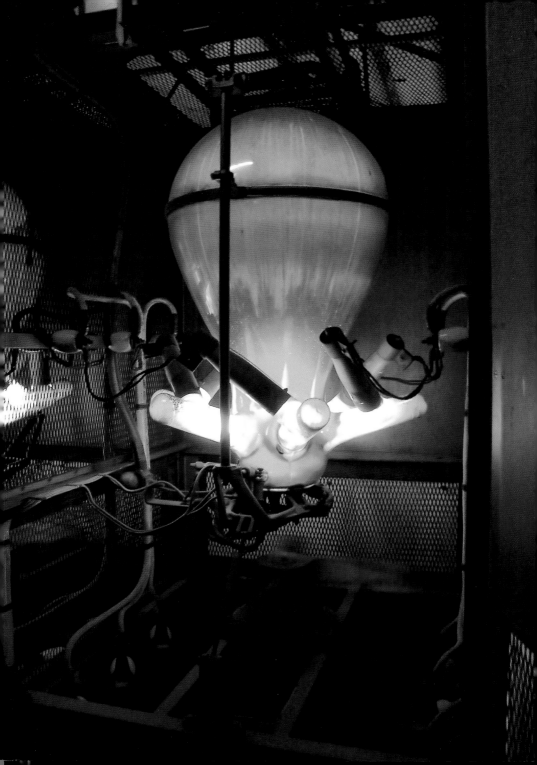

Above The rule book constantly mentions the importance of whistling... however no mention is made of **whittling!** *DU*

Below 'Granny's Cottage' aka 'The Shanty' was an original IOMT&EPCo Laxey station building, when the station was located more or less opposite the car shed. Removed to this location as the line expanded across Rencell Hill and later the Glen Roy River, for many years it served as a store until demolition in 2012 to make space for the substation. *DU*

to construct a proper Laxey interchange. Various ambitious proposals existed, even one for an advanced underpass which would have met up with the first Snaefell terminus near to the present SMR car shed, not only providing a desirable MER/SMR interchange, but to connect with the Laxey to Ramsey section, which was the final part of Bruce's strategy.

The Second Laxey Station

Changes to the layout of the terminus occurred in 1896, when the original station building was resited to a point some ten yards or so past the existing substation. It is generally assumed that a couple of crossovers were in place on this stretch of track whilst it served as the 1896 terminus. The bridge that carries the MER over lower Rencell Hill, immediately before the substation, was completely rebuilt during March 2009, when the steel girders and timber decking were found to be life expired. A much stronger structure has taken its place, which is to be commended. Take a quick glance at the instruction on the pole at Rencell Bridge, which tells MER drivers to 'whittle'! The first station building was affectionately known as 'The Shanty' or 'Granny's House'/'Granny's Cottage'. For many years it served as a store until demolition in 2012 to make space for the new state-of-the-art substation.

The Third Laxey Station

Plans for an interchange seemed to falter for a year or so, until permission was eventually gained from the church authorities for the line to pass through the churchyard; that, along with compulsory orders, ensured that the line took the simplest 'front garden' route, with Mark Carine of Groudle fame again constructing a superb bridge similar to that at Groudle, only this time the curved four-arch stone viaduct spanned the Glen Roy ravine; it was designed by the Isle of Man Tramway Company's Civil Engineer, William Knowles.

Work commenced on 14th March 1898 and was finished in four months, enabling cars to run through to a terminal point opposite the present Station Waiting Room, alongside the third and final terminus for the Snaefell Cars. When you alight in the station, have a passing look at the bridge's superb construction and design. The crenellations are a very popular feature of Manx construction at the time. Other examples are to be found in Laxey, for example, the garden walls at the Vicarage and at the printer's shop in Tent Road.

However, a contrast existed between the magnificent bridge and the poor attention given to drainage. Newell complained that a

Above Car 5 and Trailer 40 are shown from the unusual location of Rencell Hill as the trams pass the old Laxey substation in 2005. *NM*

129

Right Car 9 and its 40s trailer proceed slowly over Rencell Bridge on a typical extra working from Laxey to Douglas. Car 9 at this time still carried many original features, including the split screens, and it lacked a cab door! *RP*

Below An MER worker sits comfortably on the steps of Car 9 enjoying the sunny weather. Later on, he can be seen again in a similar pose as Car 22 crosses Ballure, clearly a comfortable spot to sit! The sign forbids potential walkers taking a short cut over the bridge, by order of the M.E.R. BOARD. *RP*

drain was needed at the south end of the station to stop the water draining through the ballast on the bridge on to the arches as the asphalt ring seems unable to throw it off… so it is working its way through the joints in the brickwork… this illustrates hasty construction and perhaps a lack of sufficient financial resources from 1893 onwards. That said, it survived without major work until 2012, when it was refurbished at a cost of £120k.

Top Car 22 is photographed from a position near to the former cattle dock, as it leaves Laxey for the journey to Douglas. Running at the maximum speed of 5mph over Mark Carine's magnificent bridge, we might wonder how many times in its 116-year history both 'old' and 'new' 22 have made this journey. *JC*

Bottom Taken in the summer of 2012, this shot illustrates the Mark Carine viaduct over the Glen Roy River, enhanced by the presence of Car 1 and 'Mr Bruce's Special Trailer' 59. *DU*

The track alignment from Granny's Cottage was slightly altered in 1898 by moving in landward by about one metre, to cope better with the curve of the new line across Carine's viaduct. Historic elements of the old layout can still be picked out: a cattle dock was made in 1903 and one of its rails is still in situ, higher than the main line. Laxey Station's rustic kiosks are presently stored there.

Several options had been mooted for what was described as a 'connecting tramway' from the Rencell Road terminus to the new Ramsey line that opened in 1898, if the direct route that we have today could not have been achieved. One plan saw the line cross the Glen Roy on a viaduct but then veer to the left, pass through land occupied by the Working Men's Institute and emerge at road level, then cross the road by means of a level crossing where the post office stands today and end near the petrol station. The line would have continued parallel to the main road.

Another plan involved an underpass along approximately the same route with the line ascending right by the site of the petrol station, whence it would continue through a cutting alongside the roadway. The various plans involved removing some of the adjacent bank formed by the gardens of several houses and the Vicarage. In the event, these schemes were unpopular and the obvious alternative of taking some of the church grounds and the mine captain's lawns proved acceptable, enabling the tramway to be a through line and no longer a 'connecting' route.

The Arrival of the Line at Laxey Station

The line had seen considerable activity in July 1894 in terms of settling land and running rights. The new 'Tunnel' cars 4-9 were frequently on test. Major Cardew and Colonel Rich visited the line several times and inspected the Groudle to Laxey extension thoroughly on Friday 27th July. The colonel was satisfied, though expressed concern that pointsmen equipped with flags and lamps at night should be employed at facing points at the termini. He sought protective guards at either side of the road crossings and notices about the danger of touching the live overhead wire, all of which highlights the pioneering untested technology.

Bruce and Saunderson did not object; they were in no position to. Major Cardew reported at considerable length and delved deeply into aspects of the electrical infrastructure. He was generally satisfied, provided that adequate record of the earth return circuit's performance were kept and Colonel Rich's safety recommendations immediately implemented. The inspection hurdle was over and the line could begin to earn much-needed revenue from the very next day.

The formal opening took place during the afternoon of Saturday 28th July. Doubt exists about which cars were used. A photograph of the supposed inaugural train shows Car 4 with a new trailer. This picture long hung in the MER offices; interestingly, Car 4 boasts two innovations: the title 'Douglas and Laxey Electric Tramway' and a destination board of 'Laxey'. The car set is poised for its historic journey alongside the wall at Derby Castle. The photo was always assumed to have been taken on 28th July, but legend persists that No 4 never made the journey as it suddenly suffered a technical failure. A further photograph survives with another 'Tunnel' Car on Groudle curve with trailer 19 on the first journey; trailer 19 survives today as 37. Of course, it is possible there were several 'first' cars, with dignitaries and invited guests.

The arrival of the official party was a huge occasion in Laxey: according to the Manx Sun of July 30th, the line was opened 'amidst rejoicing, display and enthusiasm'. The Isle of Man Times of 4th August filled its front page with the Island's great and good eulogising the new line. Bruce could do no wrong (how his fortunes would change by the end of that frenetic decade) and his colleagues Saunderson, Dr Hopkinson and Joshua Shaw, the overhead specialist, were specially lauded. The paper reported how the combined Laxey Band and Laxey Temperance Band struck up 'See the conquering hero' as the first car drew up at the station. A liberal display of flags, stretching from house to house, lent a celebratory atmosphere to the scene; the Manx Sun noted that 'the enthusiasm of Laxonians, aided by a large sprinkling of English visitors, was unbounded.'

Across the line, an amazing triumphal arch was erected with 'E.T.C. Welcome to Laxey Glen' on one side and 'Shee dy veagys, glion Laxey' (Peace and Plenty to Laxey Glen) on the other.

Bruce was cheered and made one of his amusing speeches after being welcomed by the Rev J M Spicer of Christ Church. Dr Farrell made an oration in Latin, which one could imagine was a slight letdown and had limited appeal unless he thoughtfully provided a translation, but it probably helped to focus the collective mind on the free buffet that awaited the crowds.

Expectations of instant success were realised, as reported by the IoM Examiner of August 11th. On Bank Holiday Monday, 'So great was the influx of visitors by the electric trams ... that hotels and refreshment places were 'eaten out'... the popularity of the Electric Tramway is likely to keep things brisk for some time to come.' Under the title of 'Railway Wonders', the Ramsey Courier of August 13th 1895 reported a 'fact to strike wonder into those who scoffed at the electric railway to Laxey: on one day last week over 30,000 persons travelled from Laxey to Douglas. This represents revenue for one day exceeding the gross receipts of the two Manx railways in an entire week.'

In late August 1894, villagers petitioned and were granted a special tram every Saturday morning at 7.30am 'for the convenience of persons from the parish of Lonan attending Douglas Market', to run until further notice. Other benefits noted in the press include increases in the value of property. A thatched cottage near to Rencell close to the tram station would have fetched only £80 in early 1894, but in August it realised £247. Such was the way that this unique railway opened up and changed the village of Laxey and its inhabitants' lives, a fact recognised by the entrepreneurial owner of Farrington's boot Stores in Douglas. To win business from Laxey, 'on all purchases of 10 shillings I will pay their tram fare one way; and on purchases of £1 I will pay the return fare', as reported by the IoM Examiner in April 1896.

Purchase of the Douglas Bay Tramway

Other interesting developments at the time included the Douglas & Laxey Coast Electric Tramway Company's successful bid for the Horse Tramway - it cost them £38,000. The company changed its name to 'Isle of Man Tramways & Electric Power Company Ltd' on 30th April 1894, so the company title on the 'Tunnel' Cars as they appeared when new was destined to be short lived. It must have seemed that the next stage was the electrification of Douglas Bay so that the service from Laxey could run directly into Douglas's centre, via the port, but as we saw earlier, fate held her own ace against this ever happening.

The Great Laxey Flood – 1930, the Annus Horribilis

We have seen the damage vented upon the MER's fortunes by the fire at Laxey Car Depot. 1930 proved to be a genuine annus horribilis on the terrible night of 17th September. The whole Island had suffered a series of storms in the preceding days, but at 8pm that night, a freak rainstorm held the Island in its grip almost until dawn of the following day. Widespread damage was caused. Rainwater drained off the Island in torrents, the like of which is rarely witnessed. Castletown Harbour was laid waste and the rains swept away Pulrose Bridge's centre section. Ramsey reported 4¼ inches of rain during the storm. The greatest concentration of damage occurred in Lower Laxey. The speed of these deleterious events can be gleaned from the MER's clipped and terse staff account:

It must have been terrifying. The course of the floodwater had naturally attempted to follow streams and rivers. The weir referred to above was constructed for the IOMT&EPCo in 1899 by Robert Newell, the Assistant Engineer, to serve the new hydro-electric plant. A turbine house was also constructed to the rear of what is now the Shore Hotel on the Glen Road near the harbour.

The weir quickly became so silted up by debris, including the carcasses of cattle, that the river simply broke its bank and took to the Glen Road. In the process, hundreds of yards of the riverbank were ruined; virtually all local houses were flooded and over four thousand tons of rubble lay strewn across the area. The river bridge at the power station disappeared and the station was rendered useless. In the days before house insurance was commonplace, many people were ruined; they lost their possessions and could not afford structural repairs to their properties. All this came at a disastrous time for Laxey's economy: the mines had finally closed down in 1929, after a

Accident Report 17th September 1930

Midnight: ......McLean went up to the weir and opened the centre sluice. Very little water in the river.

12.30am: ....Skillicorn passed the weir; not much water.

12.40am: ....Skillicorn passed Mines Dam and noticed nothing unusual.

12.45am: ....McLean was up at the weir and called W Gilmore at Riverside Terrace.

12.50am: ......Both automatic gates had opened at the weir. About five minutes between the opening of the gates, which indicates exceptional rise in volume of water.

1am: ....Gilmore arrives at weir. Killip and his son open the sluice gate of the Mines Dam. The water was rushing in so violently that the level rose 18 inches in 5-10 minutes, and flowed over the protecting wall, flooding his mill.

1.05am: ....W Gilmore sent to the weir to open the screw sluice.

1.15am: ....Big flood but everything alright.

1.25am: ....Barnes left Douglas on special car, summoned by McLean.

1.30am: ....Gilmore and Kermode noticed portion of MER boundary wall at river endhad been washed away; water entering Power House.

1.40am: ....Gilmore and Kermode heard screaming.

1.45am: ....Boiler House door burst in and Power House flooded; Kinrade's house above highway bridge was flooded.

1.50am: ....Water rushing down Glen Road.

2.00am: ....Boiler House flooded to a depth of one foot.

2.15am: ....Walls collapsing where water had been coming over on to road. Water rushing down from Manx Quarries. Road being destroyed in places, houses flooded.

decade of turbulence and decline since the miners' strike of 1919. A whole series of lawsuits was entered against the MER, citing their weir as the principal cause of the swollen river abandoning its proper course.

Incidentally, Laxey was prone to such flooding; the Mona's Herald of October 19th 1841 carried an article informing 'Considerable damage was sustained by the embankments and dam-heads at the Laxey paper mill, and the lower parts of the village were completely inundated ... sheep, pigs and cattle were carried away...so rapid was the rise of the river'. 1930's events were definitely an echo of 1841.

Opposite page A detailed account from MER records of the looming disaster that became the Great Laxey Flood with its terrible consequences for Lower Laxey and its population, as well as the MER.

The MER to blame?

The case against the MER was first set down in the Chancery Court in Douglas on 3rd November 1930, but actually got underway on 7th January 1931 before Deemster La Mothe. Robert Newell appeared in court, though he had left the MER for Londonderry in 1916. He testified how he had followed Joshua Shaw's plans. Modifications had been made twice to the weir (the second time being in 1910) as problems had arisen in getting a 40ft head of water to drive the hydroelectric turbine plant. It might have been assumed that the whole affair could be attributed to an 'Act of God', which was the line of defence taken by Percy Cowley, who incidentally became one of the line's greatest advocates in the troubled 1950s.

A Manchester consulting engineer, Mr. A C Dean, testified that the floodwater peaked at 3,200 cubic feet (90 tons) per second, and it would therefore be unreasonable to assume the weir should have coped. The case ran until February when the Deemster ordered the MER to clean up the rubble and debris left as a bitter reminder of the flood. The written judgement was handed down on 11th February and perhaps surprisingly held the MER entirely responsible for not keeping the river bed clear after it became silted up through the action of their weir, which impeded the natural flow of water, forcing it to drop any sediment it was carrying. The Court ruled that the considerable costs incurred in the case should be borne by the MER. The cost of the repairs undertaken by the Highways Board to Glen Road reached £3,472 – a huge sum for the MER to find. It is no exaggeration to say that the repercussions of 1930 lasted a long time in terms of profitability and viability. Any hope of acquiring some new cars to take the burden of the main service, performed by Cars 19-22, had now been dashed.

The power house survives and has been put to various industrial uses over the years. The refurbished turbine house is currently in use by Laxey Commissioners as a warehouse.

Laxey

The name 'Laxey' finds its derivation in the Scandinavian Laxa(a), meaning 'salmon river'. The 'a' (or 'aa') signifies 'river' and 'lax' means 'salmon'. Salmon still migrate upstream from the harbour in Old Laxey favouring the Glen Roy tributary. A good vantage point in the late evenings of autumn is the stone footbridge within Laxey Glen. The meaning of 'Salmon River' conjures up an image of a tranquil day's fishing in the sun and Laxey is indeed peaceful, charming and relaxing.

Laxey Station

Perhaps more than anywhere else on the line, Laxey Station exemplified the line's timeless qualities: the station, its trackwork and general layout altered little in decades. The original wooden refreshment rooms were lost to fire in 1917 and after that, refreshment facilities came and went, the café currently being located in the station building. The former Laxey Station tea-shop, situated between the Waiting Room and the Mines Tavern, and enjoyed by generations of visitors, was condemned on health grounds in May 1999. Popular couple, Dorothy and Bill Kneale, were compelled to close the café after working there, in Dorothy's case, for thirty-seven years.

In recent years, Laxey Station has presented a rather care-worn appearance, though it has always exuded period charm in keeping with the Victorian and Edwardian atmosphere of the railway. Its delightful canopy of mature rook-filled trees still gently sway in the wafting breezes, although there are fewer of them after a cull deemed necessary to accommodate the refurbishment carried out in the winter of 2013-14.

Above A wonderful view of Ratchet 31 and an 1893 trailer waiting to depart Laxey in July 1966. This car, like her sisters, gradually fell into disuse after a series of relatively minor faults in the 1970s. Last running in service in August 1979 for just three days, Car 31 was retired to Laxey Car Shed, but - allegedly being the nearest Ratchet to the exit doors - was extracted in 1992 for overhaul to represent the 28-31 class in the 1993 MER Centenary celebrations. No. 31 never ran well but was reprieved again when a truck swap with Ratchet 17 took place in 2001, enabling the tram to operate to Laxey successfully and then to Ramsey in 2002 (see photo of Car 31 at Walpole Drive). However, on her final outing, electrical problems afflicted the car and she had to be coaxed gently on the return journey to Douglas by Motorman Nick Pascoe. **RP**

Left The new post-Nationalisation livery looked moderately acceptable on a big saloon, but ruined the vintage lines of Car 1, seen here at Laxey operating on overhead wire duties. Weighing scales are in evidence as is the north end of the station building, which was for many years given over to the Laxey Woollen Mills outlet. **RP**

The traditional, long and gentle curve of the MER and Snaefell lines through the station, and the MER's two crossovers, have disappeared. In their place, the new track from the viaduct to Laxey No.1 crossing (the A2 road) consists entirely of grooved rail in two curves and three straight sections, with the mountain line running parallel to the MER. The appearance and riding effects are quite different from previously. In terms of appearance, there is greater space between the running lines to create safer operation; there is still relatively little space between the MER's landside track and the Mines Tavern, though sufficient

Above Sister Car 2 is also seen at Laxey in one of those so-called 'timeless' scenes. The MER in fact constantly changes; this location and the tram are witness to that. At this time Car 2 carried a drab livery, long before restoration occurred once its historic importance was eventually realised. The kiosk was open selling Woodbines, Manx Bonnag, Manx flags, old-fashioned sweets and other essentials, including MER postcards. *Jim Copland (Photobus)*

to obviate accidents; the concrete and brick 'anti-pedestrian' section here effectively discourages the former practice of people standing with their backs to the pub wall to avoid the trams - a very dangerous practice. The points leading to the old goods shed and the former siding have passed into history, although a new siding has been constructed between the station building and the pub.

Despite enthusiasts' fondness for the 'old' station, it remains true that the track was indeed life expired. Tramcar flanges ran in mud and there was little contact with the head of the rail. Accidents trapping walkers had occurred, so renewal and reorganisation were urgent. Health & Safety were concerned to know what steps would be taken to prevent obvious dangers and any reoccurrence of previous accidents: the present arrangement is the result. The new crossovers have been re-sited outside the station, even though the designated trailer crossover by Laxey No. 2 crossing at Dumbell's Row lies on a difficult sharp curve. Rumours circulating in summer 2014 about the re-installation of crossovers in the station in the forthcoming winter are groundless, as any attempt to pursue this would be perceived by H & S to be a retrograde step and raise questions of competency.

The new track from the Glen Roy viaduct to Laxey No.1 crossing (the A2 road) consists entirely of grooved rail. New traction

Left Laxey Station was just about as far as handbrake only cars would travel, unless they were desperately required to go north. On 25th August 1971, Car 14 was doing what it did best in the company of Trailer 54, providing seven extra services during the day between Derby Castle and Laxey. **RP**

Below On the same day, a few minutes earlier, looking towards the Mines Tavern, we can see Ratchet 14 crossing over before the crew carries out the gravity shunting manoeuvre that would see Trailer 54 re-attached to Car 14. This no longer happens in Laxey Station, with all shunt moves taking place outside the station. **RP**

poles are of solid appearance and are topped by a conical silver finial; these have been used as far as Laxey No.3 road crossing (the A2 by Princes Motors). A few old green poles remain. The new ones would benefit from a lick of green paint … hopefully a task on the 'must do' list. The entire station area has been covered with unappealing grey gravel, which accumulates in the rail grooves merely by the ordinary passage of visitors' feet accidentally kicking it there. This has necessitated an improvised extractor implement used by the stationmaster.

The verdict? People regret the passing of the old and familiar, especially as it is felt that Laxey Station looks slightly unfinished. Hopefully it will be tidied up and a surface more in keeping laid. Safe and continued operation must dictate how change is to be planned and sympathetically executed, so that the MER is not denuded of decades-long atmosphere. For example, the two rustic gablets (kiosks) have been removed from their century old,

Above Tramcars were often renumbered as part of Enthusiasts' Events in the 1990s, as a way of re-creating lost photographic opportunities. The real 'Paddlebox' 24 perished in the Laxey Fire in 1930 and only one photograph is known to exist showing the number 24. So here we have sister Car 26, taking on the role of 24 in 1997, ably driven by the late Peter Richmond, a former Ramsey MER driver and SMR Summit stationmaster. 1894 Trailer 37 is working with '24'. Long time stationmaster Ian Hughan talks to the driver. *Alan Corlett/MER*

Right With the MER goods shed and Mines Tavern in the background, two open cars together present a rare sight nowadays at Laxey. These are Cars 26 and 33 on 6th June 2007. *NM*

or longer, position. They survived the changes, stored by the former cattle dock near to the substation. Once a well-loved feature of the line at Garwick, Laxey, Dhoon, Ballaglass and even Ramsey, they had long since been disused, but did add to the decorative charm of the setting, as part of MER history. Fortunately, they are now being restored at Kirk Michael on the island and we are assured they will be returned in a restored state to their rightful position. It would also be pleasant to see the scrollwork on traction poles returned and of course when it becomes possible to paint the galvanised poles, that will be an

Top On 1st November 2013, Car 6 was teamed with 'Umbrella' Trailer 51 on Ramsey service. Seen here at Laxey there are few passengers, although some had enjoyed a bracing journey from Ramsey on the 'back half'. Autumn leaves cover Laxey Station in this untypical end-of-season view. **CP**

Above At night the MER takes on a magic all of its own. Awaiting departure on 28th July 2010 are Car 21 and Trailer 40. Functioning lights on the 40s trailers are now a rare sight, as a result of minimal evening operation in recent years. **DU**

Above 1st August 2014: A beautiful evening photograph of Trailer 59 on the new siding with green set Car 16 and Trailer 60 on the departure stand about to leave for Douglas. **DU**

Above On 30th July 2014, Car 19 arrives in Laxey, now wearing a much more attractive livery than its austerity one seen previously, although the jury is out with regard to the position of the '19'. The white fencing protects the points equipment that gives access to the new siding. **DU**

Above A miscellany of colours is visible in this view: in traditional colours, Car 32 limps into the siding with Winter Trailer 58, after a controller fault developed on a journey from Douglas to Laxey. Green Car 16 is with grey Van 10 and red Van 4 on their way to Ramsey for mini-UDE work between the Plaza and Lewaigue, and finally SMR 1 sports the original blue livery. 3rd August 2014. **DU**

improvement. Why waste the opportunity to create a successful blend of vintage, heritage and modernisation.

A new modus operandi at Laxey sees Derby Castle arrivals unloading adjacent to the Snaefell cars, which is an improvement. Cars now depart from there to Ramsey and a sign on the seaward side proclaims as much, but causes confusion, as it stands close to the southbound line for Douglas! The loading stand for Douglas has been set back a little to the north of its former position.

The 1932 mixed-gauge interchange siding, which gave access to neighbouring MER metals for SMR cars on accommodation bogies for onward transfer to Derby Castle, has been lost. It was no longer used after the construction of the new SMR shed with workshop facilities in 1995. A token additional section of grooved rail immediately adjacent to the seaside SMR track looks odd as of course it leads to nowhere: there is no crossover to access the MER's three foot rails.

Steam enthusiasts' reminiscences of the IMR's St John's Station often include comparisons with Laxey, which can be quiet and peaceful, until the simultaneous arrival or departure of MER and SMR cars, creating their own momentum in staff and passengers alike. In this sense, Laxey retains its charming sleepiness and its ability to hurry and bustle as necessary.

The 1926 MER Rule Book places responsibility for the 'Appearance of Stations' firmly in stationmasters' hands, who 'must take a personal interest in the appearance and condition of their stations. The platforms and plantations should receive constant attention and the lavatories daily inspection and be kept in PERFECT SANITARY CONDITION'.

For a historic glimpse of the station on film in 1945, try to catch the Frank Lauder film, 'I see a Dark Stranger', which was shot on the Island, and a scene at Laxey shows the star, Deborah Kerr, boarding 'Paddlebox' Car 26 at Laxey.

Laxey Station Booking Office

Laxey Station's buildings deserve some scrutiny. Topped with a green-painted corrugated steel roof, with 'Laxey' outlined in huge creamy-white lettering, this is now a café and ticket office. The building is one of the few rustic buildings still in existence on the MER, having started life as the first Snaefell Station and Waiting Room. The conservatory extension - the stationmaster's domain - looks like a hasty afterthought; it was revealed once more during removal of vegetation during refurbishment for the MER Centenary in 1993. The interior of the Waiting Room was turned into a seated cafeteria in 2001. The former Woollen Mills outlet is now the kitchen.

Fortunately, the charm of the old Waiting Room has not been destroyed. Several period pictures of bygone days illustrate the original Refreshment Rooms, which consisted of a wooden pavilion, first constructed in England, then brought to Laxey and re-erected. The Manx Sun of July 8th 1899 reports a special licensing session to consider the application of Mr Bowling of the Station Hotel, who was having to turn lunchtime diners away due to lack of space and sought a licence for the pavilion too. 'According to the Electric Tramway Company, in August the average traffic stopping at Laxey Station is 5000 people per day. Some visitors missed their cars through having to wait.' This splendid wooden pavilion was destroyed by fire in 1917 and never rebuilt.

Christ Church (Laxey Station)

Christ Church celebrated its 160th Anniversary in 2014. It was originally built because the centre of population had shifted from Lonan to Laxey. The cost of construction was £550 and the location was the prominent position at the southern end of the grounds of the mine captain's house. The foundation stone was laid by the Bishop of Sodor and Man in March 1852. I recommend a look inside the church where you will find a peaceful welcome and you will surely admire the beauty of the church. The Manx Sun of May 31st 1856 noted, '…when the timber planted around the church grows up, it will form a striking and picturesque object in the beautiful glen of Laxey.'

Above Christ Church Laxey is perhaps a building we would not expect in a tramway station. The church celebrated its 160th Anniversary in 2014. At the time of construction, the location was a prominent position at the southern end of the grounds of the mine captain's house, whose land was eventually used for the MER. *CP*

The Mines Tavern

The Mines Tavern was previously known as the Station Hotel and was owned by the MER until Nationalisation in 1957. The building has an interesting history: it was former Mine Captain Reddicliffe's House, part of which was demolished in 1898 to allow construction of the Ramsey line. The land between the pub and the church formed the garden. The stables at the rear are historic too; they once accommodated horses for the Glen Road freight tramway (The Great Laxey Mines). Of interest is the narrow gap between the southbound track and the wall of the Mines Tavern.

Right Winter Saloon Car 22 with matching 40-series trailer is seen entering a quiet Laxey Station in the 1970s. They are shown between the southbound tracks and the wall of the Mines Tavern – a 'pinch point' for the public where several accidents have occurred over the years. Various methods were used to discourage pedestrians here including laying sections of rail, as seen here. Unusually the door to the right is open for access - it is no longer used. The Mines offers locally sourced real ales and a beer garden which is a pleasant place to wile away an afternoon as tramcars shuttle back and forth. *Peter Burke*

Below Car 25 carried out its final passenger journeys during the 1993 Centenary, after which it appeared on a variety of duties including Ramsey P-Way Car and also weed-killing duties mainly on the Northern Line between Laxey and Ramsey. The weedkiller tank is carried by Wagon 8. *IH*

The 1903 Goods Shed

One other significant building, sited on the land beyond the pub, is the former Goods Shed of 1903, which functioned as a store for many years. Points were reconnected and lowering of the interior trackwork took place during the 2003-4 winter, giving the shed a proper connection to the main running line again; however, this was removed in the 2013-14 regeneration work.

Top Trailer 48 stands alone outside the Mines Tavern and is about to be manhandled into the old siding by the Goods Shed as its matching Motor 7 takes a party of enthusiasts on a short trip to Dhoon Quarry and back. *DU*

Left Winter Photography: 2nd November 2013 and Car 2 stands on the Goods Shed siding - the last tram to do so before the reconstruction of Laxey Station over the 2013-14 winter. The Goods Shed is open as valiant efforts are made to extract Tower Wagon 12. *CP*

Bottom Handbraked cars were already comparatively rare visitors to Ramsey by the early 1960s, although they occasionally went 'up' if necessary and only in the hands of an expert motorman. On 31st May 1967, Ratchet 29 and Trailer 50 arrive at Laxey after the long journey from the north. If only…! *RP*

Top 28th July 2012 and Car 33 with Winter Trailer 57 are framed perfectly in the Goods Shed siding at Laxey, once a common place for cars and crews on Specials to wait for their return journey. The 'Leaping Salmon' in the foreground is an attractive decorative piece made by the Laxey Blacksmith. This photograph is no longer possible as the gardens are being modified and the physical connection to the siding from the main line has been removed. *CP*

Bottom The blacksmith's yard to the rear of the goods shed used to display artefacts from farms around the island. Trailer 43 awaits its next turn of duty back to Derby Castle. This area has now been cleared and the extension of the track that 43 occupies is used to store vans under restoration by the Laxey and Lonan Heritage Trust. *NM*

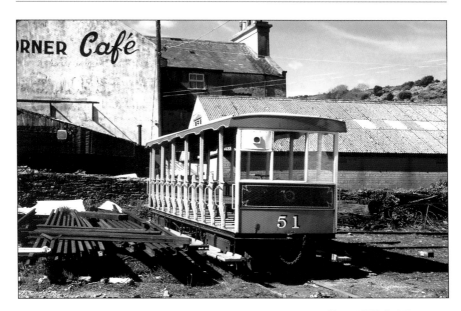

There is no overhead connection. The siding from the main running line to the blacksmith's yard has also been disconnected. The display of some of the Island's ancient industrial artefacts that once stood here has given way to an open space which is intended to become a display about the history and operation of MER wagons. The siding limit contains MER wagons, including, at the time of writing, recently restored No.16 in historically accurate olive livery. A small team of Laxey & Lonan Heritage Trust volunteers has already accomplished an excellent restoration on No.10, their reward being Wagon 10's official re-launch into service as part of the 2014 Railway Events.

Above 1893 Trailer 51 has featured several times on these pages but always in its 'umbrella' form. Prior to its 1987 modification, like sister cars 49-54, its seasonal usage had diminished to just a few weeks each year. Here it is seen as a conventional bulkhead trailer on the Laxey siding in the 1970s. *JC*

The Snaefell Mountain Railway

Although the history and operation of this amazing line to the summit of Snaefell is not a main feature of this book, we do need to see how the SMR cars and their unique line add to the atmosphere of Laxey Station.

The first SMR car for the summit only carries staff and supplies to the Summit Café and usually departs by about 8.45am. The routine at the depot usually means that the crews wash the cars' windows and generally spruce up that day's allocated vehicles outside the Snaefell depot. Two or three mountain cars roll down from their depot to be ready for the first scheduled departure at 10.15am, excepting the 09.45am departures during TT. These trams operate without trailers and their area is the shadier part of the station, where once a wooden awning over the concrete steps protected intending passengers from the rain. It was removed long ago but the indentations in the concrete steps give an indication of its location.

The SMR operated for most of its history from 1895 without the need for a timetable; however, the cars are now timetabled and their scheduled departure and arrival times marry up with whichever MER service is in operation. The MER's 'feeder' service is essential to SMR success. One of the finest times to arrive is on the first car from Derby Castle, when the whole station springs into action. Perhaps a majority of passengers disembark at Laxey, many intending to travel to the summit. As soon as the low road car departs for Ramsey, the first Snaefell departure takes place. Excellent views of the Laxey Waterwheel on the ascent, and Sulby on the descent, are enhanced by the opportunity to see the seven kingdoms: they are the Cumbrian Mountains to the east, the purple hills of Galloway to the north, Snowdonia to the South and to the west, Ireland's Mountain of Mourne in the north and Wicklow Mountains in the south – and, of course, the Isle of Man, the kingdom of man and the kingdom of heaven!

The trucks and ends of the SMR cars differ from their counterparts on the MER. The fell braking system is clearly visible at both ends of the mountain cars. Fell-braking was formerly used on the descent of the mountain, but refurbishment in the late 1970s with ex-Aachen equipment rendered it subsequently an emergency-only feature of operation. The distinctive 'Hopkinson' bow collectors (two to each car) perpetuate the same system of current collection that the coastal route initially adopted as far as Laxey, but abandoned when the extension to Ramsey was undertaken and the whole coastal route was converted to trolley-pole operation. They represent a device from the dawn of electric traction and remind us of the pioneering nature of the stock of both the SMR and MER

Douglas Arrivals and Snaefell Departures

As the first coastal car-set arrives from Douglas, the stationmaster emerges from his office to supervise onward travellers over the MER Northern Section to 'Royal Ramsey'. The capital of the North has revelled in the Royal sobriquet since the visit of King Edward VII and Queen Alexandra in August 1902. Having taken a note of the conductor's passenger count into and out of Laxey, he allows the MER car to depart, whilst the mountain car loads simultaneously.

Once the first SMR car is ready, he strides in the direction of the new pole-mounted SMR control box to set the lights. This done, with a ring of the distinctive ex-Aachen warning bell, the first summit-bound car clangs forward, in parallel with the MER rails through the station, across the A2 and, momentarily adjacent to the MER as far as the point of divergence near to Dumbell's Row. The mountain line begins its ascent for the 'Health-giving trip and Mountain Breezes'. The SMR cars take the right-hand track in contravention of normal running patterns, officially because ascending cars keep to the soft, outer part of the line's formation. Although that is true as far as the Bungalow, the last - and most testing - section to the summit follows a spiral curve to the right, and descending cars run on the soft section. Another

Above Taken on 28th July 2009, this is not a posed view, but occurred naturally as SMR Cars 2 and 5 awaited loading and departure for the journey up the mountain. MER Car 6 was just arriving from Douglas and MER Car 1 was waiting to be driven up to the siding. An unusual feature of Laxey Station is the meeting of two railways with similar numbering systems, offering an opportunity such as this or even cases where trams with the same number can be seen next to each other. **DU**

Right An SMR view for SMR aficionados! This is the 08.30 daily departure from Laxey of the tram for staff working at the summit hotel. The water tank is attached to the Summit end of SMR 6. 9th July 1970. **RP**

Manx riddle! Manx Electric and Mountain line gauges also differ, the mountain line being 6" wider, to accommodate the unusual calliper-style grippers at both ends of each car, an arrangement that allows descending cars to grab the centre fell rail.

Once service cars on both roads have slipped away, then peace reigns supreme once more, disturbed only by the rooks' squawking in mid-flight over Christ Church and above the crennelated viaduct bridge with its ochre tiles over Glen Roy; fortunately, the mid-morning sunlight still filters through the trees and sylvan Laxey is bathed in a glorious glow: ash, beech, pine and even date palms, all flourish here.

I hope you have enjoyed your journey on the MER so far. Enjoy Laxey - but please come back to the MER for the journey on the Northern Line, the jewel in the crown of the island's tramways!

Chapter 4

Laxey
to
Cornaa

Chapter 4:

Laxey to Cornaa

Departure for Ramsey

The ride over the northern section of the MER coastal route begins in Laxey Station, on to 'Royal Ramsey - passing through the garden of the Island', as a sign once informed passengers; the poles that carried the sign remain in situ. Traditional operational patterns meant that the timetabled output was Winter Saloons 19-22 followed by Tunnel Cars in the order of 5, 7, 6 and 9, with more exotic cars confined to the Laxey section or used on the Northern Line only on High Days, as it were. A deliberate attempt to even out the mileage occasions a variety of cars operating the scheduled service; many would not see the light of day otherwise.

A small ceremony accompanies every Ramsey-bound car as it leaves Laxey. The conductor declares the number of passengers on board to the stationmaster; the legend 'Stand clear!' echoes the past, as do two toots of the whistle; the release of the power car's air brake forces a small cloud of grey dust up from the tracks. On series points only, our car set embarks on its long journey north and soon issues a warning to motorists on the A2 'New Road' that it possesses the right of way by hearty prolonged use of the air horn.

An unmistakable feeling of the dramatic commencement of one of the great railway journeys is with us every time we leave Laxey Station; like the quiet start of a favourite symphony whose every note we recollect, so it is here as every movement of the cars is reassuring but exciting. And we instinctively feel that, however magnificent the seven miles to Laxey was, the next eleven to Ramsey are even better.

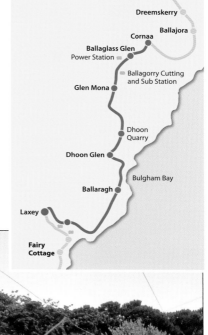

Above Taken on 10th July 1970, we see Car 5 and Trailer 41 at 16.30 departing for Ramsey, as the set commences its 11-mile journey over the Northern Line, that separate undertaking of unrivalled scenery through the Manx Switzerland and ancient glens, as MER publicity proclaimed it! *RP*

Top The map shows the first half of the Northern Line from Laxey to Cornaa.

Laxey Station – New Road – Dumbell's Row – Ham & Egg Terrace

Still employing series only running, the A2 is traversed cautiously as the motor car vibrates from the gentle hum of the motors. This crossing is known as Laxey No.1 to MER staff. The MER tracks gradually veer away from the mountain line as we clunk over the points of the trailer crossover installed in the winter of 2013-4, advance over Mines Road - Laxey No. 2 crossing - onto the new straight alignment (and scene of the ancient Deads from the Great Laxey mines some generations ago) and make our slow

Right The practice of using an open tram as Wire car dates back decades on the MER and indeed carries on today with the use of Car 32. Seen with home made plastic screen protectors around the cab ends is Car 27 near Ham & Egg Terrace. A problem with these additions is that the conductor can't easily deal with the trolley in the case of a de-wirement. Normally the ladders are fixed beneath the underframe but this doesn't really work on a Paddlebox car and so they are attached with string to the brass handrails. Car 27 is currently stored in Laxey Car Shed minus bogies and unlikely to see service again. **IH**

but sedate progress towards Greens Motors (formerly Prince's Motors and Manx Motor Auctions).

The track layout of today after No.1 crossing differs from the past. After the SMR opened in 1895, its terminus changed in both 1897 and 1898. The original terminal point stood immediately next to the Snaefell car sheds (the 1995 shed now stands on the same site as the original), which presented a problem for passengers arriving from Douglas at the MER station near the present Laxey Car Shed. It was quite a walk and the inconvenience detracted from holiday-makers' relaxation. Extensions were made to the MER and SMR lines as further land was acquired. The acquisition of Dumbell's Row enabled an 1897 extension to the mountain tracks, which brought them to a re-sited terminus at a point almost exactly where the SMR double tracks conjoin into a single line to or from Laxey Station.

The SMR station building stood between the current ascent curve on the right-hand track and the MER tracks that sweep across Dumbell's Row towards Ramsey. This building was removed and re-positioned in Laxey station in 1898. Another single line became the final extension for the Snaefell cars from the 1897 terminus right into Laxey Station as we see it today, with a new terminus adjacent to MER arrival and departure points, thus facilitating convenient passenger interchange for the first time.

Below 27th July 2009 and another Poles & Wires car combination! Trailer 52 has been used since the late 1940s as a P-way flat to move heavy items such as rails. In the early years the practice was to remove the body from the underframe in winter, then re-affix it for summer use as a passenger trailer, which now seems bizarre! The Simplex, numbered 40S280, was built in 1966 for the National Coal Board site at Kilnhurst on the outskirts of Rotherham, and is now utilised on the MER. It seems to have never had a defined role, but has proved useful over the years performing various tasks. Although looking somewhat tatty and rusty in this photo, the diminutive 'Yellow Peril' was in fact painted with the rust effect and the body is in surprisingly good condition. *DU*

Palm trees, flowers and a Laxey Commissioners' Notice Board mark the area where the 1897 Snaefell car station stood and now provide a 'country garden' image for Laxey's Café (formerly Browns), which itself dates from 1912. The café stands on 'Ham and Egg Terrace' - the sole remainder of a whole row that once extended up the Agneash road and catered for the crowds visiting Laxey in times past. History has it that local entrepreneurs occupied the whole approach to the waterwheel from the station, providing refreshments, although the residents of the terrace were famed for their Sunday lunches and 'Ham 'n' Egg' specials, an early version of the all-day breakfast! This activity was not without its hazards though: Lily Brown and four other residents were prosecuted in 1914 for 'touting' for business; they were fined five shillings (25p) each.

A feature of this part of Laxey – the statue of the Laxey miner - was sadly removed in May 2008 on account of developing rot, initially in various limbs but latterly throughout the wooden structure. However, an anonymous Laxey resident, who recently died aged 97, left money in her will for a replacement, which is being constructed in Bali by artist and sculptor Ongky Wijana; the artist could not extend his Manx work permit. It is intended to have a wall plaque commemorating the thirty-two miners who lost their lives at various times in the Great Laxey Mines. The plinth and column are reminiscent of Victorian commemorative monuments erected in honour of governors in the colonies.

Some excellent views of SMR cars beginning their ascent or approaching the level after a half-hour descent of the mountain can be obtained here, especially on warm days if you take advantage of Laxey's al-fresco dining area; a brief glimpse of the new SMR shed is also available through the trees behind the tracks.

The Lady Isabella, the Laxey Waterwheel

Perhaps the most famous symbol of Laxey is the 'Lady Isabella' - the great Laxey water wheel - nestling in the glen to the right of Agneash Road. It was designed by the mining company's wheelwright, Robert Casement, under the direction of Mines Captain Rowe, who also built the local brewery, the flour mills and 'Rowe's Pier' down at the harbour. The wheel was built in 1854 to pump water from the Laxey lead and silver mines, remaining at work until the 1920s. Being the largest water-wheel in Europe has ensured its preservation as a tourist attraction. A series of graded walks to suit all tastes and walking ability is well-signposted and a visit inside one of the former mines reveals one of the many tramways and railways that the Island, and specifically Laxey, once boasted. A series of celebrations was held throughout 2004 culminating on 26th and 27th September to mark the 150th Anniversary of the wheel, ownership of which is vested in Manx National Heritage.

A few facts about the wheel make interesting reading: Its width is 6 feet and circumference 227 feet; the length of the axle is 17 feet and its diameter 21 inches; the weight of the axle is 10 tons and the crank 2½ tons; the number of buckets is 168 and the capacity 24 gallons; the normal working speed is 2½ - 3½ revs per minute, and the official horsepower is 185HP. Before we leave the 'World's Biggest Waterwheel', who was the Lady Isabella? She was the wife of the Honourable Charles Hope, third son of the Fourth Earl of Hopetown and appointed Governor of the Isle of Man in 1845. He married Lady Isabella Douglas, eldest daughter of the Fifth Earl of Selkirk, in 1841, which therefore gives the waterwheel Scottish connections too.

Greens Motors – Mrs. Casey's Staircase & The Greaves

A siding was first installed here during World War II for loading and removal of mine waste from the "Deads" alongside; it was later removed, but exactly when is uncertain. A new siding was put in for the operation of Loch (IMR Loco No.4) in 1993, when the loco hauled MER trailers 57 & 58 to Dhoon Quarry in a recreation of the use of steam locomotives during the construction of the Ramsey line. A new siding was laid in 2014.

Our car, still on series points, passes over the former washing floors and the Great Laxey mines Railway and, accompanied by the screech of metal on metal as the bogies turn sharply on this very sharp curve, our tram gains its own right-of-way having journeyed over the A2 again by way of Laxey No. 3 crossing. We have passed the site of the former Isle of Man Road Services bus depot, which ceased operation in 1969. Much argument has

Above 1979's 'Millennium of Tynwald Day' was a very special occasion with celebratory events held all over the Island. The opportunity was taken for a procession of MER cars through Laxey Station, the first time such an event had been held. Ratchet Car 18 is seen with John Matthews at the helm, firmly holding onto the handbrake column as his only means of braking. The specially made 1979 boards can be seen on the roof: from left to right, they showed the Three Legs of Man, the Railway's official transfer and the 'Centenary of World Electric Traction' logo. On hilly Sunnycroft to the right stands 'The Greaves', the well-known guest house run by Mrs Patsy Quirk. *JC*

Centre A superb shot of Ratchet Car 14 against a backdrop decorated by the daily wash hanging in the garden of 'The Greaves'. Note the IOM Road Services building which functioned as offices and accommodation. Also of note is the original Mk1 Ford Transit Van. *JC*

Bottom The daily housework and wash completed, Mrs Quirk, a keen observer of the trams over the decades, admires rare 1894 trailer 37 and chats to its Laxey crew, including Stanley Cannell, aka Agostini. *JC*

taken place over this site and its potential to developers; at the moment the issue lies dormant. The extant building itself dates from 1933, itself being a replacement for the first Road Services depot behind the Commercial Hotel (now the Laxey Health Centre), which was a fire victim, with one bus being lost. The doors were altered after WWII to accommodate double deckers and the nearby house known as Snaefell View (because, allegedly, the mountain could be seen through a crack in the end gable!) was bought and functioned as a waiting room and inspector's office. The house was demolished twenty-five years or so ago.

Looking up from the tram, across the main road, we can see 'Mrs. Casey's Staircase'. These eponymous steps from the roadway up to Sunnycroft were indeed used by the elderly Mrs. Casey, who was a regular MER passenger even in her nineties. She frequently used the winter service and was helped from the stairs to the tram by the conductor. Nestling in the bushes, we see a board advertising 'The Greaves' B & B, which overlooks the MER and SMR; from the garden on a clear day Snaefell summit can easily be picked out. The scenery from here can be breathtaking. On Saturdays, as you sip tea and eat real home-made cakes in the garden, wisps of smoke from Ant and Bee on the Mines Railway below reach your nostrils in this idyllic location! Breakfast is accompanied by the sights and sounds of the mountain railway waking up.

The Great Laxey Mines Railway

A fascinating 'new' line has appeared, or been resurrected at least, and is easily seen from the tramcar between Dumbell's Row and the garage. This is the 'Great Laxey Mines Railway'.

The line possesses a fascinating history and space permits only some minor detail here. The Lewin Engine Company of Dorset built the locos. They were delivered directly to Laxey Harbour and worked the main line from the crusher tipplers and washing floors, running north-westwards from 'Little Egypt' along the north bank of the Laxey River, under the roadway and MER to the main mines' adit. The distance was approximately three-quarters of a mile. They also worked the network of tracks deep into the mines, until 1919, when a strike for better conditions and enhanced wages began; it was destined to last three years, by which time the flooded mines' fate was sealed: without a market and any money to reopen existing fields, or develop any new ones, the Great Laxey Company went into liquidation in March 1922. A smaller scale effort led by Robert Williamson (of the Williamson catering business) and a workers' co-operative, eked out a meagre existence for a further seven years, until total closure came in 1929. The spoil heaps were gradually removed, much of them by the MER. A great part of the ballast around Ballaglass and Cornaa used to be made up of Laxey Deads.

In many ways, the reappearance of the Mines Railway mirrors the resurgent Groudle Glen Railway. It is incredible that two railways which had vanished from the Manx landscape should now provide entertaining trips out for enthusiasts and the general visitor alike. An anonymous donation of £50k was allocated to build a replica of one of the 1875 steam locos 'Ant' and 'Bee' that operated on the line after manual and horse labour was abandoned.

Great Northern Steam Services of Middlesbrough were appointed to construct 'Ant' and 'Bee' replicas. The intention was to have at least one operational before the end of 2003, but that did not happen, one of the problems being certification of the boilers under new European Union rules. The boilers were returned to the manufacturer in December 2003 for completion of the engines. 'Ant' was collected by Richard Booth (of Groudle's 'Annie' fame) on 7th April 2004. She was steamed on 8th May and the evening of 13th May saw Ant run through the tunnel and along the extent of the line. At this time work was still in progress on 'Bee', and the whole project was coming together after considerable frustration, when the Railway Inspector agreed to passenger operation of the railway. After a few safety issues had been resolved, it was possible to implement plans for operation; a small passenger coach was built by Alan Keef of Ross on Wye for this purpose, arriving in July 2004.

Several replica tipper wagons were built and could be seen in the Smithy's yard by the old Goods Shed in Laxey Station for a time before being moved to the line. Their capacity is two tons and they are typical of the two hundred identical wagons once in operation. 'Ant' was steamed as part of the Railway Enthusiasts' weekend in July 2004, when demonstration trains hauling wagons attracted large crowds. At that time, Bee was still awaited from the manufacturers as was the passenger wagon. On 12th August

Bee was delivered and steamed on 28th August for the first time.

Passenger services were finally operated every Saturday during September 2004 and the railway was officially opened by Heritage Trust Chairman and Garff MHK Steve Rodan on 25th September 2004 as part of the anniversary celebrations of the Lady Isabella. 550 passengers were carried on the first day – and the carriage only holds about ten adults! Since then a second carriage has been constructed and delivered to the line. Considerable work on the railway's infrastructure, such as drains and the actual location of the terminus in the area near the adit, has taken place right to the present day. Electric lighting, for example, was installed in the tunnel by former MER electrician, Miles Corlett.

Considerable 'adornment' of the line adds to the visitor experience, including magnificently painted boards by Cyril the Signmann of Fairy Cottage. The boards at either end of the line are informative but also genuine works of art. Several Manx Electric relics have been placed around the area of the Mines Railway engine shed and elsewhere; some discarded MER wheels are strategically placed here too, having come from Car 32 during its major overhaul. The Mines Railway is run very professionally by genuine enthusiasts who can answer all your many questions. It has now settled down to regular, popular and deservedly successful operation. Every member of the team is to be congratulated on the creation of a further visitor attraction, which complements the history and heritage of Laxey. The line is beautiful and offers a real experience to visitors of an important part of Laxey's past.

Return of the Snaefell Mine Waterwheel

A hugely ambitious plan has seen the former Snaefell mine waterwheel re-erected on the Valley Gardens (the former Washing Floors) at Laxey. This took place in September 2003. The components were collected from the llywernog Mining Museum near Aberystwyth, the IoM Public Lottery Trust picking up the tab. Once planning approval had been gained from the Village Commissioners, discussions took place with the Department of Agriculture, Fisheries and Forestry, as the plan was to use water from the Laxey River to turn the wheel. Work was simultaneously carried out to cost replacement rim segment

Above Car 21 and heavy Trailer 57 are seen approaching Laxey from Ramsey on 7th April 2009. This area was once occupied by the Great Laxey Mines washing floors. The waterwheel in the foreground is The Lady Evelyn which is the old Snaefell Waterwheel. The heavy growth of trees now blocks the once impressive view of the Great Laxey Wheel. *DU*

castings and other components. Booth Kelly of Ramsey Shipyard offered to prepare the axle free of charge; other donors and sponsors are listed on a large information board next to the junction of the New Road and Captains Hill.

A vast amount of work had to be carried out. Imagine, for example, just one aspect: the wheel pit of the 42 feet diameter wheel, which had powered the crushing machinery. To clear the pit, part of the footbridge had to be removed as well as the stone wall on the down valley end; then the rough infill needed removing, by use of a mini digger, but the digger required a pile of infill to climb back up. This infill could not be removed by conventional digger so Captain Steven Carter of The Laxey Towing Company was brought in with a dragline! And this was just one small part of work which revealed hitherto unknown facts… one being that the bottom of the pit is some twelve feet below the river and yet there is virtually no seepage.

The grand opening of the Snaefell Waterwheel took place on Sunday 20th August 2006, when it was christened Lady Evelyn. It was set in motion by Mr. Anthony Hamilton, Chief Executive of the Department of Local Government. A family fun day was held in Laxey for this historic day. As the scope for further detail is not available here, I would refer readers to the excellent account of the work in the pages of the Laxey and Lonan Heritage Trust's regular newsletters. The wheel is a tribute to the commitment and dedication of members of the trust whose work significantly enhances the village of Laxey.

Laxey No. 3 Crossing - Little Egypt - Minorca

And now we return to our journey northwards on the MER. I am reminded of some words of the late Mike Goodwyn, which remain with me ever since one of those thrilling 'Motorman Experiences'. I paraphrase his description as, 'Railroading into the raw, into the great unknown', words which fill us with expectation and delight in the early stages of our eleven-mile trip to Ramsey.

With Laxey Station and the former mines' washing floors on the right, passengers with any passion in their hearts begin to understand Mike's words. On its private tracks again, the car's motors briefly 'sing' in parallel points until the motorman allows brief coasting past 'Little Egypt', where the mines' spoils could be viewed standing like the Egyptian pyramids at Giza until around 1930. The tone of the motors changes to a more strained pitch as the car requires full power for the advance to Minorca.

The four traction poles 385-388 were erected in June 1999, after the wires fell down one morning, as motorman Harry Christian was in charge of the first through northbound train of the day. A spectacular dewirement led to the demolition of the overhead, bracket arms and wires. Single-line working was instituted for several days. In honour of Harry, this short stretch of track is still known as 'Harry Christian Alley'.

An accident occurred just north of Pole 386 with Car 20 on 3rd October 2007, fortunately without injuries and without damage to the tram. Car 20 was on Ramsey service without a trailer, the customary practice in the late season when passengers are few. Car 20 derailed its Douglas (rear) end bogie. In a strange coincidence, the same car derailed at the same point some four years previously. The track was notoriously poor at this location, which is sometimes referred to as 'Old School House' because the former National School was located just above the Ramsey line

Next page Open Motor 33 with Trailers 46 & 51 squeal round the sharp curve of Laxey Crossing No.3. This was before points and crossovers were ever dreamed of here. The use of two trailers is exceptionally rare, but over recent years has become a somewhat more accepted special event. In previous years, this was normally the work of 'lightweight' trailers, so that the photographs would resemble stock moves when two lightweights were moved to Ramsey for winter storage. During 2010 several trailers were sidelined with wheel and axle problems, which left little option but for Trailers 46 & 51 to be used. 1st August 2010. *DU*

at this point. The overgrown remains of the path from the MER to the school are only just discernible nowadays, but probably not for much longer. The only remaining part of the school is a section of wall which can be glimpsed more easily when travelling southbound on an open car from Pole 388.

A set of 'alien' poles has been lying on the ground adjacent to pole 387 for some time now and seems to have been forgotten. A narrow pathway crosses the tracks at pole 392. Quirky but

Above Our journey to the north begins ... once the tram has traversed Laxey No.3 crossing by the former Princes Motor garage and the run along the washing floors has started, many enthusiasts refer to the trip as 'railroading in the raw', a phrase beloved by 'amg' (the authority on the MER, Mike Goodwyn). Car 18 is seen in the hands of expert motorman Jimmy Yewdall on a rare working north of Laxey. Note the white valance without a number and the brown footboards applied in the winter of 1982/83. **IH**

Above A scene which has changed significantly over the last ten years or so. The foreground is now the home of The Great Laxey Mines Railway. Car 21 and Trailer 46 are seen working the 16.00 Ramsey to Douglas on 7th June 1969. The conductor can be seen in the typical uniform of the day, the MER-issue brown dust jacket. This seems a rather odd place to be walking down the side of a trailer as surely all the fares had been taken. Maybe he just fancied some air! **RP**

Above Car 20 with an unidentified 40s type trailer and van 16 are seen above Minorca with the 16.30 Ramsey to Douglas on 31st May 1969. The scene here is very different today with trees in far greater prominence. **RP**

quaint paths exist along the entire line, harking back to times before the line's construction, and in most cases they link a farm with a bigger public right of way, in this case to Old Laxey and the beach. Speculation runs that a cross-over was once located here until the 1930s but there is no written or photographic record available.

A century of operation and tradition has left its unique mark, which is often noticed in names that mean very little to the modern passenger or even motorman. One such example is 'Hen Pen Corner' immediately after Little Egypt. It was thought that the name's origin had long been lost to history, but Maurice Faragher, retired MER Engineering Superintendent, advises that this name came about because of the plots of land that sloped down towards the tracks and which can just about be glimpsed on the landward side of the car amidst the lush vegetation. In bygone days, local Laxey folk used the plots as allotments and also kept some poultry. One particularly well-known local, Shimmin, allowed his hens and geese to wander unconcerned and free onto the tracks, hence the name of 'Hen Pen'.

A typical MER bridge over Minorca Stream - just below Minorca itself - by poles 402-3 was constructed by Mark Carine. A Test

House was built here in 1899 to verify the current and voltage from the old power station; it had fallen into ruin by the mid 1930s and was demolished in approximately 1968 for building stone. In wintertime, its position can still be noted through the denuded trees.

Minorca Station

The tram begins to climb the gentle enough 1:38 gradient towards unusually named Minorca, represented by a conventional tin shelter whose nomadic wanderings have seen it in use previously at Halfway House, or Baldromma, on the Douglas to Laxey section. It is the first of several variants on a similar theme to be found between here and Ramsey. The shelter was repainted in July 2002, but lost its name board for a time until 2009. The station has been spruced up with tarmac walkways and adorned with flowers, in sharp contrast with its decrepit appearance on old photographs. Minorca viaduct with its castellations bears all the characteristics of the Glen Roy model and is surely another of Mark Carine's examples. This is a regular halt in summer and

Below Car 1 and Royal Saloon 59 are spotted in 1956 as part of an LRTA organised trip, with flags attached to the roofs. At the time trips like this were very unusual on the MER. Car 1 is carrying the simplified austerity livery and unshaded numeral, whilst No. 59 carries the Manx Electric Railway Co Ltd livery it has had since the late 1940s. The houses to the right of the tram are now virtually concealed by trees and bushes. The stylish station sign is unusually not attached to the shelter.
Vernon Linden

Top Tunnel Car 9 and Trailer 46 are about to coast across the superbly engineered bridge at Minorca. Although constructed on a straight section, the bridge's underside boasts spectacular spiral brickwork. The castellations are in typical MER style as designed by Mark Carine, the most famous example being the Laxey Viaduct. **DU**

Bottom Car 32 is seen from the steps at Minorca tram stop on 30th July 2009. The steep and arduous steps lead up from Minorca Hill Road. A proud looking Harry Christian is seen in the smart uniform issue of the time with an Isle of Man Transport logo. **DU**

Opposite page How many times do you see Cars 1 and 2 pass each other? North of Laxey? Not many! Car 1 and Trailer 51 are seen descending from Minorca, whilst Car 2 and Trailer 60 are in full parallel 'points' up the gradient before stopping at Minorca to collect passengers. Director of Transport Ian Longworth can be seen at the controls of Car 2. Incredibly the youngest tram in this photo is Trailer 60, dating from 1896! **Aaron Boyce**

Above Although much has been written about the MER in the late 60s and early 70s with rose tinted glasses (it is true that the line still possessed much of its original function and exuded an antiquated charm), this photo from 7th July 1973 portrays a different image. The infrastructure and trams were in a very run down condition. In just two years the line to Ramsey would close. The shelter here at Minorca shows the old double window, now just one window. Although clearly a nice sunny day in July the intending passenger is taking no risks and wears a head scarf and coat. To the right can clearly be seen the 'extension' to the wall in differing style. Car 20, Trailer 48 and Van 13 provide the 10.00 Douglas to Ramsey scheduled service. **RP**

is located a short distance from the main A2 'Bayr Rhumsaa' - the Ramsey Road - and near enough to King Orry's grave for a short walk, however there is a daunting flight of steps from the side road to the station. The name of Minorca was reputedly given in honour of a local Laxey sailor who had taken part in the siege of Minorca in 1756 – a battle which the British lost, leaving the island ruled by the French for the next seven years.

King Orry's Grave

An interesting visit can be made from Minorca to the romantically entitled 'King Orry's Grave', which is in fact the Island's largest megalithic tomb. It lies in the garden of a private cottage. The Cairn, which consists of a conical shape of ancient stones that signifies a grave, is twelve metres across and four metres deep. The chambers were once used for burials. This is a fascinating site for those interested in the Neolithic history of Man some 4000 years ago and probably shows a site dedicated by farmers to their ancestors. Traces of flint have been found here from the ancients' ceremonies. To set the myth to rest, the Orry kings were not in fact buried here, but at Iona, Furness Abbey and Rushen Abbey in the south of the island.

Minorca – Laxey Old Road

The gradient becomes steeper above Minorca but presents little difficulty to the cars yet, as the route weaves its way past new residential property that, when built, reflected the strength of the Island's financial economy. In 1999, some of these new residents, unfamiliar with the joyous sounds of electric traction passing the bottom of their landscaped gardens, rashly voiced their disapproval of the noise inflicted upon them. They were soon advised in the Manx Press that the MER was there long before the area was deemed desirable for modern villas by the Island's rich, fashionable and famous. After leaving Minorca, trams rarely stop until Dhoon Glen, so this stretch of approximately two miles represents the longest period of almost continuous parallel points running encountered on the system. Passing through Minorca and onwards allows passengers to enjoy more fine views of Laxey Harbour, the beach and surrounding cliffs. It is not usually long before the realisation dawns on passengers that the views on the approach to Laxey from Douglas were lovely, but even on the early part of the northern line, they are undoubtedly spectacular.

An instruction to the motorman to whistle is often found in apparently obscure places; the toot is probably more of a warning to wild goats nowadays than people, but it is essential that any members of the public, especially ramblers, are made aware of an approaching car. A glance to the right at Pole 424 reveals a crumbling wall and a steep gravelly pathway; this is an old packhorse road from the north, known as Laxey Old Road nowadays but formerly Puncheon Road. A 'puncheon' is a large liquor cask, which creates an image of infamous Manx smuggling. Old Laxey and Laxey Beach, right up to Preston's Crossing can be accessed via this route. Take a look at the old gate here on the seaside line; where did it lead to? There is no evidence of a garden or that it gave access to any farm, so it has obviously been disused for some time. The hinges still remain on the stone pillars.

The gradient profile is 1:27 at this point and it barely fluctuates between that and 1:28 through to Skinscoe at traction Pole 458. The car tackles the challenge with motors singing, though the discerning passenger will recognise and relish the restraint of that harmony even on full nine parallel points: the real test of this ancient equipment is underway.

Above Car 7 with a 40s type trailer and an unidentified mail van at Bonner Corner on the long climb to Bulgham Top. Power is normally brought back to series points here for the tight curve. Car 7 is seen in the early 1990s in a smart looking livery. Of interest at this time were the brown roof and steps, a paint scheme tried sporadically to hide the trolley dust which marks the roofs after a few weeks in service. The whistle on Car 7 was rather unusual at this time in being placed on the front of the dash panel and painted the same colour! *IH*

Laxey Old Road – Bonner Corner

Soon a classic Manx vista of great beauty begins to unfold, which does not belie 1920s' MER publicity leaflets that described the route as 'The Manx Switzerland'. The tracks emerge from wooded hillsides to be surrounded by leafy growth and ferns, with a forward view revealing a sea that really does sparkle here in the sun. Looking back across the valley, the pretty whiteness of cottages and farmsteads dotted here and there, and individualistic groups of houses descending towards Laxey gives an impression of the height above sea level that the line has already successfully achieved. If you were on board as the car approached Laxey, you will have probably noticed the distinctive Glamorgan House at South Cape; the house stands clearly visible now across the valley from the area north of Skinscoe. Equally beautiful is the view further south to Garwick Bay and its smugglers' caves and Clay Head towards Douglas.

As we reach 'Bonner Corner', stretching from traction pole 434 to 440, one of the line's places of great historic interest, the tranquility of Laxey Station is now just over 1½ miles and about eight minutes behind us. Bonner Corner is easily noticed by the passenger as the motorman briefly reduces power to five points of series on the controller for the car to round this sharp corner, then 'notches up' once the car has safely negotiated it. This area gained its name from the famous Bonner wagons, though what actually happened back in 1914, when a well-known accident took place, might differ critically from the tradition that has prevailed ever since then.

Above Still a popular combination, an immaculate looking Car 1 and Trailer 59 are posed by yellow gorse in May 2005. Gorse can be seen all over the MER, especially on the often windswept northern section. The trams stand on a newly ballasted section at Bonner Corner. This was part of a private hire for TRAMS magazine. **NM**

The Bonner Wagons and the Infamous 1914 Accident

Back in 1899, Alexander Bruce, the formidable driving force behind the incredible venture that became the IOMT&EPCo, sought a way of thwarting apparently excessive financial demands on the part of the Ramsey town commissioners. The route had opened only as far as Ballure in 1898 and then through to Ramsey Plaza (the current terminus) in 1899. He purchased four road-rail wagons from Toledo, U.S.A., but in the event, only three seem to have arrived, to transport goods from any part of the town to the railway 'without the assistance of tramlines', and especially to transport coal over company metals to the Ballaglass power station from Ramsey. The wagons were intended to return with setts from Dhoon Quarry, and facilities were laid in at Derby Castle and Laxey to make use of the wagons there too. The wagons had been produced according to the patent of an American of Scottish / Irish parentage, Colonel Joseph Claybaugh Bonner, variously an inventor, industrialist and friend to politicians.

The beauty of the vehicles lay in their ingenious but simple 'twin ramp' equipment that allowed them to be used as road or rail vehicles. The rail wheels were positioned lower than the road ones and the transfer was effected by shunting the wagon onto a siding, where ramps at both sides of the track enabled the Bonner wagons to be raised and the rail wheels released. After being 'de-tracked' or 're-tracked' at any given point, then horse power of a conventional or electric kind could be applied to move them. The Bonner wagons had undergone trial operation for two months in the early part of the 1898-99 winter in Toledo, running on the Toledo, Green & Fremont Railway and the Toledo & Maumee Valley Railway, performing a successful round-trip of thirty miles each day. Insufficient business was given as the reason for their discontinuation. Further operation in Detroit on the Detroit Citizens' Electric Railway and the Detroit & Pontiac Railway took place probably from January to June 1899; all the relevant histories of the above-mentioned lines omit reference to the wagons, which would suggest their innovative and experimental nature.

And now back to the Island ... where the Ramsey Courier of 2nd June 1899 noted the order by the IOMT&EPCo of 'special cars (sic) from America', amid the other news of the fortnightly commissioners' meeting of 30th May, which was chiefly characterised by the disagreement between them and the company over the percentage of operating receipts the council expected from the electric railway in lieu of permission to build. The railway needed coal for the power stations and needed to transport it efficiently, which could have been done with the Bonner wagons. However, the old chestnut that Bruce ordered the wagons in order to circumvent difficulties with the commissioners is not necessarily true, as the minutes of the meeting of 16th May had already noted the order for the wagons. The dates are important here. Much more likely is the view that the company was in the vanguard of new technology, especially from the U.S.A. as it is no exaggeration to say that the line was variously inspired by American operation.

The Light Railway and Tramway Journal of 1st November 1899 records that the wagons had been undergoing an 'experimental trial' on the Island. The first test run was made on 14th August 1899 but no doubt many similar runs, probably after dark, took place. Very few photographs exist of the wagons, but one of the famous ones, posed in Laxey Station, showing them being pulled by a member of the 'Ratchet' Class 14-18, was probably taken during this first run. A second photo shows the same car carrying out a road / rail transfer at Derby Castle. It seems that Colonel Bonner visited the Island in early September 1899, which illustrates the importance of the experiment for him to travel over. Hopefully it was worth the £536 that the sale of the wagons produced for him. The photographs only ever show three wagons in tow - but not necessarily in use - as it seems they were specially posed. It is reasonable conjecture that these were the same wagons that operated in Toledo and Detroit. They would have had to undergo some rebuilding in the period between finishing service in the U.S.A. and arriving on the Island, of course. The essential simplicity of construction would have allowed a relatively easy rebuild from standard to the three-foot gauge of the MER.

It is commonly accepted (though again there is no supporting evidence) that the Bonner wagons entered normal service on 1st September 1899. Problems had arisen with noise disturbance to local residents in Ramsey, as it had become the company's practice to load coal very late in the evening after the service had ceased. Complaints fortunately led to a re-think and the Ramsey Courier of 5th September, reported that the company had special staff placed at Queens Drive, Ramsey, at 9.30pm the previous night, where coal had already been placed. The staff were 'filling wagons' and in sharp time the coals were drawn away by 'Black Maria', leaving the residents able to sleep undisturbed.

This account, however, appears to relate to entirely conventional wagons, rather than the transfer of coal-carrying Bonner wagons from road to rail mode. This raises the question of why the Bonner wagons, supposedly newly in service for just this type of work, were not being used for the very work they were intended and purchased for. It is undeniably fascinating to ponder just how conceivable it might be that the 'Black Maria' referred to was the Andrew Barclay built steam locomotive, which was used during the line's construction and finished up in use on the construction of the Baldwin reservoir. After all, the MER's homemade locomotive Number 23 did not enter service until 1900. Readers might assume we could refer to records, but unfortunately the company records of the time are often sparse and inconclusive – or no longer exist. Further similar accounts in the Ramsey

Courier (notably from 17th October) bemoan that setts from Dhoon Quarry 'have to be carted from the station to the quayside', because the extension had not yet been built. Of course, this should not have been a problem, had the Bonner wagons been in proper, regular use.

As is widely known, the IOMT&EPCo collapsed in 1900. Three Bonner wagons were indeed listed in the Liquidation Stock List of 1901, though this is the last date on which any definite reference, whether written or pictorial, can be found for the wagons as rail vehicles. An article in the Light Railway and Tramway Journal of March 1904 has extensive coverage of all the (by then) MER stock, though not a mention is made of the Bonner wagons. A fascinating MER Goods Rolling Stock Daily Return from 1911 lists all freight stock and even dismantled trailers (so it happened even then, too!), yet no mention is made of the unique wagons. The inescapable conclusion is that the Bonner wagons were decommissioned almost immediately after the expensive experiment with them was concluded.

Several reasons spring to mind. Despite the undoubted excellence of the concept, the rail bogies had no brakes, which presented a danger on a steeply graded line like the MER Furthermore, the bogies had a short 6 foot wheel-base and inside axle bearings, with only rudimentary suspension, which perhaps gave a ride that was too solid. The wagons rode very high, the top edge being approximately 7 foot 6 inches above rail level. Some form of motive power would have been necessary during the road / rail transfers. Taken together, it seems that the MER, with its perpetual twists, turns and difficult gradients with few straight sections on it, proved the wrong line for a short wheel-base, poorly sprung, top-heavy wagon which lacked brakes, especially on long 1:24 gradients during the descent from Ballaragh into Laxey. Nice idea, but wholly impractical!

The legend runs that the wagons' brief history ended on 24th January 1914, when a collision occurred on the corner above Minorca, involving the destruction of two trucks and serious damage to Loco 23 into the bargain, causing their name to be associated ever more in ignominy with this section of track. The fate of the third wagon that was unused, but allegedly still in existence, on that fateful day is shrouded in the famous MER mist of history - probably because of its lack of historical basis. Tradition has its peculiar attraction, but factual history - where its jigsaw can at least be assembled - is far better. After the accident, press reports described the wagons as 'ballast wagons' carrying twelve tons of stones. The description is certainly not apt; the load appears excessive, as each Bonner wagon's maximum was three to five tons, but it should be borne in mind that the weight of different types of loads varies for the same bulk. Apparently, a brakesman was thrown off his wagon during the accident; however, the wagons were quickly re-railed.

All this raises issues that point to the use on that day of conventional wagons, as there was no requirement for a brakesman on Bonner wagons. If the wagons concerned were indeed quickly re-railed, it would suggest that only minimal damage had been sustained and at least the trucks would still be operable. It is simply incredible that excessive loads had been deliberately dispatched southwards, down into Laxey, with obviously inherent dangers.

A further twist to this story is provided by a Permanent way report completed by Robert Newell, the P.W. Superintendent, dated 1903, in which he refers to the 'Bonner Curves', no less than eleven years prior to the accident that apparently gave its name to this location. Common sense suggests that the Bonner wagons had already disgraced themselves, perhaps even on 'Bonner Corner' curve (and elsewhere) almost immediately after their introduction, which might explain why there is no mention of them in the liquidator's fleet list as well as in Newell's report. Another conjecture is that the MER never owned the wagons' frames and therefore they would not have appeared on the liquidator's list. It may well be that MER tradition and legend have some of the essential facts correct (about accidents and incidents of de-railing on curves), but the dates are well and truly blurred. Whatever the explanation proves to be, if ever found, this beautiful spot will no doubt be known forever by the name of 'Bonner Corner'.

Bonner Corner – Skinscoe – Ballamoar

As we leave Bonner Corner, the 100hp underneath the car (110hp in the case of Cars 32 and 33) is fully required as it labours up the rugged coastline. The line turns slightly inland on the approach to Skinscoe, land which was formerly owned by Rushen Abbey in the south of the island and commonly known as 'Abbey Lands', and parallels 'Strooan ny Grogee' (Bobby's River) until this is traversed at Ballamoar, where the line sides are covered with gorse and vegetation, so much so that the lineside area at Ballamoar is heavily overgrown. The area we are travelling through nominally possesses three rarely-requested stops: Skinscoe at Pole 458, which serves the farm only and therefore has no public access apart from by the MER, and Ballamoar 'Down' and 'Up' at Poles 462 and 465 respectively. The idea that these two stops served separate parts of the farm rented out to different people is inaccurate; both stops served only the only farm but were separate stops for north and southbound travel. The contemporary availability of such close stops at mere farm gates more than a century after the line's inception shows how farming communities in this often bleak location utilised the service in times gone by, and occasionally do so nowadays, too.

Above & Right During 2009 a 'viewing platform' was installed at the top of Bulgham Bay, to cater for frequent stops on enthusiasts' tours. This rather smart addition to the MER was brought into use during special events in 2010 but isn't allowed to be used on normal service, which understandably causes confusion when passengers wish to alight here. An MER style board was recently installed simply stating 'Bulgham'. However, this now resides at Derby Castle. The newly installed platform is seen complete with name board on 16th April 2010 **DU**

Ballamoar - Ballaragh - Bulgham

The Ramsey-bound train is now conquering its steepest continuous gradient of 1:24, as it rounds a further curve to reveal one of the most beautiful views the Island can offer. Up towards Bulgham Bay and Ballaragh top, the line defies natural difficulties to present passengers with unequalled, glorious scenic views of

Left The section at Bulgham where the bulge burst in January 1967 has a plain wall and iron fencing to give the appearance of security, although the fencing is merely decorative and masks the line's proximity to the cliff face. Car 19 running single motor is caught in glorious sunshine. The tram appears to have been stopped for a photo with contented passengers visible along with an interested if bemused conductor! Of interest on 19 are the oil lamps required by statute and a memory from earlier times, a throwback to when the cars electricity supply could be somewhat sporadic. The wiper was at this time a relatively new addition and in a rather odd place. The moquette used is somewhat garish but no doubt the comfortable saloons are appreciated by the passengers. *Jim Copland (Photobus)*

a Manx mini Switzerland. Ballaragh - 'The Place of the Rocks' - has the ability in pouring rain or glorious sunshine, to create deeply atmospheric, eerie and delightful effects.

If the car does not have to slow for the many feral goats that stray across 'their' land in these parts, then the first reduction to series running will be as the car negotiates the new Ballaragh crossover at pole 488, almost three pole lengths to the south of the former crossover; the Ballaragh stop is situated by Pole 490, where wooden sleepers have been placed between and next to the tracks to enable intending passengers to use the stop safely. This location provides some favourite photographic opportunities. It must rank as simply one of the most breathtaking views incorporating a tramway anywhere in the world.

From Ballaragh, on clear days the distant Maughold lighthouse and peninsula are visible. The magnificent view out to sea stretches all the way to the Cumbrian coast and hills. You might be lucky enough to spot Corney Fell, Black Combe and even Blackpool on exceptional days. Considering the wildness of this spot, it is perhaps surprising that no shelter has existed here since demolition of the old one as far back as 1973.

Just a little further north lies Bulgham Bay. 'Bulgham' is a diminutive of the word 'Bolg', which appropriately indicates a place subject to gusts or blasts of wind. Bulgham Bay took its name from the promontory. Work on the building of the line originally began here on 15th November 1897. The road was closed for three months while it was diverted up to thirty foot

Top Winter Saloon 22 and Trailer 43 make steady progress on the ascent to the summit. They are seen passing Ballaragh on 7th July 1973. The shelter for the very few passengers who might use this stop, did not survive much longer *RP*

Middle The word 'rare' is often used for different combinations and workings on the MER. However this has to be one of the rarest, taken on the morning of 26th July 2006. Winter Trailer 57 was used the previous evening on a private hire and in the process of running round at Dhoon Quarry ended up with the Ramsey end bogey leaving the rails. The tram spent the night at the Dhoon before being rescued the following morning by the Wire car, Tunnel Car 7. At the time, the old Car 7 was nearing the end of its life and its deplorable state is clearly seen in contrast with the immaculate appearance of Trailer 57. *NM*

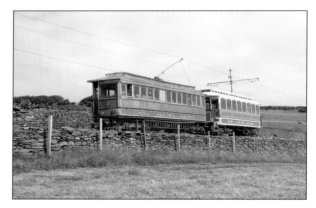

Below Car 6 and Trailer 40 head south at Ballaragh. During 2008 the Ramsey line faced imminent and potentially permanent closure, being open for only fifty-eight operating days. Single line operation necessitated a loop at Ballaskeig and various 'wrong line' moves to avoid the worst of the track. One of these moves is seen here. Note the disconnected crossover. *DU*

inland to allow the tram tracks to be built on its old drystone walled embankment. At one point the tracks were laid on a partly cantilevered shelf, which can be seen near to the summit. This was undoubtedly a flawed construction that should at its very start have aroused fears for its structural reliability. A plan to build a 45-yard viaduct had been briefly floated but was abandoned and so the original road's retaining wall was used to form the support for the tramlines.

During the line's re-evaluation exercise undertaken by Robert Newell in 1903, his comments about the cantilevered tracks greatly perturbed the new Board. Douglas Cooper, their consulting engineer, took the Highway Department's advice to move the tracks onto solid rock and make a consequent change to the road, by cutting back the cliff. Once again the road was closed, this time supposedly for six months, although the work that began in February was not finished until October 1904, after problems caused by a minor landslip. In his report, Newell makes clear he believed that catch points should have been inserted on this section of line (in fact, right from the climb to Minorca to the summit), though that idea regrettably came to nothing.

Above RMS Locotec was awarded the contract for much of the track replacement on the northern line. This extensive work required four locos to be brought to the island to assist with the work, although only three were made operable. With much of the work completed, 2009 had a much more buoyant feel to it than 2008 although there was a feeling that the MER had only just survived. This survival was celebrated too by the staff at RMS Locotec, who duly took part in that summer's special events with several staged runs. One of the most unusual was the working of 'Pig' with Trailer 51 and MER works Car 34 from Laxey to Ballaragh crossover. The lettering in the cab of 'Pig' stated a maximum speed limit of 90 mph! The new Ballaragh crossover is situated slightly further south to that previously installed. **DU**

Above Since the line first opened to Ramsey, its promoters have always advertised the health-giving virtues of riding in the open cars. When sights such as this can be taken in, it is no surprise that the open cars are always enjoyed. Few places in the British Isles can offer such clear blue seas as this, so with the clean air in your lungs, sit back and enjoy the view. It can only be imagined what people from the dark satanic hard-working industrial cities in England must have thought on their holiday travels when taking in such panoramic views. A typical MER consist of Winter Saloon 22, 40s trailer and mail van. **RP**

Right An incredible photo taken in the summer of 1974. What are the chances of taking this photo today and not getting a single road vehicle in the shot! Winter Saloon Trailer 20 and a clean looking 40s trailer have nearly completed the formidable climb to the summit of Bulgham. The sheer beauty, remoteness of the location and ingenuity of the MER's builders can be appreciated, as can the determined effort to move the line further inland in 1903: note the position of the wall. Ballamoar and Skinscoe can be made out and it is hard to imagine how much traffic could ever be generated from here even in the line's heyday. **RP**

Bulgham Bay: The Bulgham Bulge Bursts

Bulgham assumed historical importance on the fateful day of 20th January 1967, when part of an already suspect bulge in the masonry of the dry stone wall embankment at the southern end of Bulgham gave way at 2pm in the early afternoon, just after the 1.15pm Douglas to Ramsey car, Winter Saloon No. 21, had run over the ravine. Surveyors from the IoM Highway Board had already visited the site on 17th November 1966 to examine the wall under suspicion. It was obvious that gradual movement was taking place on account of water pressure building up behind the wall.

There were genuine expectations that repairs would prove uneconomical and that this would be sufficient excuse to shut the line down for good; those were times that had already witnessed a political onslaught against the MER's continued operation north of Laxey. Despite the obvious difficulties, however, and perhaps against the prevailing political odds, both the service and repairs quickly got underway.

Further more serious structural falls occurred on 28th January when the entire wall collapsed, but even by that time, MER cars had already established a pattern of operation. 'Stranded' northern cars 7 and 21 provided the service from Ramsey to Bulgham, where passengers walked to waiting tramcars south of 'The Great Divide' (or 'The Gap'). Other tramcars cars were transferred to the Northern section as the summer season approached, including Power Cars 14 and 16 and trailer 36 - if only we could ride those cars regularly nowadays to Ramsey! Car 14 had until then been regularly used by the Permanent Way gang between Laxey and Bulgham.

This temporary operation, which also necessitated some minor modifications to the timetable to allow passengers to walk 'The Gap', proved very successful, until the re-inauguration of the through service on 10th July 1967. By that time, the cliff and its face had been stabilised by the Italian technique known as "Reticulated Pali-Radice". This patent piling system, carried out by Fondedile Foundations Ltd., involved positioning a latticework structure of some 116 three-inch diameter piles into the unstable land in four parallel double rows. Liquid grout was poured into boreholes. A scheme of interlocking pre-cast units replaced the parapet wall and the job was rounded off by some additional extra-deep vertical piles, creating a section filled with concrete. Once this was successfully tested and shown to be secure, the overhead was re-erected and at 07.00 on 10th July, the first through car (ironically No. 21, which had been moved to Derby Castle as soon as the physical links had created a through line again) set off from Derby Castle for Ramsey and Car 22 departed Ramsey at 7.15am for Douglas. The MER had resumed its interrupted service and the lack of any great publicity showed the customary commitment to 'simply getting on quietly with the job'. Incidentally, the use of steam in the construction of the line meant that a temporary shed was constructed, supposedly at the south end of the Bulgham wall, more or less in the spot that Newell wanted a refuge siding.

Further problems at Bulgham - 1983

A principal task of the MER's Chief Engineer is responsibility for the maintenance and preservation of the route. When Maurice Faragher was appointed to that position in 1983, his was a baptism of fire: an incipient slip at the north end of the Bulgham embankment (further north than the 1967 troubles) was giving cause for concern. A bulge had appeared in the retaining wall giving rise to doubts about the stability of the rock material below, which seemed to be shifting partially as a result of the drainage from the road above. Immediate steps were taken to remove loose material, which revealed the foundations of the original road before the track was set further back on the landside in 1903. Holes were driven down to a depth of 20ft, then old rails were positioned and concreted in to form a new retaining wall. Resin-bonded reinforcing rods were added to give greater strength, the area then being filled and concreted, and the wall rebuilt along the original line.

In 1995, parts of the rock face adjacent to the road at Bulgham fell away, but caused no damage to the MER; the road was temporarily closed and two hundred tons of fallen rock, including a large part that had to be deliberately blasted away, was removed. The rock face was treated by Divetech and covered by netting to prevent direct falls onto the road. In 2001, REDS of Rugby were employed by the Department of Transport to inspect the cliff faces here and on the Marine Drive between Douglas and Port Soderick. Descaling work has been carried out regularly at these locations.

The storms of early January 2005 caused considerable collapse of rock from the cliff face onto the roadway at Bulgham; 2½ tons fell in February, which necessitated traffic being diverted over Ballaragh for several weeks. Unfortunately remedial work did not prevent continued falls, so the road was closed again for several months for stabilisation work to be undertaken. The rock is thin to medium bedded mudstone or siltstone and is weak, which means erosion in poor weather is likely.

The preferred method of stabilising the rock face features rock bolting, utilising stainless steel rods of 20mm diameter, drilled into the rock face, grouted and stressed. These act as anchors for the safety netting, which is comprised of stainless steel mesh bolted to the rock face at 3m centres, which are held by further rods at the top, these being of 30mm diameter bolted into the rock and surrounded by a concrete block. The new netting is much more effective in preventing rock falling onto the roadway and endangering traffic. In total 1,760 metres of rock drilling on the rock face took place; 8,000 square metres of mesh was used; 6,400 metres of steel support cable applied; 214 anchors located and over 800 rock bolts. The clean up removed 130 tons of rock and debris: the total cost was £423k.

So, as well as being famous for its views of mountainous scenery and those invigorating breezes so beloved of old MER advertising, this area is infamous for its landslip problems. Alight from a car at Ballaragh or the new Bulgham stop, one day and take a look for yourself. Take a deep breath as you peer over the edge and down to the clear blue sea of Bulgham Bay, and do not be too troubled that the apparently solid looking bars running along the parapet wall's top are really only angle-iron railings there to reassure passengers by resembling a solid bar. The cliff-edge provides an exhilarating viewpoint, especially when you ponder the true nature of the line's location. It is a glorious spot, well able to rival the scenery of the old Douglas Southern Marine Drive route to Port Soderick. You are privileged to be present if it is one of those especially bright, glorious mornings, when the limitless, broad, azure sky dazzles and, dancing on the water's shimmering surface, is reflected in the crystal-like waters, which in turn throw up soft, woolly tufts of gentle white surf, as the sea breaks on the rocks. This magical place possesses a sense of natural timelessness; merely being here is therapeutic.

Left During the summer of 2007 trailer 37 made several sorties on the Ramsey timetabled service, thanks to the enthusiasm of yardman Nick Pascoe to vary the cars seen on service. Saturday 28th July 2007 was in fact the third consecutive day that Car 6 had worked with Trailer 37. This genuine 1894 combination was much appreciated and made a great sight, seen here directly over the 'bulge' at Bulgham. The repair work undertaken here in 1967 and in the years since is clearly seen underneath the passing tramcars. *DU*

Bulgham - Summit Curve

Repairs have recently taken place to the stone wall separating the main road and tramline between Bulgham Bay and the summit. Between Poles 500 and 502, a new section of wall was built and adjacent to Pole 509 are steps rising to the road, although the right side exit is blocked off. Other work involved underpinning to part of the retaining wall of the tramline; a short section of track was removed by pole 498 to allow the work to be carried out. The different colour of the ballast from the surrounding area marks the spot. In July 2009, a new viewing platform was constructed for the MER adjacent to Poles 507-8. Its designated use is for tram tours which might stop here to admire the stunning view. During Enthusiasts' events, trams stop here for a couple of minutes. Experience shows, however, that people walk right up to the original wall rather than standing on the viewing platform. It is not considered a regular stop although MER drivers regularly pick up passengers here!

The gradient very noticeably relaxes from Pole 504 onwards; the sound from the motors underneath the car gives way from the constant but even growl to a more confident, higher pitched musicality with a consequent increase in speed: whichever car it is, it feels as if it is powering ahead much more quickly towards the summit than during the long, testing climb just passed so successfully.

A little further towards the curve around which the line disappears from view is the highest point: 588 feet above sea level, higher indeed than Blackpool Tower. We are now some ten miles out of Douglas, which was left forty-three minutes ago. It is a quite incredible daily achievement, summer and (occasionally) winter, for vintage tramcars of a minimum of 109 years' age, especially if you consider that almost anywhere else such cars would be utilised only as occasional museum pieces. Listen to the harmonious hum of the motors as the gradient relaxes towards the summit and a definite acceleration and bite is noticeable from the motors below, like tamed but straining horses enjoying their second wind. As the tram begins to round Summit Curve, the exact highest point is then achieved, halfway between Poles 515 and 516.

Immediately after pole 514, keen-eyed passengers might notice a plaque set into the rock on the landside. This monument commemorates Mike Goodwyn. Although Mike joined the MER as a motorman in 1989, his career had taken him to many parts of the world and had been as varied as the man's interests. Some regulars to the Island recall him managing the Sefton Hotel in Douglas; others, whose memory stretches to the darkest days when the line was nearly lost in 1976, remember Mike as a key driving force behind the retention of the line and its survival. In fact, Mike was much more than this. He was the renowned authority on the MER as well as the Island's other railways and, even when detractors disagreed with him, they nonetheless acknowledged his love for the MER was genuine, profound and total. The MER was his motivation in life.

Mike's knowledge was unsurpassed; his books about the MER and other island tramways are remarkable for their incisive display of knowledge. Mike suffered a major heart attack in 1995 which prevented him working as a motorman again, but we enjoyed his company instead on the back platform, as Mike became the regular Ramsey guard until his untimely death on 5th October 1999. A round trip with Mike soon revealed his depths, as the tribute to 'amg' in MTR 79 p47 notes: "He was in the true sense a Renaissance Man, Mechanical Engineer, Scientist, Artist, Writer, Wit, Mimic and Raconteur."

Mike's funeral was a fine affair. After the church service at Ramsey, the coffin was transferred to a hearse and moved to Ramsey Station, where Cars 20 and 37 awaited. The coffin was placed on specially converted trailer 37. Car 20 was fitted with black drapes for the journey and left the station at 1.30pm. It was driven by MER craftsman Jimmy Yewdall, commonly regarded as the finest motorman prior to his retirement. He was in the expert company of former Chief Engineer Maurice Faragher, and Alan Corlett - at that time Events' Coordinator - acted as guard. Many people lined the route for a final sad goodbye. Transport Chief Executive, David Howard, met Cars 20 and 37 at Derby Castle in the company of the Minister, Mr. David Cretney. The hearse took Mike's coffin to Peel Cemetery for internment. A preserved Douglas Corporation AEC Regent III, suitably carrying black drapes, travelled with the hearse. The headline of the Isle of Man Examiner for 19th October summed up this extraordinary funeral: "A fitting final journey for world authority on trams".

Above Mike's Car 32 and Trailer 61. No. 32's accepted matching trailer is in fact No. 62. However, pictures over the years show that Cars 32 & 61 have spent several seasons operating together. When the trams were last repainted, it was decided that Cars 32 & 62 would have the red and white livery whilst Cars 33 & 61 adopted the red and cream livery. This photograph therefore shows the odd combination of a white-roof motor with cream-roof trailer. It will also be noted that No. 61 has painted clerestory roof windows, whereas No. 62 does not. On 11th May 2004 this rather bizarre scene was captured: Car 32's compressor had failed, and the pair was driven back to Derby Castle empty on the handbrake, in the hands of the conductor. A far cry from when amg used to drive Car 32 on the handbrake in service to give the smoothest possible ride! Without a compressor, and therefore no air for the whistle, the gong had to be used for the journey, rekindling memories of Ratchet cars. An idyllic setting here at summit curve with gorse bushes growing wild on the cliff tops. *NM*

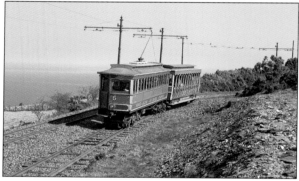

And so it was that on Wednesday 14th August 2002, Cars 5 and 47 transported a party to the line's summit, where a plaque was unveiled, with the intention of acting as a memorial to Mike Goodwyn as well as marking this particularly magnificent feature of the line. The plaque was designed by Alex Townsend of the MERS, who successfully combined the dual purpose of the plaque with an inscription taken from the closing lines of the chapter on Motorman Training in Mike's book 'Manx Electric'. Accurate and very tasteful depictions of two vehicles close to Mike's heart are included: MER Car 32, his favourite tramcar upon which he lavished attention, and Mike's North Western Road Car Bristol L5G (AJA 118).

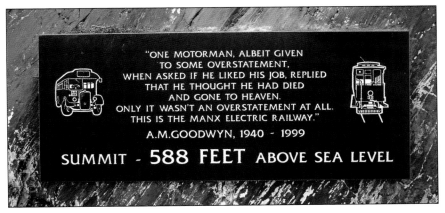

"ONE MOTORMAN, ALBEIT GIVEN
TO SOME OVERSTATEMENT,
WHEN ASKED IF HE LIKED HIS JOB, REPLIED
THAT HE THOUGHT HE HAD DIED
AND GONE TO HEAVEN.
ONLY IT WASN'T AN OVERSTATEMENT AT ALL.
THIS IS THE MANX ELECTRIC RAILWAY."
A.M.GOODWYN, 1940 - 1999
SUMMIT - **588 FEET** ABOVE SEA LEVEL

The inscription runs:

'ONE MOTORMAN, ALBEIT GIVEN TO SOME OVERSTATEMENT, WHEN ASKED IF HE LIKED HIS JOB, REPLIED THAT HE THOUGHT HE HAD DIED AND GONE TO HEAVEN. ONLY IT WASN'T AN OVERSTATEMENT AT ALL. THIS IS THE MANX ELECTRIC RAILWAY.' A.M.GOODWYN, 1940 – 1999 SUMMIT – 588 FEET ABOVE SEA LEVEL

The plaque was produced by David Gregg, monumental mason of Tromode, Douglas. It measures 36 inches in length (915mm) and 15 inches in height (380mm).

Before we leave this section of our journey, there is another enigma left to us by Robert Newell. He makes a tantalizing reference to a quarry at Bulgham in his 1903 Report on the Condition of the Permanent way. Writing about the poor ballast on the section above the 'Bonner Curves', Newell states it was mostly 'Bulgham Quarry rubbish and is a poor class of stuff as it holds water and pulverises under the action of the cars and weather.' He can hardly be referring to Dhoon Quarry, but the location of the one at Bulgham is unknown.

An avid reader of MER publicity - and timetables - over the years will recognise the emphasis that has always been placed on the 'Invigorating Trips on the Open Cars' or 'Health-giving Sea and Mountain Breezes'. If you have crested the Bulgham Summit on

Above If one person ever epitomised the Manx Electric Railway, then it was A M Goodwyn, or simply 'amg'. The plaque at the summit of the line is an appropriate memorial for a great character to whom the MER is indebted. A leading member in the battle for the survival of the line in darker times, he played a pivotal role in the 1993 Centenary celebrations, still regarded as one of the best railway events ever hosted. The plaque refers to two of his greatest passions, his preserved bus and the MER. The plaque's sentiments so simply expressed encourage us to spare a few thoughts for 'amg', a particularly poignant moment when riding his favourite car, No. 32. *NM*

Opposite page centre Car 5 and Trailer 44 head north after conquering the most difficult section of the route. Beyond Summit curve, they can now coast a little down to Dhoon Glen. This set was working D2 diagram departing Douglas at 10.40 on a sunny but cool 16th April 2010. The motor carries the unique 'Raad-Yiarn Lectragh Vannin' lettering, but it is starting to look somewhat work stained here, after spending the previous winter based at Ramsey where, with various seats removed, it was used on works car duties. At this time the car was 116 years old and helping out on P-way, before a busy summer on service again. Car 5 has since received a heavy overhaul and once again looks immaculate as befits a tramcar nicknamed 'The Shrine'. *NM*

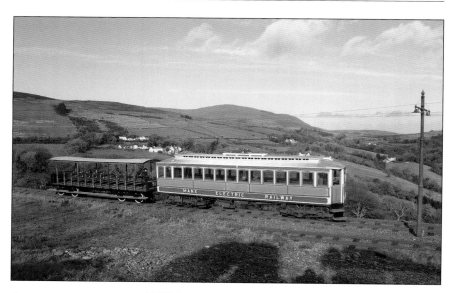

Above One brave soul has taken on the challenge of riding Trailer 51 in November! An unusual pairing of Car 6 and the most open trailer is captured on 1st November 2013. The use of lightweight trailers is exceptionally rare even at the height of summer. In low winter sun, the pair heads back to Douglas and is about to negotiate summit curve and then coast down over two miles to Laxey. With views across towards North Barrule, this is one of the most picturesque parts of the route. *CP*

Right From the inception of the line right up to the 2000s, if you were to describe a 'typical consist' on the Ramsey service, then this would be it. For over a century, the Winter Saloons have made the Ramsey line their own. Seen in the summer of 1974 are Saloon 19, Trailer 43 and Van 12. The yellow gorse is very much in blossom here with a glorious panorama beyond! *RP*

an open power car, or more likely, an open crossbench trailer, then you will be able to verify the truth of these MER claims. You might also recollect at this point the words of the famous Manx author, Hall Caine, who likened riding parts of the line (surely including this area) to the then new Sorrento to Amalfi coast road. He claimed: 'It is in parts only second to it in beauty… the safe and commodious cars are great contributors to the education and happiness of the thousands who make the Isle of Man their annual resort'. It should perhaps be added MER motormen display considerably more care than daring Italian coach drivers on the Amalfi coast road.

Summit Curve - Dhoon Glen

It is not hard to imagine the popularity of Manx glens for Victorian and Edwardian visitors, who had temporarily escaped the drab cobbled streets of northern satanic mill towns. A glen like Dhoon must have seemed charming and idyllic. Such was Dhoon's fame in the 1880s, long before the MER reached here in 1898, that a regular attraction was to sail here from Douglas in the 'Inney Wooar' pleasure boat. 8000 people came by boat in June, July and August of 1895 and incredibly 42000 came by road, a not insignificant feat in those times. Tree planting continues today as part of the management of the glen with ash, wych elm, alder, sycamore, birch and mountain ash to be found here.

For anyone standing just around the curve that marks the Bulgham summit, the swish of the trolley pole and the ringing hiss of its bronze wheel on the overhead herald the appearance of a car. The motorman usually applies five series points for a brief couple of seconds to pull the car out of the curve and enable it to start its powerless glide down to Dhoon Glen. The hardest part of the whole journey to Ramsey is already over.

The thick, tall trees to the right of the car grow up from the steep sides of the glen below. In the line's early days, the IOMT&EPCo rented the glen and charged 4d (1½p) for admission, with almost half being paid to the owners; incidentally similar charges were made at other glens, such as Garwick. Fortunately, this is one area of life that has become less expensive: Manx National Glens all have free admission. The name 'Dhoon' probably derives from 'Dhowin' meaning 'deep', which will immediately strike a chord with visitors, considering the steepness and depth of the glen. On the other hand, it might find its origin in 'Doon', meaning 'a

Top left 22nd July 2009 and Winter Saloon 22 is running 'single motor' to Ramsey, which became an unavoidable occurrence: so many trams and trailers were withdrawn with defective wheels and axles, that there was little choice at times but to run single motors until the affected cars could be fixed. Car 22 looks somewhat tired as did many of the trams at the time. Thankfully there are now adequate serviceable trailers and the fleet is looking much more presentable year-on-year. No. 22 has the air whistle attached to the front at this time, but by 2014 it had been repositioned underneath the cab. Bus No. 44 on the right is now re-registered as E17 BTS becoming No. 350 in the Blackpool Transport Fleet. The sign warns of the wild goats that roam from here to Skinscoe! **DU**

Top right With nine 'points' on the controller, the motorman of Car 16 has left Dhoon Glen to ascend the steep gradient to the summit. With all the shutters down, we can assume that the weather is not as clement as it might look. This was a 'special' from Ramsey to Douglas on the 15th July 1970. It is somewhat ironic that number 1 in the charts that week was 'In The Summertime' by Mungo Jerry, with its eulogy of the golden age of long hot summers that we happily recall! One can only presume that the gloveless driver would be glad to get back into Laxey after the breezy ride over Bulgham and down the hill. There used to be an unwritten accepted order in which the MER allocates its tram cars. Once the enclosed cars had been used, then the order would be 32/33, 25/27/26, 16 followed by the ratchets and Cars 1 & 2. **RP**

193

Above Friday 1st November 2013 was a day for rare workings: Trailer 60 is on Ramsey service with Car 20 on the 10.40 working. This view of Dhoon Glen shows perfectly some key features of the stop, including the new shelter installed in 1987 complete with station sign. The white building has long been a cafe. Chairs and tables are stored in the shelter, supposedly to keep goats out but quite successfully preventing passenger access too! The archway to the left was the former entrance into the MER owned glen, and a glimpse behind the bricked off wall shows the turnstile still in place! It's hard to imagine the days when a turnstile was needed for intrepid walkers, possibly staying at the MER owned Dhoon Glen Hotel until 1932, when it was destroyed by fire. *CP*

fort'. If this seems unlikely, it isn't: north of the glen lies Doon Veg, meaning 'little fort', and which is part of the area known as Kerroodhoon, owned by the family of Skillicorns in the nineteenth century.

Although Dhoon Glen is not for the fainthearted, amateur ramblers should not miss the deepest glen on the Island, which contains forty-four acres. As soon as the tram disappears, and you begin to descend the steps next to the tram tracks of Dhoon Glen Station, rural quietness falls and prevails. A steep yet attractive descent leads along a route of perhaps the finest sylvan settings the Island can offer, all the way down to the sea. The variety of birdsong here is amazing and an occasional accompaniment to the sounds of nature is the sweet hum of a tramcar's trolley-wheel on its swishing pole, which soon subsides as the tram continues its journey and nature peacefully reasserts itself. The path hugs the river the whole way. You will see the old lead and zinc mine workings (which were active until the middle of the 19th Century) and the stone wheel-case, which is preserved. This housed a 50-foot wheel to pump water and lift the ore from the shaft beside it. It seems the mine never really proved a good business venture.

Left Dhoon Glen on the 4th June 1969 and Car 19 and Trailer 44 have just stopped to pick up an intending passenger, having departed Douglas at 16.00 and scheduled to arrive at Ramsey at 17.15. The old waiting shelter dating back to 1898 lasted until 1985. Car 19 has the double headlamp complete with oil lamp on the front. The pronounced sag in the body that the winter saloons suffered at the time is very obvious here. **RP**

The silence of Dhoon is remarkably pure and is created by the elimination of low-pitched sounds of traffic from the busy A2 by the density and height of the trees, though the tinkling sounds of the river babbling away are perfectly audible before being visible. The waterfalls provide an ideal accompaniment to sandwiches and a flask as the lunchtime hour approaches. It is well worth the struggle of an energetic 600 foot climb back, punctuated with occasional rests to observe the ferns, brackens and moss that also nurture innumerable coloured fungi in season. This is exactly the kind of magical Manx setting for your musings on traditional local tales of the 'little people'. This glen undoubtedly holds something special for all the seasons: in spring, carpets of bluebells and anemones shine with blue-white hues; summer is a cool, refreshing musical paradise amid dense foliage that occasionally allows golden bursts of sunlight to penetrate, and autumn a refuge of delicate pictures of orange and yellow, as the soft peaty ground is enriched with that year's decaying and dead leaves.

For those who succeed in reaching Dhoon Beach, they find a secluded and majestic stony place ideal for sunbathing and picnics, with high rocks jutting provocatively and climbing steeply from the very sea; these are known as the 'Dhoon Flags', and are a very special feature of the area. Remember to allow sufficient time for the relatively steep ascent back to the tram tracks, but be mindful of the Manx attitude towards time, Traa-dy-Liooar, which translates as "time enough" - don't hurry, just enjoy it and keep the memory safe. You can always take a breather on one of the wayside seats and muse upon the views or catch sight of a fulmar petrel nesting on the steep ledges and gannets diving for fish out to sea.

Above One of the fascinating characteristics of the Manx Electric Railway is how the landscape changes so quickly. Within a few minutes, the cliff tops of Bulgham have been left well and truly behind as the MER takes on the feel of an inter-urban trolley wending its peaceful, if twisting and winding, way through the countryside. Car 22 and Trailer 41 are seen near Burn's Crossing as denoted by the flag attached to pole 540. 19th May 2006 **NM**

Dhoon Glen – Dhoon Quarry

Back at the tram tracks, the Dhoon shelter is one of the MER's wooden examples and was erected in 1987. One of the attractions of stopping here in recent years was certainly to sample the delights of the café known in different incarnations as 'Jean's Place', 'Henry's Halt' or simply 'Dhoon Café'. The café building was the original ticket office for the glen and remains of the former turnstiles were uncovered during refurbishment in 2006. In 2009, Dhoon Glen halt became a compulsory stop; regrettably long since vanished is a rustic building including a stationmaster's office - again a sad illustration of how the line's patronage has declined and not always just in its recent history.

The car park opposite used to be occupied by a hotel owned by the MER, but which fell victim to the blight of fire - another rather tragic MER (and Manx) tradition - early on 3rd April 1932. A certain mythology builds up about such events: in this case, the story runs that the licensee, Reginald Cain, had already moved his furnishings and belongings into a barn further up the field behind the hotel some time before the fire started. The fact that he and his wife were out visiting relatives in Douglas seems to have heightened suspicion. We will probably never know what the real story is. The hotel was built by the IOMT&EPCo and reflects their early intentions to branch out into other concerns. Licensed hotels and refreshment rooms were also built at Laxey, Douglas, the Bungalow and SMR Summit, as well as here at Dhoon Glen. It appears that plans even existed for the company to build a new brewery to supply these premises, though the plan was fated to collapse as a result of the financial storm clouds gathering and threatening to burst over the Company's future. Some remains of the hotel's foundations can be found amongst the luxuriant plant growth at the rear of the car park, should anyone wish to look for them. Just as the insubstantial insurance monies failed to fund replacement trams after the 1930 fire that destroyed Laxey car shed, so in 1932 a replacement hotel could not be financed. The structure was beyond repair and its remains were removed from the site. If you park your car here or take a break by tram, take a look at the interesting arboretum.

One of the Manx Electric's undoubted attractions is its constantly changing scenery. After the harsh climb towards the summit, the turn away from Ballaragh and Bulgham heralds a change towards a much more bucolic landscape after Dhoon Glen, as the car rolls through pleasantly wooded valleys in the shadow of North Barrule. The list of stopping places on an MER conductor's list illustrates the rural nature of a service once dedicated all year round to its surrounding farming communities: we pass Burn's crossing at pole 540, then Dhoon Manor with a farm gate as a halt; this is Dhoon Farm at Poles 549-550. This area is usually referred to by MER staff as 'Dhoon Platt'. A section breaker is located on the seaside overhead at Pole 539, but not the landside. Stencilled pole numbers are only partially inaccurate on this section. The modern plastic discs are correctly numbered, but the old painted ones on every fifth pole occasionally deviate by one hundred lower than they should be. This is another feature of the MER, which might confuse some, but is obviously a long-standing feature of the line, which every member of the driving staff, P.W. and Poles & Wires gangs knows about.

Some of the farm crossings, such as Dhoon Platt now have sleepers laid across the tracks. They are used by locals and the placing of old sleepers there makes crossing the tracks much easier and safer, as well as more economical than tarmac. Dhoon Quarry and sidings deserve a special visit, to try to capture the essence of what the MER was like in its heyday. The fifty-odd

Top Car 19 and Trailer 40 rattle through Dhoon Quarry with the 13.45 Ramsey to Douglas on 7th July 1973. The track at this time was unchanged from its heyday, when heavy use was made of this site for transportation of stone brought in by a narrow gauge railway and an aerial ropeway. The tracks to the right can just be made out. The double necked headshunt offered access to the sidings as well as the aerial ropeway. On the left was the site of the crusher on the track which would later have a facing point added as part of the Steam on the MER celebrations in the 1990s. The loading dock on the left was served by the narrow gauge railway which traversed the road by the extant Smithy now used as stores. **RP**

acre granite quarry that lies north of Dhoon Glen gave rise to a well-developed area of great importance to the MER; its alludes to the grandeur of a different age. Little action seems to occur here now, other than an occasional train passing through. At the time of writing, the selection of vehicles stored here varies; it might include Dreadnought 21, former trailer No.45 (although this often resides in Laxey Car Shed), and two tipper wagons, as well as former RMS Locotech diesel engines. The site had been greatly used during the 2008-9 relay of the track. Quantities of rail were - and still are - stored here, as well as discarded points and other relics ripped up after a hundred plus years of use.

The intertwined history of Dhoon Quarry and the IOMT&EPCo. - superseded by the MER - is illuminating for what it tells about this innovative company. Prospects of financial

Bottom A delightful looking Car 1 and 40s trailer pass through Dhoon Quarry on a rare working to Ramsey on 24th July 2005. The amount of times which Cars 1 and 2 work to Ramsey in a year is rarely into double figures, with most of their time spent between Douglas and Laxey or on private hires. The impressive remains of Dreadnought stone wagon No 21 can be seen on the left, at this time in use as a heavy ballast hopper. This modification was removed in 2008. **NM**

Above The deplorable state that the railway was allowed to fall into by 2007 can be seen perfectly here! 'Shrine' 5 and Trailer 47 are depicted on 26th July 2007 climbing out of Dhoon Quarry amongst tracks overgrown with grass and weeds, reminiscent of pre-nationalisation days. The new stacks of sleepers are a hopeful sign. The 'dish' that Dhoon Quarry sits in can be seen well here. Car 5 has usually been the first choice tunnel car after the Winter Saloons have been allocated and usually clocks up a high annual mileage. *DU*

profitability from developing the site must have played an important part in Alexander Bruce's determination to reach Ramsey. He leased the Dhoon and Dhoon West quarries from 1895, shortly after the 1894 opening of the line as far as Laxey, and brought men over from Dalbeattie, the Scottish granite centre, to develop and work the site. The quarries provided setts for paving of the route of the Upper Douglas cable line (another IOMT&EPCo. project), but Bruce's keen business acumen anticipated profitable exports to the mainland. A line ending at Ramsey harbour and meeting up with the MNR would facilitate this venture; exports did begin prior to the line's inauguration.

The company constructed special 12-ton bogie stone wagons, known as 'Dreadnoughts'. They stood in special sidings waiting to be supplied initially by two-wheeled horse carts each with a capacity of 1,700 lbs. They were quickly superseded, however, by the construction of a 2' 0" gauge tramway from Dhoon West quarry through a narrow tunnel to the MER sidings, and an efficient aerial ropeway system that carried output from Dhoon Quarry to the sidings. The Highways Department some time ago converted the tunnel's mouth into a drain, which is located immediately by the stores building and remains clearly visible. Mike Goodwyn had searched the area for the tunnel's exit into the quarry itself but that proved fruitless, though it must remain, as the quarry is flooded now, but the water level rises and falls, proving there is a feed out at some point.

The quarries were first closed in 1900, a casualty of the Dumbell's Bank collapse, but they were re-purchased by the fledgling MER in 1903. Rail haulage of stone gradually became less profitable in the 1920s and ceased completely in the 1930s. No longer a hive of activity, the Dhoon generally presents a very quiet and rural aspect, although personally I much prefer the presence of works vehicles, 'bits and pieces' and artefacts that prove the line is alive; they give it atmosphere and generate a nostalgia that heritage railways should tap into. Sadly the remains of disused cars and the 'Creosote Cottage', which stood behind the loading dock and was demolished in the winter of 1979-80, are only a distant memory from a visit decades ago or a photographic reminder.

A rickety, blackened and well-rusted tin shelter was erected at Dhoon Quarry at some time in the dim and distant past by the quarrymen, who would have needed protection from the winds that bedevil the island in the winter. As the entrance faced north, a viewing hole was made in the south side so that intending passengers could see the Ramsey bound cars (if the wind drowned out the sound of the car!). Positioned close to the point where the road and tracks cross, it survived until 2003, although not under the care or ownership of the MER. Its continued survival was impossible as it reached a stage of imminent collapse. Perhaps unsurprisingly, no new shelter has appeared.

The remains of two short poles alongside give the impression that a place name board was once displayed here, but that is not so; until 1981 a pole-mounted box housed the "traction telephone" which was replaced by radio-telephone equipment on the cars themselves. A single line ran alongside the shelter and next to the roadway; it is not known when it was removed but apparently it was long before the former sidings adjacent to the seaside line. Unfortunately accurate dating is not always possible with the MER; quite often records were not kept and even when they were, much has been destroyed.

The sawmill that can be seen in many old photographs was demolished in 1973. On the landside of the tracks, over by the roadside stands the former Smithy. This was leased off until 1992 but is now a P.W. store; note the time-table pasted to its door for the line's few patrons in this area. Perhaps the most interesting alteration to the layout of this part of Dhoon Quarry was the construction of a new siding, along with watering facilities, in 1992-93 in readiness for the MER's 1993 Centenary celebrations. These jaunts featured IMR Loco No. 4 'Loch' in steam on the MER, pulling winter trailers 57 and 58 as far as the quarry, a highlight for enthusiasts that was repeated for subsequent centenary celebrations. The water tank for Loch, painted up with 'Dhoon Quarry' on the side, was subsequently removed and for a time resided at Ballasalla Station on the IMR.

Overhead wiring for the siding used to run only from the points by poles 556-557 as far as the MER's only wooden traction pole (take a look: a small rowan tree is growing from the top!) but was extended to the temporary turnout put in to create a second passing loop in an emergency or special operations during the meagre 58-day period of single line Ramsey service in 2008. The turnout has since been removed.

Below It's very difficult when looking at Tunnel Car 7 from this period to say anything positive. The use of power cars in the winter for P-way and overhead duties has been a problem on the MER since its inception. The sole dedicated freight car was Loco 23, which never had its own bogies and after World War II has never had a permanent function. It therefore fell out of service, necessitating passenger cars in use for freight and the harder work of moving ballast on the line. Car 7 was weakened by pulling the ballast hopper and being stored either outside on the line or in the roofless Laxey shed. It is never acceptable to do this to a unique tramcar over a hundred years old: this was the situation facing Car 7 on 17th February 2005. The photo shows the now lost practice of hanging a ladder on the side of the car. The future wasn't looking good for Car 7 and within a few years it was withdrawn from traffic. Fortunately it was completely rebuilt and carries a build date of 2010. Such is the extent of the rebuild to the body and trucks that it is virtually a new tram. **NM**

Dhoon Quarry Gallery

Dhoon Quarry holds a mystique for many enthusiasts. There is always something to see and many items of rolling stock have rested here, either for an hour, days, weeks or even years. The industry which took place here is hard to imagine now, with its tranquil setting and quietness which can only be found in the Isle of Man. workers would have spent their entire lifetime working here, possibly even commuting to and from work. They would have waited in the old ramshackle shelter which was demolished in 2004. It is always worth a look here to see which vehicles are there, and if any remains of track, cranes or aerial ropeway can be found!

Top Seen in October 2005 is the formidable ballast hopper built by the MER on the underframe of 'Dreadnought' 21, a remarkable survivor which could have a book written just on itself! As part of the constant track renewals being undertaken at the time it was felt that a ballast hopper would be beneficial. Following conversion in 2000, duly increased in 2001 to the large proportions seen above, claimed to be S.W.L 6 ton - Standard Weight Laden, Car 7 was allocated to works car duties and needed extra under frame structuring for pulling this around. When loaded it was quite a feat for it to pull and ballast at the same time. *NM*

Right With track work becoming an ever increasing problem, outside contractors were used in large numbers for the first time. RMS Locotec won the contracts and duly set up camp at Dhoon Quarry. The use of their own vehicles greatly changed the fleet of the MER, with reduced reliance on MER power cars. No.21 was converted for another life, this time as a flatbed vehicle but fitted with air brakes, as can be seen. The work was undertaken in the rather unusual location of the siding at Ham & Egg Terrace (Dumbells Row) in Laxey during winter 2008. This meant there were now three MER flatbed vehicles in the form of 21, 45 and 52. 21 has the added advantage of being able to safely transport heavier loads such as rail, due to its air brakes. Bearing in mind that many power cars lost their air brakes, it is rather ironic that for the first time in its life 21 had air brakes fitted. *NM*

Bottom In the former loading dock, where the famous 'cresote cottage' building was located are three very unusual locomotives to be seen on the MER. They were all purchased from Bord Na Móna, the Irish Peat Company. The locos from left to right are LM363 in unpainted yellow and never named, 'Zippy' LM370 and 'Bungle' LM373, none of which were ever used as locos but did work as a generators. The fourth loco, named 'Pig' LM344, has been used extensively and still operates on the railway, whereas the three seen in the picture are all stored at the Weardale Railway in County Durham, where 'Pig' was stored shortly before returning to the railway. The tippler wagons behind were purchased in the 1990s and used for various ballasting jobs. Originally used on the Lochaber railway near Fort William in Scotland, they are only really suitable for short journeys, and are currently stored. *NM*

Above Ruston and Hornsby HO48 'Bertie' came to the island in 2006. Built for the Ufton Lime pits in Warwickshire, it was loaned to RMS Locotec by Irchester Narrow Gauge Museum. The loco has a powerful 150 horsepower Gardner engine and proved very capable and well suited as a diesel works vehicle with its well built dimensions. It was also popular with enthusiasts and had a starring role in the 2008 enthusiasts events, including the last passenger use for trailer 62. Also seen is the unfortunate trailer 45, which was in the process of an overhaul in 2004 when the decision was made to demolish the car body and use it as a flat wagon, therefore effectively scrapping an 1899 built tramcar as recently as 2004. The red 4x4 vehicle in the background is actually an MER vehicle and is used to access the remote parts of the line. *NM*

Left Although the vast majority of trams simply pass through Dhoon Quarry now, with few reasons for the normal traveller to alight, the crossover here is frequently used. It not only offers the opportunity for a look around the interesting site but is also the first crossover after ascending Bulgham Bay. On Tuesday 25th July 2006 26+57 attempted to cross over as part of an evening private hire. 26 had safely used the points when winter trailer 57 attempted the move by gravity shunting over it. However the tram derailed, with its rear bogie off the rails. This resulted in the passengers being shuttled to Laxey in two trips on car 26, including working wrong line as the crossover obviously could not be used! 57 spent the night at Dhoon Quarry and was rerailed early the next morning before returning to Derby Castle with car 7, which was then allocated to works car duties and far more used to spending time at Dhoon Quarry. *NM*

Bottom As well as having a useful crossover, the siding at Dhoon Quarry is also a ideal place for a photo stop tram to get out of the way of service cars. On a simply superb sunny day, 26+42 are seen in the siding on 27th July 2007. Motor 26 was originally delivered as a trailer before and carried the number 42, which can still be seen on the inside bulkhead. Therefore this hire had the novel factor of using two trams which have carried the number 42. The curvy ends on trailer 42 are clearly seen in this view and the immaculate condition of these trams at the time. Both trams are now stored. *DU*

Top Dhoon Quarry often features in photographs of the MER. It seems to be a favourite place for tour trams, although it passed through long periods of dereliction. High profile events in recent memory include Steam on the MER in 1993 and afterwards. A water tower was specially constructed and the site was given a sanitising makeover with much of the decaying remnants of old wagons being removed. Now used as a base for P-way operations (new rail is delivered here), the scene is a picture of cleanliness. The grass and track are pristine. Car 26 looks magnificent in this setting. **NM**

Bottom Car 19 and Trailer 48 are about to cross the road by Thalloo Mitchell that gave access to the Dhoon Quarry site. The farm gates on the right are one of various unsighted hazards on the Railway which require great vigilance on the part of MER motormen. **DU**

The Former Weighbridge

For those who recall it, the former Weighbridge, an item of unique interest in the tramway world on the Island, was removed when the current siding was remodelled and relaid. During lifting, it sustained damage and was destroyed. This device, a Pooley Wagon weighing machine, was rare on tramways but common on steam railways, the most famous manufacturer being Henry Pooley. The MER machine at the Dhoon was No. 10293 and though rarely utilised, was none the less a unique part of the line's architecture.

Dhoon Quarry - Ballellin

The tracks rise from Dhoon over a brief 1:24 gradient to Thalloo Mitchell crossing, which leads by a tarmac road to the farm; notice the magnificent rhododendron bushes at the trackside here, which are the remains of those brought from Kew before World War II. 'Thalloo' is another Gaelic word for 'land', though the word should properly be 'Tolta'. The place name means 'Michael's Hill'. The track follows an easier gradient of 1:100 to Brown's Crossing by Pole 568. This crossing was relaid with new rail in June-July 2006 and was then given a fresh layer of tarmac.

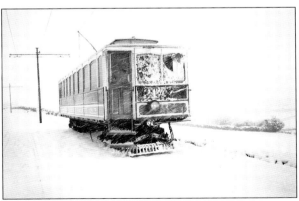

Left The MER as visitors and locals rarely see it. A severe snowstorm on 14th April 1998 saw all road traffic halted but the MER's Car 21 still running and maintaining a much needed service. This snowy scene was photographed by Motorman John Matthews at Brown's crossing on the northern line, with conductor Nick Pascoe on the back, who had fitted a special trolley wheel designed to break up ice on the overhead.
John Matthews

Magnificent scenery accompanies the car's relaxed progress on the run inland down to Ballellin at Pole 579, with spectacular views of the northern mountains gradually opening up to the left. Photographs of cars specially posed between Brown's Crossing and Ballellin, and on the section round to Ballig (Pole 590) are especially sought after by enthusiasts on 'photostop' runs during

Special Events, simply for the excellence of the rural location, which shows the trams in their natural unspoiled setting to great effect. Such views are quintessentially the same as a century ago.

A common feature of the line and 19th Century farm and road construction on the Island, is a set of ornate square-based pyramid pillars (properly known as 'piers') at farm crossings. A good surviving example is located on the landside just before Ballellin farm by Pole 576. Others similar pillars survive at Ballafayle, for example. 'Ballellin', which enjoys various different spellings, means 'Allen's Farm'. An unusual feature of Ballellin farm is the cattle tunnel under the tracks just after the farm crossing. It is easily passable, which shows it is still occasionally in use. This is a superb spot to take a photograph in the late afternoon, when once again we can create an image of the MER that has changed little over generations.

Numerous farm crossings exist on the Northern Line. Listen for the distinctive air-whistle warning, which the driver operates by a small fixed floor button on the driving platform, as they are traversed, instigated by stencilled instructions on a nearby traction pole, though that instruction is a mere formality, as expert motormen habitually know when to announce their car's presence.

Ballellin - Ballig - Ballasholague

Passengers can learn much about MER driving technique over this section. One important lesson about handling an MER car is when to use full power - for example, to get up from Dhoon Quarry to Brown's Crossing - and when to allow the car to coast, as it will all the way down to Ballig. A journey on the MER reveals many places with names beginning 'Balla-', and this area is rich in such place names. It is fascinating to know meanings, because they usually reflect the history of the place, whether owners' names or perhaps local geographic features. 'Ballig' is not the original name; it was 'Rencullen' meaning 'Holly Division', but the farm has been known as Ballig, 'Farm of the Hollow', since the early eighteenth century.

Occasionally the underfloor sounds of your MER car will liven up as full series points are applied to keep momentum round the contours of the line, but then coasting will be allowed. From

Above Paddlebox 16 and heavy Trailer 43 pose at Ballellin whilst on a rare working of an open car to Ramsey on 2nd August 2008. With limited running to Ramsey that year, the opportunity to run 'exotic' cars was restricted to just a handful of occasions – in this instance when Motorman Gary Moore requested an open car. The set is noted working wrong line. *DU*

Ballig, the car rounds a curve which has been used as a ballast store on land overgrown with thorns. Access has been cut into the thorns on the roadside and the ground then roller-flattened and smoothed out. This work revealed the Rhenab flowing down under the MER's rails towards Glen Mona.

Severe storm damage was caused here during the night of 7th - 8th January 2005 when five large pine trees fell across both the main road and tram line causing severe damage to the overhead wires, poles and fittings which were bent beyond repair or destroyed. The wires were brought down between poles 578-83 between Ballellin and Ballig), and those in the region of 588-592 from Ballig to Ballasholague were badly twisted and fit for scrap only. Operation of the winter service was impossible with these obstructions here and elsewhere, so service was suspended until the summer season began on Monday 21st March. Repair work saw use of a diesel locomotive on loan from the IMR in the company of 'Tunnel' Car 7; they stabled at Dhoon Quarry each night. The day after this terrible storm, the wire at Corkhill's Crossing - Pole 607 - was cut to allow free movement of traffic along what became a substitute for the main Laxey to Ramsey Road that was blocked with fallen trees; all this recalls Mike Goodwyn's words aphorism about railroading into the raw.

Our car now glides down to Ballasholague, which should be known as 'Balley Shellag', 'Willow Farm', where you will not find a shelter, but there is a stop sign located at Pole 602. The track here consists of old rail and is one of the poorer sections on the Northern Line. It is estimated that good coasting should generally enable a car to cover approximately 45% of the entire route from Douglas to Ramsey without the application of power. The Rule Book is also clear about 'Economy of Power', which is rule No.13 for motormen: 'Advantage must be taken of every opportunity of saving current by careful coasting on down gradients. With a little practice a skilful Motorman will be able to judge the gradients and the weight of his Car, and so avoid using power any longer than is absolutely necessary.'

Corkhill's – Glen Mona

The next crossing is correctly known as either 'Corkhill's' (its more modern name) or 'Looney's' and occasionally nowadays as 'Barony View' from the name engraved into the wall below the rather splendid gilded eagles – well, perhaps it is only gold paint. The Corkhill family farmed the Ballagorry land to the north of here. The reference to 'Barony' is Barony Hill, which was formerly the property of St. Bega's (St. Bee's) Priory in Cumbria. A stone circle and tumulus known as Carnane Breck crown the hill. A short descent over the new tarmac across 'Jones's Crossing' (not a stop, if it ever was), past four poles northwards brings the car to Glen Mona station. Also known as 'Rhenab Glen', this a favourite halt for ramblers, who can once again fortunately enjoy the hospitality of the Glen Mona Hotel, after

Right During the 1990s, following the success of celebrations of various railway centenaries, the vogue was to renumber trams to recreate scenes that hadn't been seen since before the 1930 Laxey fire when several trams were lost. One tram that survived, but was withdrawn as far back as 1902 and then converted, was 1895 Car 10, becoming Freight Car 26, which is now preserved. As the 1990s' transport extravaganzas progressed, it became more difficult to recreate lost cars. It was thought that the appearance of Car 10's front might be replicated on a tunnel car with a split windscreen. The only one at the time to carry this feature was Car 6, rebuilt in this style following an accident which required mainly new cab ends. Whether a tunnel car with a split screen really looks like a member of the 10-13 class, is left to readers to decide! The pairing of Car 10 (6) & Trailer 45 is seen on the approach to Corkhill's Crossing from Ballasholague. *IH*

Above The unmistakable gilded eagles at Corkhill's Crossing, aka Looney's, guard the entrance to the impressive 'Barony View', a private residence. Car 22 and Trailer 44 with whistle 'peeping' make their way southbound over the crossing. An idyllic setting as we look down towards Glen Mona. *DU*

a period of some uncertainty about its future. The house nestling behind and below the halt is known as 'Archallagan', which is also the name of the pathway from the side road that branches from the A2 to this spot.

Glen Mona

Walkers using the MER to reach the glens will not be disappointed with Glen Mona, which is a much easier walk than Dhoon. Two of the pools in the glen are known as 'Linga Phynnodderee' (the name of a fallen or malevolent fairy) and 'Linga Glashtin' (a mythical creature or water spirit), to support the ancient belief in hairy satyrs and goblins. The route down to the ferny glen follows a clear track to a footbridge over the stream at the bottom of the hill. Take the narrow road to the left overlooking the valley. You will see the stream in gentle descent towards Port Cornaa. Approximately half way along the route, opposite a cottage, stands the entrance to 'Cashtal-yn-Ard', which is signposted.

Formerly known as 'Ballachrink Cairn', this is now the largest Neolithic Age long barrow on the Island. It dates from about 2000BC, and comprises a series of tall stones standing upright in a curve with flat stone slabs to form a forecourt to the graves.

When it was built, it is believed to have covered an area of 500 square yards. This ancient tribal burial place shows clear evidence of the remains of a pyre at its centre, all of which seems to indicate that cremation was the preferred method for the burial of the tribe's dead.

The size of the structure and its historical significance makes it an essential visit for people interested in the history of Mann. You can also access this site by road from Brown's Crossing and it is well signposted. Back to Glen Mona: after reaching the

Right An empty Car 19 towing Trailer 40 glides past Glen Mona, operating the 15.15 Douglas to Ramsey on 7th July 1973. The unrestricted tree growth over the Manx Electric Railway and the Isle of Man as a whole has unfortunately limited sight and enjoyment of great swathes of the beautiful landscape. Photos from 30-40 years ago show this whole area to be clear of trees and offering unrestricted views of the surrounding countryside. The travelling public often wonders what the view from the tramcar would look like without being 'hemmed' in on certain sections of the line today. **RP**

waterfall, the path carries on until it leads to another stream about a mile further on, where Glen Mona meets Ballaglass Glen. A turn here to follow the stream inland through the thickly-wooded glen is memorable for the way the tiny stream, having descended from the mountains, hisses and murmurs over the many tiny rocky waterfalls, providing constantly oxygenated water for the innumerable small fish, which dart for cover as long human shadows threaten. The path crosses a road and not far beyond can be seen Ballaglass Station. Perhaps it is worth pointing out that all MER tickets make breaks of journey very easy. The availability of a variety of Rover tickets enables all the glens on the route to Ramsey to be visited at leisure over a period of days. Indeed, their attraction brought passengers in such great numbers in bygone days when people were content with more innocent holiday pleasures and the MER's timetables noted that 'All the charming glens en route are in magnificent foliage'.

The glens still deserve a visit, because their development was inextricably connected with the Manx Electric, and because of their enduring charm. It is not possible to understand and appreciate the coastal route without understanding the simple pleasures previous generations of passengers experienced. Relive some real MER history and stop off at Dhoon, Glen Mona or Ballaglass to recapture the flavour of a long-lost era.

Glen Mona boasts a clean if small station building, the area being greatly improved by the addition of plants and flower boxes. The Victorian stone post-box edifice, like the one still in existence at Ballajora, has now been lost to the memory of history. It was last emptied at 4.50pm by conductor David Hodgson on 30th September 1975, the day the Northern Section closed, which prevented the continuation of the Royal Mail contract. Tram mail was never especially post marked and was rarely an object of philatelists' attention at the time, though commemorative covers of the closure and other events are now widely sought after.

Above Car 21 and Trailer 44 working the 15.30 Ramsey to Douglas on 7th July 1973. The droop in the Winter Saloons is again clearly visible here, a sign that they required significant work done on the underframes and bodies in the late 1970s after what was already a long working life. The rather odd shaped Glen Mona shelter and typical sign board are on the right of the car, as photographed. Glen Mona was a rural location with a post box, last emptied on 30th September 1975 by conductor Dave Hodgson. A footpath leads from here to the glen and also the A2 road, where Dhoon Church, Dhoon School and the old Glen Mona Hotel are located. *RP*

Glen Mona – The Garey (Dhoon Church)

Cars continue to coast down to the curve, which is now commonly called 'The Garey', but which was formerly known as the stop for 'Dhoon Church' nearby on the main road. Although the church is in the area of Glen Mona, in 1855 it replaced the original at Dhoon Bridge a mile south from here, hence the name. The architect of Laxey's Christchurch, Ewan Christian, also designed this church, which might explain the broadly similar appearance of both. 'Garey' comes from 'Garee', which means 'rough, wet waste land' or 'a sour piece of land', which is appropriate as there is a sewerage farm here! The crossover was removed from Ballagorry - the next northbound stop - as part of the 2008-9 trackwork programme and a new one was positioned at The Garey on a much easier gradient by Poles 617-8. Dhoon School is visible from this point, but the stop at Ballagorry provides more direct access. An attractive retaining wall by the landside track just before the curve was completed in late summer 2008.

Below Compare this view of Car 22 and Trailer 47, passing through an archway of trees at Glen Mona on 1st August 2014, with the previous two photos to appreciate the considerable tree growth along this section. Intending customers of the line feel very isolated here on a wet day such as this, when the tramcars' whistles and quiet hum on the overhead wire can be heard from some distance away, although local road traffic noise is deadened. **DU**

The Garey - Ballagorry

Skilful handling of the car will see it emerge from this corner on all nine points of power, to be faced with the sudden 1:28 pull up smooth trackwork to Ballagorry Farm by Pole 624. Ballagorry is an official stop, more or less in the farmyard, where hens strut,

cluck and peck in freedom, oblivious to the trams, amid a ramshackle collection of old cars, tyres and ephemera. The farm bears the surname which appears to have no connection with the place, but might be connected with land at Ballajora (see below). Cast a glance at feeder box number 25 attached to traction Pole 620, just before Ballagorry Farm when travelling northwards. These feeder boxes existed at half-mile intervals along the line though are no longer in use. The box contains a row of knife switches and terminals, and served the overhead wires with the facility of isolating a section of the north or south wires at either side of the traction poles. A third 'feeder' overhead wire can be noted here apart from the running wire. In theory, a tram can run by drawing power from this wire, but the heavy oxidisation results in an undesirable display of pyrotechnics.

Above Car 19 running single motor has just glided through the road crossing at The Garey on 29th October 2007, prior to the installation of the crossover which is now situated just in front of the tram. Senior driver, Jeff North, is conducting for a change and can now relax in the switchbox at the Douglas end. With few passengers at intermediate stops towards the end of the season, this will be a quiet journey. The winter saloon carries a version of the austerity livery formerly worn in uncertain times for the MER and also sports yellow numerals. Scuffed bodywork and flaking paint on the dash panel were regrettably a sign of the times. The fleet is now much more presentable and welcoming to visitors. **DU**

Ballagorry – Dolland - Ballaglass

The stretch between The Garey, Ballagorry Farm and Ballaglass is a regular place for crews to change over during the season, the actual spot depending on how closely the trams operate to the published timetable. Our train crests the hill and then rolls steadily through the cutting that in 1898 was originally single track only, under Ballagorry overbridge. The line is at its furthest from

the sea here, at just over one mile. The first wooden bridge was replaced in 1950 by the present modern concrete structure. Under its seaside span, the bridge now houses one of the line's electricity sub-stations incorporating a GEC/Alsthom solid-state rectifier, replacing the old company power station at Ballaglass Glen further down the line. It came into use in 1989 and has a capacity of 300kW. Refurbishment work on this substation is planned in the near future.

Opposite page Car 5 is captured through the eye of a telephoto lens working single motor on 3rd August 2014, approaching the road crossing by The Garey. Incredibly three tram stops can be seen in one photo: Ballasholague, Corkhill's Crossing and Glen Mona. **DU**

The bridge is easily accessed from the main road; when travelling north, it is located before 'Corrany' on the Ordnance Survey map; older maps show 'Corrany Farm'. The sub-station itself is obviously inaccessible. The bridge provides excellent views of the cars in this rural - and unusual - setting. You can see the dust patterns on tram roofs caused by specks of debris from the trolley wheel revolving on the overhead wires. The action of gently swaying trolley-poles is well evidenced here as is the unique clicking sound of the trolley wheel passing under the section breaker at the feeder pole. The car passes under the bridge and coasts onwards to Watson's crossing at Pole 636 by another farm gate, which is another regular halt. The Watson family had an intimate and long connection with the MER and Ballaglass power station from the 1890s to 1970. Frederick 'Pop' Watson started

Above During the winter of 2008-09, the crossover at Ballagorry was removed and replaced by a new one at The Garey, sometimes referred to as Dhoon Church. This rarely used crossover was used on 27th July 2009. The wires had been brought down at Laxey by a low loader and the power had to be switched off in Laxey. Car 21 and Trailer 46 were brought back to Laxey without reaching the northern terminus. The set was involved in this unusual manoeuvre at The Garey, which requires the trailer to be pushed up a rather steep gradient, before it can be gravity shunted back onto the motor. **DU**

Above On 25th June 1968, we see Car 22 and Trailer 41 working the 16.00 Ramsey to Douglas, having just crested the 1 in 24 summit at Ballagorry. Visible in the background is the only remaining over-bridge on the MER. In the 1990s a substation was built in the space formed by the right of the bridge and the seaward section of the embankment. In recent years, the building has become susceptible to leaks and requires investment in the near future. One of the striking features of this photo is the cleanliness of the whole scene: newly painted trams and trimmed embankments. *RP*

working for the IOMT&EPCo in 1897; he later ran the power station for its entire existence. 'Pop' lived on the landside in a house called 'Pinewood'; his son Duggie became Way & Works Superintendent, residing on the seaside of the line at 'Highfield'. Jack Watson ('Pop's' son) was of course Deputy Chief Engineer, later becoming joint manager of the MER in 1952, and general manager in 1963, a position he held until retirement on 31.12.67 after thirty-eight years' service.

Experienced Ramsey-bound drivers will always 'knock off' the power by turning the controller handle right back to its starting position before they pass under the traction pole between the crossover and the bridge. This ensures the trolley wheel does not cause a flash, as it passes over the small 'dead' gap fitted into the section-breaker. Douglas-bound drivers return the controller to the fifth series point. Switching the power off completely would make a very discernible and uneven jerk for trailer car passengers, on account of the weight and drag effect of the trailer on the power car, when power is re-applied for the car's continued climb up to Ballagorry.

It is quite possible for you to follow much of the line to this point by car from Laxey on the A2, though from Corrany, the MER diverges and it is not possible to access the line again other than by footpaths, for example at Watson's and Dolland, as far as Cornaa. A useful road route lies one mile north of Corrany. Take a right turn onto the A15. After considerable gyrations, a narrow unnumbered branch road diverts and leads to Cornaa Halt. Reversing at Cornaa, take the minor road once more to join the A15; turn right towards Ramsey (no signposts remain in situ), and the road now runs parallel to the MER past Murray's Road/Crowcreen, over Ballaskeig, and through to Ballajora, where it takes a right turn towards Maughold. The B19, however, continues from the turn to Ballajora Station to run alongside the MER all the way to Lewaigue, where it rejoins the A2. Narrow but adequate access can be made from the B19 to the halts at Dreemskerry and Lewaigue.

In the pioneering days back in 1898, the unsupervised single-track through Ballagorry cutting met with disapproval from the pedantic Colonel Rich, one of the railway inspectors. In this case, however, he rightly refused permission to operate until some additional safety measures had been implemented, and he insisted on the section's doubling at the first opportunity, a recommendation implanted the next winter. One of the safety measures was to post flagmen at either end of the single line after dusk. As the tram emerges from the cutting, passengers can take a glance back at the wide and beautiful expanse of Glen Mona, leading away inland. To your left, the glorious verdant hills of North Barrule (at 1,860 foot, the Island's second highest point) stand proudly soaring skywards. So beautiful are they that they appear in the Manx National Anthem. In winter, the often snow-capped tops of Barrule glisten against the weak sun, if you are lucky enough to experience wintertime MER riding. If the MER does operate a full winter service again, enjoy the warm, cosy ride in a winter saloon, with draught-excluders fitted to the windows, against the backdrop of an ever-changing winter wonderland.

Ballaglass is the next frequently requested halt, though just prior to it lies an interesting public footpath that crosses the track at a point known as 'Dolland' - Pole 644, where the stone remains of a dilapidated farmstead are being rapidly eclipsed by advancing trees and plant life. Plenty of rumours abound about the former occupants: the one that they moved to South Africa in the 1950s and simply left Dolland appears credible. The main white-painted

Next page The over bridge offers a good vantage point for photos but not normally ones like this! On 19th May 2006 we see Car 21 and Trailer 48 working wrong line, whilst Wire Car 7 and traditional tower wagon attend to the seaside overhead wiring. This also offers a good vantage point to show the cutting, where unsatisfactory single line working was in place during 1898. Also evident is the long held practice of replacing previously used traction poles with new ones, but leaving the old ones in situ. As most of these have been filled with concrete and then had 'collars' attached at the bottoms, it is actually extremely difficult to remove them! *NM*

house never enjoyed running water or other amenities, but did have some home comforts, including the ornate fireplace, which partially survived in the 1990s. Another rumour runs that a well-known denizen of Ramsey wanted to buy Dolland, but the complexities of Manx law in respect of potential surviving relatives of the last-known owners meant that the project never came to fruition. The house can be accessed by the farm gate before the stop, but it is a precarious path that leads to the house, which is now merely a shell with trees struggling to compete, where once people lived. The tram actually runs along an embankment from a point near to Pole 642 to reach Ballaglass, though it is not easy to detect as much on account of the trees and flora of the local environment.

Ballaglass

Ballaglass - meaning 'Green Farm' or 'River Farm' - once boasted an IOMT&EPCo. steam power station. The fast-flowing Corony stream brought water right to the station. It is quite possible to imagine by standing on the embankment overlooking the building, how coal was brought from Ramsey and simply tipped into the bunkers below. The power station was rather ornately

Below The non-matching combination of Car 2 and Trailer 60 is seen on the series of curves leading down from Ballaglass Glen to Cornaa. This twisting and steep section requires trams to negotiate an 'S' bend before Cornaa and then immediately start the climb to Ballaskeig. The old poles filled with concrete seen in this view from 3rd August 2014, have been lopped and rest on the ballast next to the replacement poles. Inside the discarded poles can clearly be seen the concrete infill! Unfortunately when these new poles were put up the tops were not covered and their fate will be much quicker than for the older ones. The public footpath here appears lost on both sides of the tracks. It does remains, but picking your way along it in places where the grass and brambles are overgrown is not easy, showing it is now rarely used. Not for the fainthearted, the long trek to the A2 is likely to be damp, difficult and 'longtail' infested! *DU*

Right Car 19 and Trailer 43 climb from Cornaa into Ballaglass Glen on 25th June 1973 with the 10.30 from Ramsey. The original traction poles look incredibly tired, but bravely carried on holding up the wires for some years to come! The collars at the bottom were a relatively new idea then and helped extend traction poles' useful life for another 30 years' service. The span pole is bowing significantly above Car 19. Once again, Nos. 19 & 43 appear immaculate. A car's roof often yields a clue as to how long it is since the last repaint. The memorable blue sign leaves passengers in no doubt as to where they are ... however by the time they've seen it, it might be too late, which is why the conductor hands the motorman a note of all the lesser stops he needs to call at. *RP*

Above Although Ballaglass shelter survived for over 80 years, there are very few photographs showing this archaic structure. The shelter is of an odd design, more in keeping with structures at the principal stations than a wayside shelter. This reminds us just how busy this once MER-owned glen was in earlier days, when a kiosk and refreshment facilities were available here. The rustic log effect is evident, a style that can be seen at Derby Castle booking office to good effect. *Peter Burke*

decorated, its walls panelled with pitch pine and the tiled floor was patterned around each piece of equipment. The exterior view today is not so different from its 1897 aspect that we cannot recognise the buildings that housed the old engine and battery rooms; an absentee is the 60-foot high iron chimney. Something of a transformation has taken place within the grounds. Major rebuilding in 1992 saw this become a residential property, with an approach road that ironically used much of the material from the demolished Ramsey Plaza. The property was advertised for sale at £2.85m as a 'luxury country house' in summer 2007!

The rather dank and dark wooden shelter at Ballaglass harks back only to 1989. It was improved in 1999 by the addition of a gate, which waiting passengers and sheltering walkers are kindly requested to close, otherwise the straggling feral goats will occupy it. They display an alarming propensity to hide there or seek refuge if they have come to grief. Several have even removed themselves there to die, particularly in winter.

A rare MER accident occurred on the southbound track in this area in 1944, when a van and trailer (believed to be No.45) broke loose from the motor car and ran back, hurtling into the glen. No one was injured. Speculation that the trailer car was repaired in wartime using inferior woods may well be correct and have determined the choice of No.45 as a P-Way flat, the car's timbers being found weak and rotten when withdrawn for refurbishment.

Ballaglass Glen

A sign proclaiming 'Ballaglass Glen' used to hang at the entrance to this greenest of glens, but collapsed and disappeared apart from a few individual letters which survive hidden in the undergrowth! A nameboard adorns the station shelter. The walk down to the seventeen-acre glen is one of the Island's most stunning, with an abundant show of bluebells in spring. A fish hatchery is open Monday to Friday all year round. More importantly, you can enjoy peace and quiet here whilst awaiting the next car of your choice. A little further along from the hatchery is old Cornaa Mill, which has been converted into a very attractive dwelling with a plaque on the wall showing the date '1503'. It is well worth a short walk to be able to see the 70ft diameter bridge span that carries the MER over the river, as it cannot be seen from any other vantage point, nor are passengers on the line really aware of it as they sit inside an MER car.

Ballaglass Glen contains other points of interest. You are bound to notice numbered posts at regular intervals. These are all detailed in a publication entitled 'The Ballaglass Nature Trail', containing such fascinating gems as the rhododendron tree in the garden of the house near to the mill being listed at the Royal Botanical Gardens at Kew as the tallest of its kind in Western Europe. Casual walkers are always likely to come across old mine workings on the Island and this is no exception. Post number 8 indicates the remains of another 19th Century mine, this time of 'The Great Glen Mona Mining Company'. It is quite easy to find one's way back to the Ballaglass Station halt or to continue all the way back to Glen Mona via the track and stone stile onto the main A2 road at the top of Corrany Hill.

Ballaglass - Cornaa

Back at Ballaglass, it is illustrative of changing visitor patterns that the idea of a refreshment kiosk here would seem quite amazing in the light of current operations - but there used to be one, although it suffered demolition as far back as 1944-45. From Ballaglass, the track begins a series of convoluted turns amid the wooded countryside of the glen to the right, and farm land to the left, on a gentle 1:100 descent towards Cornaa, though the final curve before Cornaa Station steepens to 1:24. Readers who enjoy tram photography might like to leave the tram at Ballaglass and follow the northbound track for 200 yards, where they will come across a public footpath that leads into the glen or back to the former power station and eventually the main road. At this point, you can get interesting shots of southbound trams by 'framing' them between successive poles as they wend their way to Ballaglass.

The longest section of original traction poles was on this stretch until recently; the odd disused one is to be found between the tracks or in undergrowth, and in some cases the old ones have been left in situ, so you can see what the old ones are like and how amazing it as that they remained standing so long by being stuffed with concrete and clamped at the base! This section also possesses several surviving traction poles from the 1896 Douglas Southern Tramway (the Marine Drive route), which are easily recognisable by their two ring collars and their excellent state of preservation. They are to be found dotted along the line, though their numbers are gradually diminishing as a flurry of activity from the Poles & Wires Gang continues.

Just before Cornaa, we can see some of the improvements made to the trackbed and banking during recent permanent way work. The track crosses streams which previously caused water to be held in the trackbed; new drains are much in evidence and a weak bank has been turned into a retaining wall on the landward side only between Poles 682-3 with the use of gabions, like the one referred to at Lamb's Crossing. The rail used on these curves is stamped 'BS Workington 02' and is of 85 lbs weight.

Chapter 5

Cornaa to Ramsey

Chapter 5:

Cornaa to Ramsey

Cornaa

The name 'Cornaa' has a fascinating and ancient history. Its origin is the name 'Cardle' from the Scandinavian 'Kvernardalr' with a general meaning of 'Mill-stone dale'. A 'kvern' was a hand mill. In the Runic Monument of c.1200, it was spelt 'Kurnadal', and by 1511 had become 'Cardall', the name of a 'treen' and its quarterlands, a treen being an ancient land division within the 'Sheading', which itself is a land division legacy from the Norse administration when the Island was divided into six parts. By 1637, Cornaa had become known as 'Cornay Begge', the 'Little Cornay Dale', and it was transformed into 'Cornah' by 1709. There were fluctuations in the spelling all through the eighteenth century until 'Cornaa' became the norm in the 1800s, so you can see just how ancient a place and how much history is attached to this beautiful little area on our journey to Ramsey.

Cornaa Station is elegantly framed amid trees. The shelter used to house an essential item for motormen: sand in sacks under the passenger bench so that crews could maintain the stock in the sand-hoppers under the cars' seats, an essential aid to adhesion on greasy rails. In the days when winter services operated in the evenings, it was not unusual for intending passengers at Cornaa to flash a torch or even set light to a piece of paper to make sure the driver could see them in the unlit shelter.

Cornaa halt has benefited from the wonderful efforts of local people, who have created flower beds next to both sets of tracks. A new 'Cornaa' painted board was placed in situ during the first morning of the 2009 season and the shelter has been re-roofed too. This shelter repays a visit just to look at the ancient graffiti. Some is dated, the earliest yet found being 'Audax' (the 'Bold One') from 1924!

Crews can never take the Manx Electric for granted and assume that even what promises to be a mundane, routine trip will remain so. One summer evening not long ago, in the middle of a spectacular thunder and lightning storm, an evening tram service reached Cornaa at 8.25pm on its northbound journey to be confronted by sheep and even cattle on the track; perhaps the car was unexpected as it was running long after the previous service. In such situations, the 1926 Rule Book is quite clear: The motorman must stop his car until the conductor has put the animals into the nearest closed field. The conductor should

Above The map shows the second half of the Ramsey line from Cornaa to Ramsey Plaza.

Left Cornaa is possibly one of the most exquisitely named stops and has confused visitors to the line, many thinking that it must be Manx for 'corner'. In fact, the spelling of 'Cornaa' was quite variable until recent times but the meaning is in no doubt: Mill stone dale or glen. Cornaa is a good example of a traditional surviving MER shelter and has some of the oldest graffiti inside (it's worth a look!), along with Ballajora (even better), some of which dates to before the Second World War. Operating the winter service on 3rd February 2007 is Winter Saloon 22, the newest tram at the time. Following its rebuild, it was often the first choice for winter service alongside one of the 1899 built saloons. Although no longer a feature of winter operation (the line is a seasonal operation only), in the past the Winter Saloons would have small individually made pieces of wood inserted around the window frames to stop them from vibrating and to keep the warmth inside the cosy saloon. This is a feature of operation lost from the MER. However a bundle of these inserts was recently found at Derby Castle all individually marked! **NM**

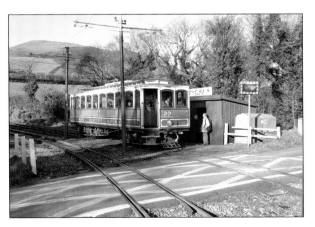

request a willing passenger to take the red flag along the line to warn the following car. A written report must be made … immediately on return to the depot.

Exactly that procedure was followed by the crew of Gary Moore and experienced guard Ronnie Hall, in charge of Car 19. The cattle virtually galloped from Watson's Crossing, past Dolland, round the curves to Cornaa and on towards Murray's Road. Certain skills and competencies, which fortunately are not required on a daily basis with passengers, included shooing panicking the perturbed beasts into a field or actually up Murray's Road. The situation was satisfactorily resolved even if the car did arrive twenty-five minutes late into Ramsey!

Walks from Cornaa

It is worth going down to the beach at Cornaa whether for relaxation or to see some of the remarkable remains of the Bellite factory. An easy (preferable) route by car would be to follow the road from Brown's Crossing just north of Dhoon Quarry. Parking is available on the beach itself where the briny air is unspoiled. Turning back from the beach, a well-trodden path leads inland. Take the bridge over the river, then head off as if you are going into the wooded area. On your left stands the mass of masonry that forms the remains of the 1890 Bellite factory. Initial experiments with Bellite had taken place somewhere in Pulrose in Douglas, according to the Isle of Man Times of March 1890 before the decision was taken to locate the factory here in the wilds. This fascinating place has allowed nature to take over where the floors of this ugly building once stood, but the side walls still show the rectangular apertures cut out where wooden beams were slotted.

Bellite was the new, miracle explosive of the Victorian age. The secret of its success lay in the fact that it would not explode when thrown into a flame or by concussion; a detonator was required because of the delicate composition of ammonia and dinitrobenzole. The factory went ahead with production but came up against very hostile reaction from residents along the coastline and elsewhere, who perceived a danger. The factory was abandoned at great financial loss in 1892 and the entire contents of the factory's machinery were sold off at auction. An advertisement was placed by Alfred Chatstal Auctioneers of Ramsey in the Ramsey Courier in September 1892 for the sale on Tuesday 6th of the 'valuable timber, plant and other effects'. Of note is the final paragraph of the advertisement, informing interested parties that the steamer 'Fairy Queen' would stop directly opposite Cornah Harbour (sic) to set down and pick up passengers from Douglas at 10.30am and from Ramsey at 12.30 and 5.15pm. Those were the days!

This tranquil area is also historically associated with the Island's 1859 Manx Telegraph Company submarine link to the mainland. The cable was originally laid between St Bee's Head in Cumbria and brought ashore at the turbulent Point of Ayre, but movement on the sea bed created such disruption to the service that the terminal point was brought to the sheltered region of Port Cornaa. The hut on the south side of Cornaa Beach could still be seen until recent years.

Cornaa - Ballaskeig

Travelling northbound once more from Cornaa, the tram is now just over thirteen miles out of Douglas. The line briefly turns south-east to avoid the highest ground ahead and commences a wide southward detour, which is followed closely by the A15. The car works hard up yet another 1:24 section towards Murray's Road crossing by Pole 699. Although the MER regards 'Murray's Road' as the stop's correct name, 'Crowcreen' ('Withered Bush') is also used, though 'Crowcreen' is properly the area occupied by the farm and all its attendant buildings to the right of the lines between Cornaa Halt and Murray's Road. The Murray family farmed this land in the late nineteenth century.

The much persecuted Quaker, William Callow, was born in Ballafayle, a little to the north of Murray's Road, in 1629. The Island authorities kept him for many months in the dungeon of Peel Castle until banishing him from Mann to London, where he stayed until King Charles II's Declaration of Indulgence allowed him to return. He is buried in the Quakers' Cemetery - Rhullick Ny Quakeryn - in Maughold, opposite which is the Ballafayle Cairn – a horned barrow without chambers or passage. The burial ground is adjacent to the Raad Ny Foillan. This latter translates as the 'Road of the Gull' and is the coastal footpath

around the Island. It is waymarked with a blue sign displaying a gull in flight and runs for ninety miles, following the coast wherever practical. There is an abundance of fascinating historic sites deserving of a visit in the north of the Island and there is no better way of reaching them than the MER! This is a beautiful and peaceful area to visit; it is easily reached by a pleasant walk from the Murray's Road tram stop or by car using the narrow road. The views are magnificent on a fine day.

This area has been associated continuously with the names of Murray and Looney. It is feasible to access this stop on foot only, as there is no reversing facility for a car. The trams now pass through one of the loveliest areas of the Northern Section; you might be treated to the sight of highland cattle grazing contentedly on the farm above Murray's Road towards Ballaskeig, as the tram gathers speed over Ballaskeig Moar. On clear days, Sellafield Nuclear Power Station is visible from this area. The road conveniently runs parallel to the MER tracks for a short distance from Ballaskeig Farm, where the crossover was removed in the winter of 2013-4. Horses can usually be seen quietly grazing on the seaside of the line, even in fine weather in the off season. If horses are outside in the fields near to the tracks, drivers will usually shut off power and might even use the original car gong instead of the air whistle as they pass Ballaskeig Moar farm, so as not to frighten the animals. Once autumn arrives and the Douglas

Above North Barrule at 1842 feet dominates the North of the Island and is the second highest peak on the Isle of Man, behind the 2036 feet of Snaefell. Tunnel Car 5 pulls Trailer 47 as they accelerate hard again after slowing for Murray's Road/Crowcreen crossing on 25th June 1973. It is clear just how hard it is for the motorman to see these crossings when a car sneaks up unexpectedly (and often without anticipating the presence of a tram), which is why crossings are all restricted to 5 mph. This is yet another of the MER's magnificent views! *RP*

Opposite page A magnificent early season shot of Car 1 with Van 4 just beginning the climb from Cornaa towards Murray's Road / Crowcreen. *Jason Cross*

horse tram service is suspended, a number of horses from the stud occasionally spend winter up here.

Ballaskeig has a long etymological history, too. It finds its origin in 'Balley Skipavik', a Scandinavian name meaning 'Ship Creek Farm'. Ballaskeig Mooar has been known as such since 1843 and means, 'Large Farm of the Ship Creek'. The land runs down to meet Cornaa Beach, and the name takes us back to those times when Cornah Harbour was a place of significance. There is in fact a shelter at Ballaskeig – though it is not immediately obvious. It lurks, small and thickly covered by ivy, just inside the farm road. It can no longer be used as it has become unsafe. The bench inside survives as do old copies of the timetable pasted one over the other.

Ballaskeig awoke from its peaceful existence and became the main passing point for trams in the brief operating period of summer 2008. A new loop was created here. The recently removed trailing crossover just to the north of pole 714 was used for cars arriving 'wrong line' from Ramsey to traverse to the seaside track. Trams heading for Ramsey on the 'correct' landside line usually arrived first and waited for the southbound car to cross and its driver to hand over the staff. Then the northbound car would depart. No inspector was required here and the system proved successful. The car heading for Laxey then proceeded slowly along the seaside track past pole 713 until it reached a temporary slewed track arrangement which had lost its physical connection to the southbound rails. The car rejoined the operational landside line. Additional overhead wiring was provided and the conductor's duty on southbound cars included 'trolleying' across to the temporary wiring through the seaside loop, then back onto the landside line at the Laxey end of the loop. One way spring levers were fitted to the loop points and drivers were required by in-the-face yellow signs to check that points were correctly set at all times before advancing further.

Ballaskeig - Ballafayle

From Ballaskeig, cars often 'tramp' in MER parlance, achieving a speed well in excess of the original maximum 18 mph, stipulated at the dawn of the line, until they customarily slow down for the crossing at Ballafayle Corteen's by Pole 731. The old farm buildings have been demolished and new attractive houses

erected. In the early days of the line until 1934, a stop was sited at Ballacannell, which is assumed to be Pole 734, although old maps mark the area from Corteen's towards the coastline as 'East Callow' and a stop - now lapsed - called 'Ballafayle East Callow' definitely used to exist in this area, most probably between Ballacannell and Kerruish. Whether or not the MER would recognise Pole 734 as an authentic stop is a moot question. There is a clearly a degree of confusion with place names in this area between 'Ballacannell' and 'Ballafayle'. I am grateful to the staff of the Manx Museum for clarifying that the eighteenth century name for 'Ballafayle y Cannell' - Cannell's Farm - was simply 'Ballacannell' and that the close proximity of this place and 'Ballafayle Corteen's' is because they are effectively borders of two halves of one quarterland and the exact delineation of property has become blurred over the last two centuries, hence the confusion over MER stops, too.

Older passengers and former boy scouts may well have enjoyed the experience of camping in one of the fields belonging to Ballafayle Kerruish (Pole 745) up until the late 1970s. A prettier and more peaceful location would be difficult to find. The house here carries the name of Kerruish; Sir Charles Kerruish was probably the foremost Manx post-war politician and a great

Above During 2008 the Ramsey line was closed due to the appalling state of the track and was only partially re-opened for the busiest fifty-eight days of the season. To facilitate single-line operation, a passing loop was installed at Ballaskeig, which involved use of the single-line staff, to protect the trams on their relevant sections. Northbound trams had to wait at Ballaskeig for the southbound tram to pass. On 28th July 2008, Car 22 and Trailer 44 await the staff from the crew of Car 21 and Trailer 48, which are returning from Ramsey. This was another period of great uncertainty in the MER's fortunes. *DU*

Above Tunnel Car 6 and Trailer 48 on a timetabled service to Ramsey pass Ratchet 31 at Ballaskeig in the summer of 2002. Car 31 is about to use the crossover and return to Ramsey. This was even then a highly unusual and rare working for Car 31 as part of an Isle of Man 50 group private hire that saw the car taken over all parts of the route including the northern terminus at Ramsey, so the crossing over at Ballaskeig has to be considered very rare! *IH*

Centre The odd combination of Big Open 33 and Trailers 46 & 51 passes through Ballaskeig on 1st August 2010 whilst working an enthusiast's special on the 16.10 Ramsey to Douglas. No. 46 looks absolutely filthy here. The motor had been repainted, but just at the Douglas end, in the style this tram carried when photographed in 1939 by W A Camwell. The little black line between the headlamp and whistle is a Velcro strip, which is used to attach an 'L' Plate when the car is used on the popular 'Ultimate Driver Experience' courses. Anthony Quayle, long time Laxey Stationmaster and popular motorman, is seen at the controls. *DU*

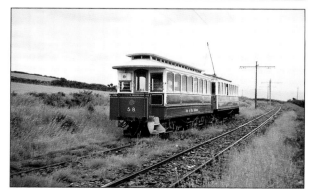

friend and supporter of the MER. He represented Garff from 1946 until 1990, when he became the first President of Tynwald. Legend has it that Sir Charles' son was almost knocked down by an MER tram, when he failed to respond to its gong. The result was another of those small but significant improvements, the fitting of an air horn to all the air-braked cars, No.20 being the first. It would be inconceivable nowadays to operate without a powerful warning horn, and the sound of that horn is wonderfully reassuring when you are waiting in a far-flung outpost on a bad day and you know that an MER car is hurrying towards you.

Ballafayle Kerruish - Rome's – Ballajora

The scenery now becomes much more open, with Port Mooar easily visible to the north-east and beyond the picture-postcard massif of Maughold Head and its pristine white lighthouse. Port Mooar or 'Big Harbour' was once a little fishing community. Iron mines were also operative in the period 1840-70 and ships loaded up with ore in this bay. It is the traditional site where Culainn, the Magic Smith of Man had his smithy and forged weapons for the old Gaelic heroes. The Port was also made famous by the description in Hall Caine's 'The Manxman'.

Opposite page, bottom Seen in typical mid-1980s condition is an unrecorded pairing of a Winter Saloon and Winter Trailer 58. The use of winter trailers in service used to be regarded as a last resort. The open trailers have always been preferred except in inclement weather; however in poor weather, MER patronage is low and so trailers are not usually needed: a Catch 22 situation. Their use now is normally on private hire work (or unusual combinations) and this is where the 'big' trailers come into their own. They have 'Brill' trucks which, given their low mileage, means they always offer a smooth ride. On the Douglas end platform, the handbrake columns have been coated in white plastic to protect them, although this gives a somewhat 'tacky' image coupled with the Isle of Man Railways lettering. **RP**

Left Car 20 and Trailer 47 at Ballafayle (Corteen) with the 16.00 Ramsey to Douglas. A sign spotted in November 2014 indicates that the new housing here is to be referred to as 'Ballafayle Callow'. Photographs showing the shelter here are quite rare because of the remote location and probably its lack of glamour. Shelters here and at Ballaskeig are unusually set away from the railway and are actually on roadways heading down to the local farms. This often caused confusion as to who owned them, although it is believed that these were in fact constructed by local farmers in a similar style to other MER ones. They were supposedly maintained by the MER. The shelter seen here was demolished in 1979. **RP**

Top During recent repaints the numbers on Winter Saloons 19 & 20 have for the first time been moved into the middle of the dash panel as opposed to the middle of the tram. The trams have a rather odd look which thankfully will not be repeated. On 31st October 2014 on a rather overcast and gloomy day, Car 19 is seen storming round towards Ballafayle Corteen on its way to Ramsey. As well as the traditional headlamp with two conventional tungsten bulbs can be seen the light on the bulkhead just through the door, which would provide limited illumination in the early days when on all-day working deep into the forbidding winter darkness. **DU**

Bottom In terms of sheer beauty the MER has no competition. Here in a typical country setting we see the narrow roadway that leads up from the MER to the house of Sir Charles Kerruish (1917-2003). 'Charlie' was Speaker of the House of Keys from 1962-90 and the first President of Tynwald. He was a longstanding and vociferous supporter of the 'Electric'. Car 19 is operating the Ramsey bound service on 7th May 2004. At the side of the road are found ubiquitous yellow gorse bushes and cherry blossom trees. Dirt from the trolley wheel is evident on the roof of No. 19. **NM**

Car 21 and its 40s series trailer travelling south between Ballacannell and Ballafayle, with a smiling Motorman Jeff North. *NM*

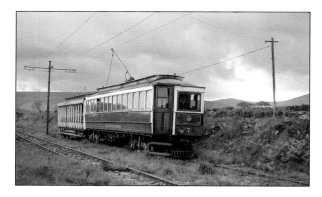

Our car coasts onwards through from 'Kerruish' towards Ballajora. The car whistle is vigorously sounded at the approach to Rome's crossing, so named after Francis Rome, who lived nearby in 1916, according to the Ramsey Courier. He was a member of the Rechabite temperance movement. The new wooden landside shelter is entirely in keeping with the line, although it remains unpainted and is once again not an MER structure. The original shelter was placed here by local people some time ago, though the MER staff did once put it back together again (and generously painted it) after storm damage. A new retaining wall adjacent to the shelter has recently been completed and the stability of this area is helped by the use of former MER rails on both land and seaside of the tracks. A new attractive shelter and waiting area has been made adjacent to the southbound line by the owners of 'Croit Rance' (Rance's Croft), the house located on the seaside of the tracks a couple of car lengths beyond the crossing. The surname was a common Maughold one and features on stones in Maughold Churchyard.

The tram hurtles on now, as the land becomes flatter. More expansive fields present prettily contrasting colours, from deep green in the cattle-grazing pastures to the rich yellow of ripening wheat, oats and barley, wafting in the breeze. Some of the fields, bedecked with wild flowers, including unique orchids, extend almost to the sea, but are broken by a final arrogant thrust of harsh moorland heather that separates them. The coming approach to Ballajora provides excellent views of Maughold Head again, as well as soft and elegantly domed hills around the village, which spread as far as Dreemskerry. It is a wonderful panorama (the best on the Island?), which a skilful photographer can capture.

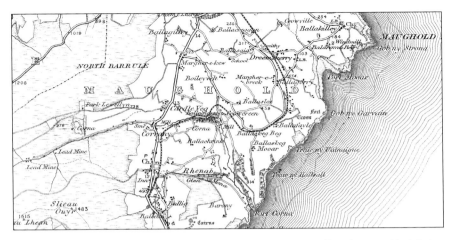

Ballajora

Ballajora halt is next. The -jora element comes from the same root as the Scottish Dewar, meaning 'the custodian of a relic who held it in respect of his office'. Ballajora probably derives from a farm held by the keeper of St. Maughold's Staff. It could, however, also mean 'Farm of the Stranger'. The origins of some place names are not immediately clear - and indeed in this case, when and why it was called Ballajora. The 1906 map of the island (held ironically by the National Library of Scotland) shows the MER station here but refers to the area as 'Ballagorry', possibly because the line itself cut through 'Gorry's Farm'. This suggests that the station's name of Ballajora refers rather to the general area that the line was intended to serve rather than the exact location of the station and that it began to be referred on maps by its current name at a later date perhaps in the 1920s.

Above It was surprising to find that the area now known as 'Ballajora' did not appear as such on the early maps. Manx place names and land delineation in the remote northern landscape remained changeable until recent times, which also often caused quite different spelling formations. The numerous villages - or rather tiny farming hamlets - cannot have provided many passengers for the line.
Reproduced by permission of the National Library of Scotland

Left Car 22 and Trailer 43 travelling south approach the road crossing at Ballajora on 25th June 1973. The conductor can be seen deep in conversation with the motorman. Although not carrying an oil lamp, the bracket can be seen just to the right of the second lower lamp. The trams are now wired so that every time the trolley is on the wire the lights are automatically switched on. This wasn't the case in 1973 and the trams often ran during the day with external lights out such as here. It was during the mid 1980s that the wiring was changed, since when all cars run with the headlights on continuously. **RP**

Above Ballajora has one of the largest waiting shelters away from the principal stations at Douglas, Laxey and Ramsey. Ballajora has always been a popular stop over the years, with many schoolchildren using the stop when winter services operated. Local roads are narrow and awkward for buses and larger vehicles to negotiate. In an almost timeless rural setting, we see Car 32 single motor next to the well maintained shelter, complete with double windows and hanging baskets. Inside the shelter is a large bench. Perhaps only the rather large fire extinguisher on Car 32 detracts from the scene. 30th July 2009. **DU**

A glance at his watch to check his car is sixty-three minutes out of Douglas and our motorman slows down for Ballajora Station, having covered almost fifteen miles of the journey. Old motormen had another system of checking time, by allowing five minutes for every sixty poles. That is also accurate for Ballajora, which is a principal time point on the Northern Section. The relevant pole number is 762.

This is another regular halt, equipped with a fine Victorian shelter, period-style wooden bench and the 'smell' of MER history. If you happen to wait for a tram here, take a look at the rather innocent graffiti going back as far as 1923! Of interest is the tiny Victorian letter box built into a stone pier, with 'VR' proudly displayed, harking back to the halcyon days outlined earlier when the MER retained its postal contract with the Royal Mail and conductors were sworn in, and acted as, auxiliary postmen. This lucrative activity ceased with the closure, fortunately temporarily, of the entire system on that fateful Tuesday, 30th September 1975; to observers and supporters of the MER that day, it might have seemed that trams would never run again beyond Laxey. Today, visitors can still absorb some of the original feeling and charisma of the line at Ballajora; a pause here and a brief study of the environment tell the story of how invaluable the pioneering MER was in opening up the small communities that still exist so near to the line.

Maughold Village and Maughold Head

Ballajora is the most convenient stop for alighting to explore the village of Maughold and its parish church, itself reputed to be the Island's oldest. It boasts a magnificent collection of 44 Manx Cross slabs dating from the 6th Century, together with the imposing Maughold Cross in the adjacent Churchyard. All of these are well detailed and deserving of a special visit. The church and its historic collection enjoy international fame and students engaged in Celtic and Norse Studies from all over Europe visit this area. The Church and Parish are named in honour of St Maughold, who founded a monastery at Maughold Head in the seventh century. According to the Manx Traditionary Ballad, he was buried in his own church at the head. His episcopal Staff was a much-worshipped relic until the Reformation. St Maughold enjoys two feast days: July 31st is Maughold's principal Feast-Day and November 15th is the Winter Feast-Day. A fair used to be held in the church on both days. St Maughold's Well, which for hundreds of years was a place of pilgrimage for Islanders on the first Sunday after the July Feast-Day, is situated near to Maughold Head.

After you have visited Maughold Church, to continue the walk, you need follow the path in the direction of the lighthouse, then left uphill on the path to Maughold Head, which skirts round the headland and on towards Ramsey, where the coastal scenery offers unparalleled views. Don't miss the glorious spectacle of North Barrule by looking back inland and of course the mountain range that stretches to meet Snaefell. The coast of Cumbria can be seen and Burrow Head in Scotland. Continue along the easy coastal path for about two miles where it meets the Port-E-Vullen road; turn left and walk back to Maughold Church or enjoy a relatively gentle stroll up towards the MER tracks at Lewaigue or Belle Vue. Keen ramblers who seek the pleasure of fresh air and trams might find the additional 'optional' extra of a walk down to Port Mooar Beach irresistible. Once again, it is well worth the time and the route can be followed from Maughold Church along the double-hedged track, which is, of course, well signposted.

Ballajora - Dreemskerry Quarry

Our Ramsey-bound car rolls on beyond Ballajora towards Dreemskerry. The owners of the attractive pastel yellow house on the landside have recently made a gateway from the end of their garden to give access to the MER. The gate is marked 'Rivers' and is right by Pole 767. Although this is not a dedicated stop, crews stopped their southbound trams here during the 2014 season.

The official stop 'Ballajora Quarry' is located at Pole 777, where a siding once existed to serve the stone quarry. The quarry sidings here were much more primitive than at the Dhoon, comprising an up and down crossover, a headshunt and a solitary siding, which served the loading bank. As can be imagined, all quarry traffic ceased some time ago. If you make the journey by car, you will see the still functioning 'Dreemskerry Quarry' close to the road parallel to the MER at this point. Incidentally, a large amount of MER ballast used to come from this source. The quarry provided such rich business for the MER that Mike Goodwyn, using some exaggeration and perpetuating the Egyptian analogies from Laxey ('The Pyramids of Deads'), likened it to Professor Carter discovering the treasures of King Tutankhamun's tomb.

It is worth pausing here for a short visit, which begins at Pole 777, where we can look down the falling 1:28 gradient towards Dreemskerry. The crossover was no longer deemed necessary and was removed in the recent rehabilitation of the line in 2008-9. Immediately to our left stood the headshunt and points for the siding to the loading bank; all this area is now very badly overgrown with huge ferns, though it was perfectly visible in the mid-1970s, when the rails and overhead remained in situ. Walking northwards, we used to be able to pick out the wider sleepers that led to the headshunt, but that is no longer possible as they are all standard now. To our right under the pole stands one of the original IOMT&EPCo feeder boxes that still exist scattered around the system. To our left a single pole remains, hideously rusted, but offering a guide to the location of the rails, as it stands exactly in the middle between the loading bank siding and rails leading to the main track.

Some discarded pointwork from the sidings here has been abandoned amongst the plant-life, which adds a little to the line's charm as well as helping the unwary explorer to trip over. A few

Opposite page Another full winter set, this time Car 21 and Trailer 57, on 7th April 2009. No. 57 was used on service due to the lack of traditional 40s type trailers during the axle crisis. However, two days later the trailer de-railed at Lag Birragh and was taken out of service until repairs could be effected. The trams are seen passing the former site of the siding and loading bank at Dreemskerry. A crossover was formerly situated on the main line for activities in and out of the siding. Incredibly the overhead pole situated on the right still survives. This was used for the siding and it must be nearly thirty years since it was last used, an incredible survivor and reminder of the heavy freight activity which used to be so important to the MER. The loading gantry and associated equipment can still be seen under the bushes and tree growth. *DU*

Above An evocative photo of Winter Saloon 21 with Trailer 45 working the 14.30 Ramsey to Douglas on 25th June 1973, which sums up the MER in one picture. Both motor and trailer are heavily loaded and of course the big saloons were always first choice for the timetabled services. Seen to the left are the overhead poles for the siding, which leads up a steep bank to a loading gantry for stone to be removed from Dreemskerry Quarry. This was used on the MER as well as exported. Although the siding is clearly heavily overgrown, the overhead remains. Rather incredibly in 1979 it appears that the siding, embankment and headshunt were cleared, so that occasional overnight stabling of the 'Wire' car - often Ratchet 14 or 29 - and Van 12 could be arranged. *RP*

of these relics can occasionally add some charm and it would certainly be a pity if a place of such significance in the line's early history could no longer be discerned. It is less dangerous to approach the old loading bank and tipping gantry from Dreemskerry Station itself, following the woodland pathway that MERS volunteers excavated and revealed in Centenary Year. A short walk, preferably unhindered by the aggressive swarms of wasps that plague the area, leads to two lines of light track, one dual gauge, much of which remains very firmly in situ. It is perfectly possible to follow these metals for some distance in the undergrowth, but if we retrace our steps towards the MER, we come to the crude tipping gantry. Apparently there were two, but only the southernmost one in 'Jubilee track' survives with its two curled rails poking out of the lush ferns and grasses. This peculiar set-up can be seen from the MER trackside, too, though sadly now only in winter when the luxuriant growth dies back. Legend has it that a single skip operated on each road between the MER and quarry.

Dreemskerry Halt

There is some dispute about the meaning of the place name, but the majority view is that is stands for 'Ridge of the Division', or 'Ridge Quarterland Farm', as Woods' Atlas shows a band of intack land running from Port E Vullen to Port Mooar which divided the ridge at Dreemskerry and its quarterlands from those at Ballaterson (see below). Dreemskerry Halt is one of the quaintest of the smaller stops scattered along the line. It is believed that the wooden seating in the shelter came from Car 5 after its benches were removed and '2 plus 1' seating installed in 1932. The current signboard was the first to be painted and erected by the MER in many years, after the death of local residents Richard and Marion Kenworthy, who had maintained the shelter from the 1990s, the first to 'adopt' their local station halt and enhance the charm of the line's heritage. A white-painted lopped down traction pole complete with finial was placed between the tracks here in 2007 for Health and Safety reasons.

Left The delightful combination of Car 26 and lightweight 1894 Trailer 37 is seen on a gloriously sunny 5th June 2007. This was a special sent from Douglas at 10.30 to Ramsey and is seen on its return as it crosses the road at Dreemskerry. The newly installed white post and finial were supposedly installed for 'Health & Safety' reasons. Looking across towards Maughold and Port e Vullen, it is often wondered how the MER would have looked had this course for the line been progressed. With 100+ year old wooden-bodied tram cars and a view like this, it doesn't get much better for a tram enthusiast! 2007 was something of a swansong for Car 26. At the time deemed 'weak', it tended to run with a lighter trailer and 37 fitted this role perfectly. No. 26 carries the cream roof and yellow lining on the dash panel. Known as a 'Paddlebox' due to its high footboards to clear the outward swinging bogies, this is readily apparent here. *DU*

Bottom Beyond the former loading siding at Dreemskerry, Car 22 working single motor on 31st October 2014 is about to pass the shelter before traversing the road crossing and then coasting down the long straight to Lewaigue. The trolley pole on 22 looks as if it has suffered a few de-wirements! Dreemskerry shelter is a remarkable survivor. It is one of the few shelters on the MER to have a closing door! The back of the shelter is actually made of stone and is furnished with an ornate wooden bench, reputed to be from Tunnel Car 5 when 2+1 seating was installed in the car in 1932. The area is adorned with hanging baskets and flower tubs made from old sleepers. No pictures have ever been seen of this area when it was a working site and it can only be imagined when it must have been like. However the shelter suggests that it must have been of some importance with workers making their way to the quarry by the railway. Dreemskerry Quarry is still a working site and can be seen from the road above. *DU*

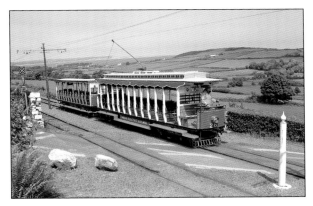

Dreemskerry - Crowville

From Dreemskerry, the line now runs on its longest straight section down to Lewaigue, pronounced 'Laig'. Immediately after the road crossing, the white painted house is the former 'Smithy' marked on the 1906 map. Two stops are listed in this section; the first is 'Crowville' at Pole 789, though experts say that the stop effectively fell into disuse in 1934 (!); it led down to the isolated farm almost a half mile away. The farm was formerly known as East Ballaterson Farm and became the residence of Sir Hugh Crow, a famous slave trader, who took part in a number of naval fights until he retired here in 1811. He is buried in Kirk Maughold. The area extending beyond the farm as far as the road is known as Ballaterson East and Ballaterson West. Old maps clearly show a lane or at least a hedged pathway running across the MER tracks to the farm; that this has disappeared over the years appears attributable to the removal of one hedge to make the field larger and the usual guilty party: use of motor vehicles instead of the railway.

Below The traditional IOMT&EPCo style is evident here too. The incredible amount of work undertaken by a railway which was struggling financially (as Bruce well knew judging by his creative accounting practices) illustrates the serious intention of taking this attractive route into Ramsey, and how hard it must have been to change the route of the line. Had the preferred route been completed, it would have offered panoramic views of spectacular scenery. *DU*

The Sea-front Route to Ramsey

The route of the line from Crowville to Ramsey as we know it was not the intended one. The original planning of the line seems to have been to a point just north of Ballure Glen, some two miles to the north of Dreemskerry, with a terminal point at the Pavilion Theatre in Walpole Road, but the Ramsey town commissioners, ever (in)famous for what might euphemistically be termed their 'individuality', proposed a new line along the shore from Port Lewaigue, to a point near Queen's Pier. Drawings by William Knowles (the IOMT&EPCo's engineer, formerly of Liverpool Tramways) show that the promenade from Port Lewaigue was to be 50ft wide, with a 4ft footpath, 20ft tramway, 16ft roadway and 10ft seaward footpath. At the same time according to Knowles' drawings, the line was to run right down to Ramsey Harbour, where it would meet the

Manx Northern Railway and provide an excellent interface between the systems. A terminal point there would have immeasurably reduced the costs of supplying the line's coal requirements and, we can justifiably suspect, it would have made more feasible any future effort by the company to take over the MNR and its circuitous route to Douglas. We certainly know that Bruce entertained the idea, as records show that the MNR actually approached the IOMT&EPCo, which planned to electrify the Ramsey to St Johns section and construct its own electric line to Douglas.

This plan was resurrected later in 1904 after Bruce's death and the founding of the MER, but the outcome then saw the sale of the struggling Manx Northern to the IMR with the final merger in April 1905. It is evident that Bruce intended to maximise revenue from all aspects of the electric line's operation and it was essential that he took economic advantage of the trade benefit that a line to the harbour would yield, as well as additional custom from local residents. Not only that, the line's natural attraction would have increased had it followed the more scenic sea-shore route and enabled passengers to alight at the busy Ramsey Pier, instead of taking a 'back-street', less attractive route.

Above The planned coastal route into Ramsey is an often overlooked and little known piece of MER history. Seen on the coast at Port e Vullen are MER style houses, originally destined to be guest houses. It is believed they never opened as such. When the Manx Electric Railway Company bought the railway and its properties from the Isle of Man Tramways & Electric Power Co Ltd in 1902, they immediately sought ways of raising revenue and the unopened guest houses were sold and turned into private residences - still the case today. *DU*

There is only one way truly to appreciate the beauty of the Manx Electric Railway, and that is from the front of an open car, preferably on a hot sunny day! It is always best to ask the motorman as it is not a guaranteed seat as passengers can get in the way. Seen from the front of Car 33 is an authentic 1893 set, Car 1 and Trailer 51, heading along Lewaigue straight on their way to Ramsey. 3rd August 2014. *DU*

The precise reason why Bruce's preferred direct route never came to fruition is once again lost in history, but we can assume that geological reasons are likely, since the land has proved somewhat unstable throughout the last century. The route outlined above required a deviation from the one actually adopted, to send it across the fields approximately half way between Dreemskerry Farm and Lewaigue. It would have made for a steady descent to the promenade at Port Lewaigue, calling at Port-E-Vullen en route, as well as providing a service to the villagers of Lewaigue.

Crowville – Dreemskerry Farm - Lewaigue

Some drivers enjoy 'tramping' their car down the smooth straight towards Lewaigue, where speeds in excess of 30 mph have been noted! The next stop is frequently used today, at Pole 795 - Dreemskerry Farm. The original Dreemskerry farmhouse was demolished and in its place, the new resurrected house is magnificent and enhances the line. Particularly gratifying is the siting of a small shelter for the use of intending passengers. The view from here is surely one of the best on the Isle of Man. Enjoy this pastoral scene across the sheltered inland valley and beyond to bring in Ramsey Bay and the Island's most northerly spot, the Point of Ayre.

The long stretch to Lewaigue culminates in another small halt equipped with a modern shelter after vandals destroyed the original in 1986. It is sad to report that considerable damage was caused through vandalism to the existing shelter in July 1999, when the station nameboard was destroyed, as well as all the guttering. A new signboard from 2009 adorns the shelter. The halt serves the few houses in the area and the popular summer camp, used mainly by Irish scouts and school parties, located in the farm buildings on the landside. This stop provides regular custom for the line during the peak summer months. The group leaders follow another long-standing MER practice of giving the conductor a note of the number of passengers and their destination. The fare is then paid as a group booking directly to the MER offices rather than the conductor. The Rule Book warns motormen of the danger of cattle wandering unattended at Lewaigue, too, and that they should exercise due caution and sound the gong.

Above One of the MER's least used stops is on the longest straight on the railway at Dreemskerry Farm (not to be confused with the farm at Dreemskerry tram stop). Formerly a farm house which then fell into disrepair, the building was bought and demolished and a new larger structure replaced it. How many houses can you buy with its own MER stop at the bottom of the garden? The new owners built a small flag-stoned area and installed a shelter for two people complete with foam cushion … how much use it sees isn't known! Seen at the rarely used stop, with Ramsey Bay in the background, is Car 7 with matching Trailer 48 on 26th July 2011. *DU*

Right Lewaigue request stop is seen to the right with a rather unusual station sign sporting a red border. The feeder box in the foreground is still a regular feature of the MER although their purpose ceased many years ago. The letters on the front of the feeder stand for Isle Of Man Tramways & Electric Power Company Ltd. Car 19, Trailer 44 and Van 16 work the 12.00 Ramsey to Douglas on 5th June 1969. *RP*

Lewaigue – Belle Vue

Lewaigue finds its origins in the Scandinavian 'Hlidvik' or 'Hlidvagr', meaning 'Creek of the slope'. 'Vik' and 'Vagr' both mean 'creek' or 'narrow inlet'; interestingly the French-Norman definite article 'Le' has been prefixed, just as it has in 'Lezayre', on the Ramsey to Peel road. It is again the name of a treen and a quarterland owned for more than three centuries by the distinguished family of Christians from Milntown, just outside Ramsey.

Our Ramsey-bound train is now less than two miles from its ultimate destination. It rides along one of the patchy sections of track that do remain here and there. These older rails herald from the Douglas Head Marine Drive and lead us almost to Fir Tree Corner also known as 'Karran's Bank' (Pole 825). Marine Drive railheads generally proved unsuitable on the MER because of their pitted heads, creating an awful clatter as the cars passed over them. Had any use of rail-grinding equipment been made, it would have shown that the rails were far from life expired; interestingly, several ex-Marine Drive ring collared poles survive in this area too, having given 119 years of excellent service - so far! This location is famous for one of the MER's rare accidents: in August 1955, single line working was temporarily in place and Car 22 heading into Ramsey had a head on collision with Ratchet Car 14 travelling south. There were only a few minor injuries sustained.

Having crested the sharply rising gradient, the car coasts back down along brand new smooth rails on both tracks to appropriately named Belle Vue, where the signboard exhorts passengers to visit Port-E-Vullen (Port of the Mill). Note the 1934 sub-station, fed directly from the public supply, nestling in the greenery adjacent to the landside track just before the road crossing.

Below Car 21 is seen at Belle Vue on 5th June 1969. The sign announces 'Alight here for Port e Vullen', a popular walk down to the coastline. The rather dreary but historic shelter at Belle Vue was removed in 2001, as it was derelict. Thankfully other MER shelters have survived and it is hoped that we will not lose the charming survivors. A more modern shelter was eventually erected here, although it has none of the original's charm. The stone pillar and Victorian post box was another well-used example on the Railway, being emptied by MER conductors acting as auxiliary postmen, who had to take great care in the summer when it was often occupied by a wasps' nest! Interestingly the road sign for the national speed limit is in place; however, there is no national speed limit and therefore no limit applies and therefore the sign is somewhat pointless! *RP*

Top Car 20 and Trailer 59 at the Belle Vue substation on 2nd November 2006. Royal Trailer 59 was on a private hire which found it operating with different motors throughout the day on timetabled Ramsey service. **DU**

Bottom Car 5 and Trailer 47 leave Ramsey and Belle Vue behind on 25th June 1973. The tram looks full and no doubt includes passengers who have amongst other things enjoyed a trip along the pier, perhaps on the tramway. Sadly this is no longer possible. Although the pier still exists, its precarious condition precludes public enjoyment of an afternoon stroll there. Hopefully one day it might be restored as there comes a point when dismantling such an edifice costs more than refurbishment. **RP**

Belle Vue and Port-E-Vullen

The name 'Belle Vue' was first used in the nineteenth century for a residence called in Manx Gaelic 'Faaie Mooar Folieu', and then to the MER adjoining halt as from 1898. The translation of 'Faaie' is generally accepted as meaning 'The flat' land or a field near or under a mansion house and one which is better manured than other fields. They are, however, by no means always flat or level, and so might be more easily understood as 'The Green'.

Belle Vue used to be the proud owner of a classic Manx Electric iron-clad shelter, like the one at Baldrine. The long-gone post box used to cause conductors problems because it was usually occupied by a swarm of wasps in summer. Great controversy was caused in 2001 when the old life-expired shelter was removed. It seems a more modern steel and glass structure was intended, but local opposition to that demanded a traditional wooden structure. As workshop staff were not available to construct a new shelter, in its place appeared temporarily a doorless garden shed of the typical B & Q kind. Whilst it was big enough at 6' by 4', and sported three windows and a bench inside, it nonetheless looked somewhat incongruous on the vintage railway and peace was restored with the erection of the current version. Although open fronted, it is attractive, featuring a sloping roof, bench seating and two windows on each end piece. Since the re-siting of this shelter, the area has been embellished with plants and sections of tree trunks, making any stay here pleasant as with all the shelters tended by local people.

Motorists can take another convenient turning from the B19 to reach Belle Vue Halt. If you are travelling on the MER, alight at Belle Vue and enjoy the walk down to the coastline from the tram stop. An unmarked left turn just before the main part of the village leads to the car park and shore at Port-E-Vullen, where you can verify how attractive this approach route to Ramsey would have been. When you survey the sweeping curves from the Lewaigue direction and then turn to face the charming view of Ramsey, two private houses loom into view. It seems from the records that they were almost definitely constructed by the IOMT&EPCo or perhaps one of Bruce's 'associated companies', perhaps in an effort to convert this area into a new resort like Port Soderick. If they followed the Douglas pattern, proceeds from one enabled the second to be built and so on.

These properties, which enjoy unparalleled sea views, were most probably destined to function as hotel or more prosaically boarding house accommodation. This would have been in line with general company practice of the period. It would have made good sense and good business, as the electric line would have provided the only transport link. Some ornamental stonework here is reminiscent of the Glen Roy viaduct and other places, such as Minorca halt, so it seems certain that considerable work and expense had already been undertaken before Bruce was compelled to change his plans. It may well be the case that construction of the route at this point was halted on account of the instability of the coastal strip as we look towards Ramsey; small land-slips and rockfalls occur especially during winter. Indeed in 1981, land erosion problems demanded government commitment to the tune of £100,000 - repairs were interestingly interpreted as a communal matter: road and railway were at equal risk. In the winter of 2011-12, the track immediately before Ballure Bridge was the subject of urgent drainage work, which also required work to be carried out on the landside of the MER in Ballure Gardens. The season opened with cars operating single line between Lewaigue and Ramsey. In December 2012, considerable earthworks in Ballure gardens were the first visible sign to passers-by of the stabilization programme underway. It seems likely that Bruce and Knowles realised the potential troubles of the area's geology along the shoreline south of the Ballure stream just in time and moved the intended line towards the safer, though perhaps less lucrative and attractive, route from Dreemskerry into Ramsey.

Belle Vue - Ballure

The first really entrancing view of Ramsey Bay is visible just after Belle Vue. On good clear days, the Point of Ayre and the northernmost plains of the Island stand out, with yachts and light craft out to sea, and the sun tints the peaceful waters a myriad of azure colours as it reflects off the sea's surface.

From Belle Vue, the cliff-edge route recalls and rivals the beauty of the descent into Laxey. We can enjoy excellent views of Queen's Pier and Ramsey Harbour, from the vantage point of 'Windy Ridge'. Sometimes there is no obvious origin of older Manx place names, but this 'English' one arose after the

Left An aspect of the Manx Electric Railway which is perhaps taken for granted is the collection of characters who peopled it: not only railway staff, but also its many regular passengers, especially the all-year-round locals and crews on the service. One of these drivers is Harry Christian, seen here on an unexpected stop near Windy Ridge just after Belle Vue whilst on a private hire with Car 32. Harry knew that there were good cooking apples to be had along this stretch and duly stopped the car in the perfect place and, with walking stick in hand, acquired a supply. A great character, a wonderful tram and a unique railway! **DU**

commencement of the MER and is appropriately christened, as strong winds really do whistle and moan across the ridge, sometimes even on summer days. However, that minor distraction is more than compensated for by one of the finest locations for tramcar photography: an MER car and trailer set, posed against the backdrop of the harbour and Ramsey famously 'shining by the sea', takes a lot of beating.

Ballure is the next historic stop. The name is probably derived from the Gaelic Ball-y-Ure, 'the place of the yew'. Originally a treen, the name is now restricted to the slope that rises from the south-east corner of Ramsey Bay, including the cliff, the ravine in the hill and the land to the west at the foot of Llergy Frissell ('Frazer's Hill'). Readers of Caine's 'The Manxman' might recall his description of the fuchsia tree in the garden of the cottage near the railway crossing, which was reputedly the largest on the Island. A huge yew tree stands there and it is tempting to think that this is the source of the name Ballure.

Public services commenced to the Ballure railhead on Tuesday, August 2nd 1898, after inspections by Colonel Rich and Major Cardew. Both were satisfied the line was safe, the only concern being the alarming lack of protection for cars working the single line at Ballagorry, referred to earlier. Both insisted upon a few minor improvements required for reversing cars at Ballure, and commented unfavourably on the general lack of finishing touches on account of hasty construction. Major Cardew appeared satisfied at least with the electrical side and expressed his interest in checking the performance of the cars and the

Above In Spring 1993, Winter Saloon 20 was given a repaint into the red and white livery with 'The Manx Electric Railway Co. Ltd' lettering along the side. Seen here at Windy Ridge Car 20 and a 40s type trailer are superbly turned out. As the name suggests, the location isn't the warmest place on the island! It is only possible to photograph Windy Ridge when on an organised tour as there are no footpaths and access is otherwise impossible. *IH*

return circuits. The fare from Douglas was 3s 6d (17½p) return, which incidentally was still the winter return price in 1965. It was not cheap for its day and one wonders how many tourists and visitors from the North of England were shocked to see fares marked-up from that price for the summer season - a practice continued to this day.

Press Reaction on Reaching Ramsey

On August 6th 1898, the Isle of Man Times reported the arrival and opening of the line. Once again, I quote an arrival story, because it reminds us that our ancestors did not take the phenomenon of this new electric line as lightly as we take 'progress' today:

'On Tuesday afternoon a remarkable development in tramway enterprise was celebrated in the Isle of Man, in the opening of the Laxey to Ramsey extension of the line which, for several years, has been running between Douglas and Laxey. The new extension is about 10½ miles long, and as the Douglas-Laxey line has a length of seven miles, the whole tramway covers a distance of nearly 18 miles, and connects by a direct route through very fine scenery the two most important and popular centres of the Island. The inaugural proceedings consisted of a trip to Ramsey by two of the new motor cars and a banquet in the Pavilion, a commodious building situated close to the new terminus at Ramsey. The run northwards along the new route opened out some new and delightful scenery. The lofty rugged cliffs that dip down steeply to the water's edge at Bulgham, fringed with the surf of a rather stormy sea; and the pleasant wooded stretch of country reaching to Ballaglass Glen, were especially pleasing features in the countryside. At each station along the line knots of people gathered to cheer the party of shareholders and guests as they went by, and each station was prettily decorated with flags…'

Further praise was to be found in that newspaper's other pages: THE NEW ELECTRIC TRAMWAY BETWEEN DOUGLAS AND RAMSEY IS NOW OPEN. Without exception the finest Excursion in the Island is a journey over this line, the Scenery opened up to view being magnificent.

Ballure Shed – Another Mystery!

The original Ballure depot, with a facility to house six vehicles, was located to the east of the seaside tracks; the access junction was located approximately fifty yards back from the bridge in the Laxey direction. No trace of the original depot building is discernible from the limited view of a passing tramcar today, but enthusiasts' investigations some time ago revealed the location of the original pit, which extended further north by a car length than the parallel track which did not have a pit. Island transport authority Martyn How removed some of the plant growth in and around the pit in 2006, revealing the fragile pit walls. Martyn followed the line of the former tracks and found some original coach bolts and a variety of other small artefacts.

A tram stop is located immediately before the bridge. If you try to find the location of the old depot, enter the gardens from this stop at Ballure, turn immediately right and follow the sunken path to the first clump of trees. The former pit can be found by turning right, towards the existing running lines, exactly at the point where the sunken path diverges uphill towards the MER and to the left to skirt the gardens. The sunken path gives a false impression that it could follow the direction of tramlines to the main line. A new fence alongside the tram tracks prevents access to the tram tracks from the gardens other than by the entrance mentioned, so you will need to retrace your route when leaving.

It has long been assumed that the original 126ft long, 21ft wide depot was removed in 1899 when the line reached Ramsey Plaza. The Plaza was then known as the 'Palace Concert Hall'. Word has it that the old Ballure depot was re-erected at Parsonage Road, where you can see it today. This, however, may be something of an urban myth ... or is it?!

In Newell's 1903 'State of the Line' PW report, he makes the comment that, 'It is time something was done with the old car shed at Ballure; we have had to put guys on it to keep it upright and now a lump of roof has gone.' We must therefore conjecture that there was undoubtedly some kind of shed still in existence at Ballure at that date. The shed's obviously weak structure after only five years of use surely points to the intentionally temporary nature of its construction; perhaps it had not been removed by 1903 because it had been converted to a store or simply because it was not a priority task; Newell's report listed major concerns such as ballasting that perhaps were more urgent, especially in view of a constant lack of enough labourers, a point cited many times.

We know for certain that a car shed had been erected at Ramsey by 1899. This northern outpost of the empire needed cover for at least two Ramsey-based trains which operated summer and winter and probably a spare set, as extra cars were supplied in summer by Ramsey depot. It is unfeasible to believe they were stored in the open station. All this indicates that the current depot is not the original from Ballure after all, but most probably a new structure erected in time for the opening of the full route in 1899 - unless the above is nothing more than a Manx 'red' herring.

In view of the dubious financial circumstances that surrounded Bruce's enterprises, it is just conceivable that a flimsy hastily-built structure was in situ at Ramsey until c1903-04, when it was removed by the new MER company and the Ballure one was re-erected with improvements at Parsonage Road, although Newell's doubts about the Ballure structure's strength would have meant this was yet another very temporary and undesirable measure. As Alan Corlett, formerly the Events' Co-ordinator for Isle of Man Transport, once correctly pointed out, however, this is also an entirely realistic possibility, because Newell's report goes on to mention that, 'A strong guy should be put to the north end of the Ramsey car shed to act along with other guys,' which might indicate another less than substantial building. It's all quite confusing: an enigma, which we are unlikely to resolve because records have disappeared ...

Ballure Bridge

Back at Ballure, a magnificent steel bridge carries the line over Ballure Glen. It was constructed by Francis Morton and Co. of Garston, Liverpool, and bears cast-iron maker's plaques on its southern abutments, as well as the name of its construction engineer, William Knowles, and the date of 1899. Morton & Co provided a lot of structural iron work for the Island. No doubt their location in Liverpool benefited them in this; for example, they made and positioned the replacement spans for the IMR Glen Moar viaduct.

Below Tunnel Car 5 with split windscreens traverses the main A2 road into Ramsey after coming off the 5mph restriction for Ballure Bridge on 24th June 1968. This would be Car 5's last summer with the split screens. During the winter of 1968-69, these were replaced by the single piece windscreen carried today. The split screens on the tunnel cars caused visibility problems for the motorman, with the pillar virtually in the centre of the line of vision. This isn't a problem on the larger screens on the Winter Saloons. *RP*

Unlike the viaducts at Laxey and Minorca, Ballure was constructed with four iron girders, arranged in pairs, each pair spanning a gap of 80ft, with a girder under each rail. The bridge received attention during the winter of 1990-91 in the run-up to the MER Centenary in 1993 and is due for substantial refurbishment in the winter of 2014-15, with the incredible sum of £1.2m being applied for from the Manx Treasury in October 2014. In 1991, the timber decking was replaced and the metal work sandblasted in readiness for a full repaint, which used over eighty gallons of the highest quality industrial paint. Over the winter of 1999-2000, the wall at the northern end of the bridge was rebuilt. In 1988 an additional guard rail was placed along the outer rails purely as a precaution in case of a derailment.

A treadle device operates the automatic lights, so that A2 traffic in and out of Ramsey cedes preference to the trams. The public is not permitted to walk along the bridge, though this is a good place to make a friendly request to the motorman to pose the car on the bridge during Photo-Stop tram trips, as photographers can vie for the best position from the gardens. The trams observe a maximum speed of 5 m.p.h. as they traverse the viaduct.

Above Although a relatively recent photo, it is now in fact a rare one as Car 26 is stored inside Laxey shed facing an uncertain future. On 27th July 2007, Car 26 operates single motor as part of a private hire, posed on Ballure Bridge for photos. *DU*

Opposite page Car 20 and Trailer 48 on 2nd July 1973. The shadows underneath the bridge illustrate its construction. When built in 1898, it was well ahead of its time and apart from routine maintenance has given well over a century of trouble free use. Health & Safety would have a field day nowadays with our previously featured workman sitting on the front step enjoying the sun, and the conductor collecting the fares on the side of the trailer! It is easy to see how accidents can happen doing this and why the practice was later banned with all fares being taken at the main stations. *RP*

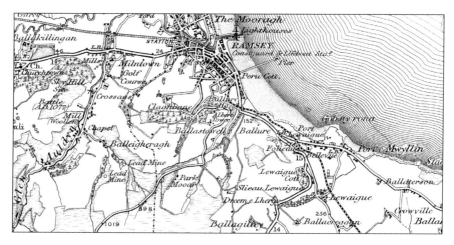

Ballure – Ballastowell

Beyond the road, once the car set is on its reserved track again, a second treadle device automatically sets the lights in favour of A2 traffic once more. A black pole sited just beyond the treadle has a re-set button that the motorman can use, should the treadle fail to de-activate the lights automatically. The system here is identical to that at Ballabeg and Halfway House (Baldromma) on the Douglas to Laxey section, though Ballure was first installed as a trolley-activated device as far back as 1936, the old equipment being hidden at the back of Ramsey Car Shed. Ballure Bridge stop also provides access through the nearby glen to the mountain road for good vantage points of the TT Races in early June, or indeed the Manx Grand Prix in late August.

One of the difficulties in researching the MER is that several places along the line are almost unrecognisable from the inception of the line in 1898-99 because of housing developments and road construction. This is partially the case with the MER from Ballure to the Ramsey car sheds. Original rule books and the 1926 revised version list the MER's many crossings from Ballure to the terminus in order as: Ballastowell, Walpole Drive, Queen's Drive, Brookfield Footpath, and Parsonage Road. And yet, since 1899, we have assumed that the stop and pathway that is located at Pole 898 is correctly called Ballastowell. Concerns were initially raised about the correct order of stops, on the eminently sensible grounds that the rule book would not deliberately list crossings in the wrong order.

The 1906 map provides some explanation: the area to the west of the MER is named as 'Ballastowell', but its extent is not clearly delineated in every direction; westwards it seems that the land close by the famous Hairpin Bend was known as 'Stella Maris' ('Star of the Sea') and the fields below there were called Ballastowell, the name itself meaning 'Stowell's Farm'. The farm was known in more recent times as 'Tower Farm'.

As far as the pathways are concerned, many ran down from individual farms into Ramsey and it seems likely that one particular route was named as Ballastowell crossing by the MER. Most probably, the answer lies near to Claughbane Walk, the road that runs adjacent to the MER after Ballure. A short distance along this roadway reveals that a pathway does indeed descend from there and crossed the line by pole 874. If one crosses the tracks there, a route once continued directly across the fields to Ballure Road, the pier and promenade. New bungalows stand on this land and so the pathway literally disappears once it has crossed the MER.

Some fields that once belonged to the farm are now covered by housing from the Mountain Road right through to Ramsey promenade. I am indebted to Manx National Heritage in Ramsey for telling me that 'The Brough Field', which should be

Below Car 16 and Trailer 43 at Queens Valley on 2nd August 2008. The unusual track slew, which sees the trams change tracks and take up wrong line running, was part of the emergency process of enabling the line to enjoy limited opening in 2008. The track had been largely condemned for the extent of the Northern Line and single line operation was seen as the only viable stop-gap, in response to the waves of criticism levelled at the Minister, Adrian Earnshaw, for allowing the intended closure to happen. Queens Valley has now become a busy and attractive location. **DU**

Above A feature of enthusiast events in the past was a quick run from Ramsey Station as far as Walpole Road before turning the tram and returning to the station. This was a good opportunity for people to sample briefly the delights of a ratchet car and for photos to be taken around the Ramsey area that wouldn't otherwise be possible. Car 31 is seen at Walpole Road on its final visit to Ramsey. Motorman Nick Pascoe required all his skills to coax Car 31 to the northern terminus and back that day. This car is now stored in Laxey with no real possibility of a return to service. *IH*

pronounced as 'Brook', lay on Ballastowell and took in the strip of land exactly where Brookhill Road was built. This road is also quite historic and features on MER postcards, specifically one that shows a train travelling south and about to cross Queen's Drive, itself formerly called 'Ballastole Road', as it leads up to the area described above as 'Stowell's Farm'. In pictures, the distinctive conical structure on one of the end houses, and the picture of the whole row of Victorian edifices, is very clearly visible, though nowadays tree growth prevents seeing the same view. A steep pathway runs from Brookhill Road and crosses the MER by Pole 898, then by steps and a narrow path reaches Waterloo Road. Probably known in Ramsey as 'Brookfield Pathway' in the 1890s, it is likely that this stop lies on the perimeter of the Ballastowell lands and common parlance accepted it as 'Ballastowell' for the greater part of the MER's history.

The final proof of where the respective pathways of Ballastowell and Brookfield lie, is found in MER Chief Assistant Engineer Mr. J F Watson's Report on Inspection of Permanent Way, dated 1936, prepared for Mr. E Barnes, the General Manager and Engineer. The report details the state of the line in quarter mile sections; besides mileposts, quarter-mile markers were in use for PW crews. In the very last quarter mile of the line, reference is made to 'Brook Crossing', surely the one by pole 898.

Other pathways certainly existed until recent times but not all were named, as we have seen during our journey. Some stops and crossings on the early MER were no more than ancient gateless shortcuts across farmland and this held true for the area from Ballure to Ramsey. The extensive building of new luxury homes at on either side of the MER and particularly the Queen's Valley development has erased all trace of ancient rights of way.

Left Walpole Road has private homes which bring very little trade to the railway. In this photo from the late 1970s, we see one of the many attractions which did bring customers to the line: the Beach Hotel offered an indoor heated swimming pool, solarium and tennis courts. Car 21 is seen wearing the Isle of Man Railways yellow lettering, which it carried for only three years from the spring of 1978 to 1981. **JC**

Below Car 1 and Trailer 41 are seen heading into Ramsey at an early hour after being dispatched from Douglas at 09.15 as a special. An 1893 electric tram sent out on specials at 09.15 is extremely rare and only took place due to the exceptionally busy crowds as part of the 2007 TT event. **DU**

Queen's Valley – Walpole Drive – Walpole Road

The MER takes a back-road route into Ramsey, though nowadays it is by no means completely unattractive (nor was it in 1899, as old photographs illustrate). The line runs from Ballure round the back of the palatial modern villas of Queen's Valley, down towards Walpole Drive, so named in honour of Sir Spencer Walpole, Lieutenant-Governor of Man, 1882-93. The exceptional single-line arrangements in summer 2008 necessitated the creation of a revised track layout at Queen's Valley. The track from here to Ramsey car sheds was considered to be dangerous for operation on the landside track, but the seaside rails were in a far better state of repair. Immediately past Pole 881, a temporary track 'slew' was constructed that delivered trams across to the seaside track, which was reached just before Pole 882. This arrangement was certainly unique for the MER, and required the overhead to be realigned. A 5 mph speed limit was imposed.

At Walpole Drive the line curves to run parallel with the road. The ornate traction poles that once stood here have sadly been replaced with conventional models. 'Mary's Chapel' or 'St. Mary's Church' was deconsecrated in the new millennium and is now a private residence. The old graveyard has been remodelled but some of the interesting gravestones dating back to the mid-16th century have been aesthetically rearranged and are available for viewing on Sundays. It is a short walk along Walpole Drive to Queen's Pier, where you can turn left towards the harbour along Queen's (formerly South) Promenade and trace the line's original planned route, which is not so far from the present-day line, but had the advantage of an attractive sea-front approach. Walking the proposed route shows why Bruce was so enthusiastic and demanding about it.

The nearest that the MER line in Ramsey ever came to conventional street running can be seen in Walpole Road. Until 2008, a glance at the landside tracks would have revealed life-expired rails. These were the original Belgian grooved rails although the groove had worn away after more than a century of virtually uninterrupted service! Incredibly, it is believed that these rails were actually bought second-hand. These rails were replaced during the 2008-9 winter; the seaside tracks had already been replaced by conventional rail in 1997-98. The purpose for laying grooved rail was supposedly a requirement in 1898 of the Ramsey Commissioners as they intended to surface the entire width of the MER and the highway to create what could be described as a 'Vicinal' setting. Manx time can be slow and the work was never completed!

The track relaying made great improvements on this section. Walpole Road had looked a mess; problems were experienced with private cars frequently parking on the tramway and leaving insufficient space for a Winter Saloon to pass. The track has been repositioned and relaid, and the level and curve made easier. The new track is some eighteen inches lower than previously. The track is well ballasted and gives an excellent ride, but the main improvement is the separation of the tramway and the roadway with a neat and attractive kerbstone. Interestingly, the gradient on the section of the line between Walpole Road and Walpole Drive is 1:20, quite amazingly the steepest on the line. The 1:23½ Port Jack section had hitherto been considered the sharpest gradient.

The area at the intersection of Walpole Road and Queen's Drive was used for a long time as a small P.W. store for rail and related items, and we have already seen that this was the site for loading the coal wagons back in September 1899. The advent of modern housing necessitated tidying up of the site some time ago. Once the route of the line had been finally decided, it was expected to end at the Pavilion, which later became Queen's Hall. This building was situated on Walpole Road, just before Queen's Drive. It no longer exists, of course, being demolished to give way to house construction. The Pavilion was the nearby Beach Hotel's pool and ballroom and one regular MER motorman remembers playing badminton there in the early 1970s!

In June 1898, permission was gained to advance further than the Pavilion into Ramsey town and the IOMT&EPCo bought the Palace Concert Hall to use its grounds for a new terminus. This plan also only just came to fruition, as Bruce refused to pay for a toll on the line, which the commissioners insisted upon. The photograph of a winter saloon with Brookhill as its backdrop, taken from Queen's Drive, has another interesting feature: a hut can be seen next to the seaside line. Suggestions are that this was an Inspector's hut, which was manned during steamer arrivals, when passengers would walk from Ramsey Pier round to this stop to board the MER. Alternatively it could be a crossing keeper's hut; we know that there were crossing keepers at Laxey and elsewhere in the line's early years.

Queen's Drive – Ramsey Car Shed – Ramsey Station

Crossing Queens Drive, the line runs along its admittedly mediocre back-garden approach to the rear of Waterloo Road, where the washing permanently hangs on ever-spinning carousels and the gardens are tended without loving care. For the line's opening, temporary track was roughly laid on nothing but soil ballast with a top dressing of stones, to reach the Palace in time for the 1899 season. As with the track in Walpole Road, good intentions to upgrade the track here and eliminate awkward curves from Queen's Drive were not accomplished for some time and the whole of the line from Queen's Drive required renewal after four years. Some easing of the curves took place in 2008-9. The principal reason why upgrading did not happen in early days was the collapse of Dumbell's Bank, which plunged Bruce and the company into a financial abyss, leaving modern day MER passengers with Bruce's 'temporary' 1899 route. Newell commented detrimentally about the rotten ground and slippery nature of the track bed on the final section causing persistent problems. In view of the coal requirements, as well as summer patronage, it seems a pity that the intended branch line from Queen's Drive to Queen's Pier also remained an item of grand

Below Queens Drive is the location for Car 21 and an unidentified trailer in the summer of 1971. This photograph shows perfectly the landside overhead pole with ornamental scrollwork. This was the only section of the MER to have grooved rail and side poles for the majority of its history. During the 2013-14 relay, grooved rail has been used in Laxey Station. The distinction between road and railway isn't very clear here, as Ramsey Commissioners intended to make a continuous surface with road and rails – work that was never carried out. **RP**

intentions only. A much-vaunted extension to reach the MNR and the quayside via Mr Cruikshank's garden to the west of Parsonage Road also failed.

As Ramsey Car Shed comes into view, we pass Pole 898, and the pathway referred to as 'Brookfield'. We are nearing the end of our journey now as we pass another unnamed and ancient pedestrian pathway. To its immediate right stands the decrepit but historic Ramsey Shed. Plans for the entire refurbishment of the station area to include a bus interchange appear likely for implementation during the winter of 2014-15, which will, to a degree, sanitise the area and remove 115 years of history.

Above Car 26 with its usual matching Trailer 56 is seen crossing Queens Drive on a 'special' from Ramsey on 5th July 1973. What makes this view particularly interesting is not the fact that Car 26 is operating a journey to Ramsey, but that as a special it has picked up a van. Was it needed so urgently that instead of going with the service set, it was attached to Car 26? Vans are never used on the MER in normal circumstances nowadays, except for event specials. It is incredible just how much use they had in the past, especially prior to the 1975 closure. *RP*

Left Car 22 and (in these photographs) rare heavy Trailer 42 depart Ramsey on 5th July 1973. The majority of the journey on the MER takes place against vistas of sheer beauty. Unsurprisingly, the approach to Ramsey often leaves the passenger with something of an anti climax! It was never planned to be the end of the journey or indeed the route into Ramsey, but 'needs must' and this area has somewhat of an unplanned backstreet feel to it! This is the area incorrectly known as Ballastowell, as shown in the text and accompanying map. *RP*

The refurbished crossover outside the car shed was laid with track from the IMR and heavily used in summer 2008 to enable trams proceeding on the seaside track to enter Ramsey Station on the conventional landside track. The motorman verified that the points had been set correctly by the Ramsey Stationmaster; a one-way spring lever had been specially installed. The trams tended to slow right down to 5 mph but not actually stop; the conductor removed the trolley from the wire as there was no crossover overhead fitted, and then placed the trolley back on the correct wires before reaching Parsonage Road. Running-round of trailers at Ramsey was unaffected by these temporary arrangements.

Seconds after the car shed, the car rolls over Parsonage Road, permission to cross having been given by the stationmaster according to the Rule Book, and our tram reaches Ramsey Station - the end of the line. This is 'Royal Ramsey - Shining by the Sea!', the northern capital of Mann, a journey of some 17 miles 6 furlongs (17¾ miles), one hour and fifteen minutes 'out of Derby Castle' in MER parlance, ten miles and six furlongs, and forty-five minutes from Laxey. The same journey, on the same cars, in the same time, on the same line as a century and more ago, and still retaining every inch and ounce of atmosphere, beauty and character from the dawn of the electric traction age. Welcome to Ramsey!

Ramsey Town

The name 'Ramsey' is another controversial one. It is commonly said that the name is derived from the Norse 'Rumsaa' meaning 'Wild Garlic River', the assumption being that this refers to the Lickney stream, which was known in Gaelic as 'Struan y Craue' or 'Stream of the Wild Garlic'. It bounds the parishes of Maughold and Lezayre. However, the name 'Ramso' was certainly in use as early as 1376 in the Chronicles of Man. It may descend from another Norse source, 'Hramns-ey' or 'Hramns-a', either 'Raven's Isle' or 'Raven's River'. Interestingly, this derivation has found wide acceptance in Ramsey itself, for example by the Ramsey Grammar School Magazine, the Raven Club and the Raven Players. The raven is a fairly common bird on the Island, but its habitat is usually in places hillier than Ramsey. One wonders really whether the raven would have been so noticeable to early Ramsey dwellers to cause them to name the place after the bird.

Ramsey Station
The Car Shed and Former Museum

The interior of the car shed was converted to a museum as part of the Island's 1979 Millennium Year Celebrations. This survived until the 1992-93 conversion of the Goods Shed into a 'Visitor Centre', when the museum resumed its original and proper function of a depot and running shed. The shed had always been used for the semi-permanent storage of rarely used equipment, such as the 1893/4 lightweight trailers which found peak summer employment only, as well as the last car home each evening and first car out on the following day. Loco 23 has been stored here on occasion. At the end of the 2014 season, the remaining stock, comprising Ratchet cars 14 and 30, Trailer 50 and Freight Wagon 26, was removed to Laxey car Shed in preparation for the demolition of the life-expired shed in the winter of 2014-5, as part of the station refurbishment (see the Laxey Car Shed section).

Left Ramsey car shed became the place for contract repaints in the mid 2000s. On 12th November 2004, we see Car 2 undergoing a repaint from the controversial blue livery carried previously for only two years, the shortest time this veteran tramcar has ever carried a particular livery. Keeping Car 2 company is Car 5, which at the time was being used for P-way work! For a long time Ramsey car shed has been an unloved building, neglected and forgotten at the northern end of the Railway, yet redolent of history. The car shed is able to hold six trams. In the peak years of the railway, the car shed was full of sets used daily, including a special set, which was often required in the early afternoon apparently. Given the numbers travelling today, this is a practice that is hard to imagine! Latterly, however, the car shed was used to store the Ramsey set and stored cars such as Trailer 50 and Freight Car 26. **NM**

Bottom Car 1 and Trailer 51 are stabled on the shed road on 28th July 2009. The need to make the shed straight and level, highlights the steep gradient which faces the trams as soon as they set off on the journey south, giving the impression that the shed sinks too low. The simplicity of design of the MER has contributed to its long survival. Simply designed trailers such as No. 51, which owe their origins to horse cars, have required little attention and maintenance over the years, especially as they clock up only low mileages in modern times. With newly overhauled trucks and sound body there is no reason why Trailer 51 cannot survive for generations to come. **DU**

Above Works Car 34 and Trailer 51 wait patiently as Car 33 and Trailer 46 clatter over Parsonage Road at the start of the long journey south. This set is about to pass the car sheds on 1st August 2010 as a special operation during the Enthusiasts' Events. There is always debate as to which is the 'youngest' power car now that 34 has become part of the MER fleet. No. 34 was built in 1995 as a replica SMR 'Maria' (sources differ on the build date with construction actually starting in 1994) and Car 33 in 1906. Generally No. 34 is not considered to be one of the passenger fleet. Although it has been used at events as a power car towing trailers, it would never enter normal service in this form and should therefore be considered only as a member of the engineering fleet. The headshunt used to gain access to the 'back road' of the car shed can be seen to good effect on the right. *DU*

Centre August 1996 and Ratchet Car 18 makes a very rare trip to Ramsey. It is seen here stabled on the Cattle Dock siding whilst its crew takes a break. Upon returning to Douglas the tram suffered problems with its ancient motors and had to limp back home on just two motors as opposed to the usual four. *IH*

The Former Goods Shed and Visitor Centre

Considerable work was undertaken in the three years prior to the 1993 Centenary. Having a museum in the Car Shed was fine back in 1979 and thereafter, but the idea of having intending visitors walk up the line and then into the precarious environment of an old running shed had lost its appeal by the 1990s. Health and Safety was beckoning! Whilst conversion of the former Goods Shed into a Visitor Centre would release the depot for its proper purpose, the result was neither a winner nor loser: it was small and minimalist, but offered some interesting photographs, basic story-telling about the line's history and some carefully chosen ticket machines and artefacts. An old controller and Christensen air-brake unit was turned into an interactive attraction by being assembled in front of a mini mock-up cab, incorporating a motorman's typical forward rural view in the region of Ballellin.

Opposite page, bottom A busy scene at Ramsey with a Winter Saloon and disabled Trailer 56 in the station, and waiting on the back road at the car shed is unique Trailer 60 in nationalised green. The access to the back road is through the use of a 'neck', where Tunnel Car 5 is positioned. Unlike at Laxey where the back road was never wired, at Ramsey this is not the case and motors can take power on this road. *NM*

Left Winter Saloon 20 sits on the goods shed road. Extracting the service car from here proved unpopular with crews especially in rainy weather. The oil lamp bracket can be seen on the front dash panel, and the steps are painted brown as are the bogies. The small door on the goods shed is opened and closed using a weight mechanism on a rope with an old trolley wheel used to guide it! MER ingenuity at its best! *IH*

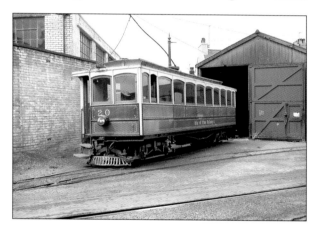

Bottom Tunnel Car 9 and Winter Trailer 57 await departure from Ramsey on 21st July 2007, the first time that these cars had ever run together. Car 9 was never fitted with air cocks and so could not tow the winter trailers. However, the air cocks were removed in the Howard era. In the background can be seen 'The Shed'. Built in 1903, it was used for goods traffic until 1966. It then remained unused until the car shed was turned into a Museum in 1979, which caused overnight stabling problems for the Ramsey based set. As there was no longer any room in the museum, from 1979 until 1991, the last car to arrive at Ramsey was stored in the Goods Shed, with the trailer abandoned to the elements and local youth in the station, a most unsatisfactory arrangement. Even undercover accommodation for the motor car was risky, as the shed persistently flooded! Unused once more in 1992, it seemed the ideal place to create a small museum as part of the 1993 celebrations. Royal Trailer 59 was subsequently incarcerated here, seeing even less use than previously. The siting of a museum at the Ramsey outpost proved less than successful and it duly closed in 1999. During 2003 a youth centre was created, called 'The Shed', which was refurbished once again in 2011. This historic building faces demolition during the Ramsey station redevelopment. *NM*

The main attraction was a scene centred around the Royal visit of 1902 and incorporated Royal Trailer 59, which could still be extracted as and when necessary for service, though it was obvious that keeping a prized treasure such as 59 at Ramsey effectively rendered it mainly useless as part of the running fleet. The Visitor Centre was given a facelift in 1999, but somehow the moment had passed; irregular opening and a lack of real focus meant that it had outlived its time, so it was converted into 'The Shed', a youth drop-in centre of little appeal.

Right The last chance to see Ramsey Station in full swing occurred on 3rd August 2014. The third road has been reinstated, complete with Mail Van 4 occupying the far end, in a scene reminiscent of past operations. Car 2 and Trailer 60 are seen departing Ramsey in the hands of Ian Longworth. With the third road back in use, several moves were undertaken over the tracks after that, for example for Winter Photography. The final such manoeuvre was staged when Car 22 arrived at Ramsey on the last working of the 2014 season, but unfortunately it could not advance any further than the goods shed without hitting an old drain pipe. This suggests that Winter Saloons could never easily access this section of track, although in Car 22's case, its slightly wider 1992 body might be responsible. **DU**

Ramsey Station Trackwork

The former cattle dock siding on the south side of Parsonage Road had its turnout to the main line removed in Spring 2004, whilst the track itself was covered over by a foot of rubble and soil. An 'improvement' was the erection of a wooden fence around the car shed area, which was originally fixed to the shed doors (this is not a joke). During the winter of 2003-4, trailer 61 went to Ramsey and was kept on road No.2, the closest seaside track, for repainting. When 'Big Open' Car 32 went to collect 61 on 11th May, the new boundary fence had to be lifted clear from its ground supports so that the doors could be opened! Trailer 61 emerged spotless and beautiful, but could not get far, as the next section of fence, which was not designed ever to be lifted, touched the trailer's running board. A hammer was quickly brought to the scene... then another section of fencing was successfully - if brutally - removed, only for 61 to be blocked

Left Car 5 and Trailer 44 are seen on the timetabled Ramsey service on 11th May 2004, next to Car 32 and Trailer 61, which had been repainted at Ramsey. Car 32 was sent as a special to collect 61. As can be seen by the roofs, Nos. 32 and 61 carry slightly different liveries. Ramsey Station has always been an unfinished project and additions such as the 'Q HERE' never really helped matters! The unwanted landscaping feature of flower beds on the third road to the left of Car 5 were introduced in the 2000 era and therefore rendered this useful road unusable. Thankfully the wires were retained and maintained, and in 2014 the tracks were cleared (by volunteers) and used again! **NM**

again. This time a saw was called into play and 61 finally rolled on to the head shunt. Those sections of the fence that could be repaired were put in good order and 32 and 61 sailed merrily away back to Derby Castle. For some time, five-ton freight van No. 14 of 1903/4 stood at the edge of Parsonage Road, advertising carriage of freight by the MER, but it was then moved (without derailing) to the old cattle dock. The van sustained some vandalism in March 2002; its sad fate was to be stripped down, ostensibly with a view to rebuilding, but not long afterwards, its frame and wheelsets, the only surviving parts, were noted languishing outside the IMR's workshops. It now resides on a grass bank at Dhoon quarry.

The station trackwork provides three roads, where originally in 1899 there were only two. The arrival (centre) road, Road 2, is clearly the busiest, as the motor car reverses and by some deft fly-shunting manages to run round the trailer to face south for the return journey to Douglas. Passenger loadings to Ramsey very rarely demand the use of a special set in addition to time-tabled services, but if two cars do find themselves at Ramsey simultaneously, then the special will usually be stabled on the road nearest the station building. The service car will occupy the centre road, the motor car standing partially over the crossover. Road 3 had long been effectively decommissioned by the siting of square flower tubs made from old sleepers. However, this track was re-commissioned without problem in July 2014 and saw use in an enthusiasts' 'Cover-every-inch-of-the-MER-track' Event, as well as during the Vintage Transport Festival.

Top An immaculate looking Car 27 runs round its trailer, No. 45, at Ramsey. Ramsey Plaza is seen towering over the station. The green door is the back of the Plaza; the front of the building is where the MER's booking office was sited. The building was demolished in 1989 and the area has since been used for car parking. Car 27 shows the typically well turned out tramcars of the period, complete with grey bogies and footboards, varnished wooden seats and a crest on the dash. The conductor is seen keeping a firm grip of the trolley rope, as he will have to turn the trolley shortly after negotiating the wires. Trailer 45 was unique in having the extra band below the number on the ends, which always makes it easy to identify. *JC*

Right Loco 23 'The Kruger' about to take up residence in the newly formed Electric Railway Museum at Ramsey Car Shed in 1979. Prior to this, the loco had featured in the Millennium of Tynwald tram cavalcade described previously. The trucks on Loco 23 are unmotorised Milnes plate frame trucks. *JC*

Shunting at Ramsey Station

Passengers alighting at Ramsey enjoy observing some of the techniques of shunting operations in practice here. Accompanied by toots of the whistle, the power car uncouples from its trailer and draws slowly forward so its Douglas-end truck is not in danger of 'splitting' the points. The trolley is turned, then the power car reverses over the crossover as far as Parsonage Road itself. The gravity shunting of the uncoupled trailer takes place next; in the meantime the motor has its trolley turned again. The stationmaster might assist with the shunting of the trailer, which is carried out with great precision, so that the trailer is left close to the rear white-painted wall of the station near to Pole 903. The power car uses one point of power to get it moving and is then held to a very low speed by the driver's judicious nips of air that apply the brakes. The motor then pauses just less than a yard from the trailer; the stationmaster or conductor holds the coupling bar in place for the motor to advance inch-by-inch and the coupling to be made.

Nowhere is this manoeuvre and demonstration of the use of the Hughes Patent Coupler device better demonstrated than at Ramsey. Mr. Albert Hughes of G.F. Milnes & Co., Birkenhead, takes the credit for the coupler that was originally designed for steam railway use. The primitive-looking coupler gear features a pendulum lock which engages the coupler bar when pushed into the mouth of the coupler. MER coupler heights do vary between cars (even those built in the same year, such as Motors 32 & 33 and their trailers 61 & 62 from 1906), so it is common practice to marry certain cars with certain trailers. There are other combinations that cannot or have not been able to operate together. For example, Motors 9, 32 and 33 used not to be able to pull Winter trailers 57 and 58, because there were no air cocks for the trailer to take air from the power car's tanks. This ceased to be a concern when the air supply was no longer deemed necessary and removed during the refurbishment of these trailers. It was David Howard's idea that the usual combination of closed power car and open trailer could then be reversed with an open power car, such as 32, towing a closed trailer.

There is no longer a dedicated stationmaster, the job being carried out by the Ramsey Bus Station Inspector, who makes his way across to the MER as and when required. After the proposed regeneration of the station area, one inspector will perform both roles.

Station Area

The station area has changed considerably since the first company days. The Palace Concert Hall provided staff facilities at the rear of the building. It was leased to the concert hall operator and later converted into the Plaza Cinema, only to be sold off by the MER in 1938. It was demolished in 1991 and the area became a car park, simultaneously providing a much more open, if unauthentic, aspect to the station area. The church at the north end of the station was called Quayles Hall and was built in 1837 for the Presbyterian Church of Scotland, later becoming a Temperance Hall and now as Ramsey Heritage Centre celebrating the rich history of the Northern capital. For some time until after the

millennium, a green shed-like structure was sited on the station, this being the local Citizens' Advice Bureau.

The first station building - the re-erected temporary wooden station from Ballure - was in use from 1899-1901 and located at the extent of the station by what is now the rear wall and car park for MER users. The booking office was close to Road 1, where specials are occasionally stabled nowadays. Four archways made for a pleasing appearance and passengers could wait under cover here. The two rustic 'gablets' (sales points for souvenirs and gifts) were at opposite ends, one separate from the main building, the far one concealed by a kiosk; palm trees also adorned the station area. From 1901, booking office and staff facilities were made in the Palace itself. These lasted until the new station building was constructed in 1964.

The End of Our Journey

Considering the technological progress of our day and the almost instant obsolescence of today's technology, it is truly remarkable that our journey to Ramsey from Douglas has just been aboard a car that could be up to 122-years-old, but is at least 109-years-old. We are experiencing the latest in Victorian and Edwardian engineering, still going strong and made to last, and we see it intact as it was in 1899, fulfilling the same function for visitor and resident alike as it did more than a century ago, although it has to be said that the MER today is principally a visitor attraction. 'Royal' Ramsey inevitably reminds us of the quaintness that once was England, too; the town boasts 'real' shops along its narrow streets, with true Manx family names adorning the headboards. It is not difficult to find a cosy café here where you will be welcomed and can treat yourself to traditional Manx fare. The Market Place survives and of course, the fishing boat-bobbing waters of the harbour ebb and flow to squawking seagulls' cries, recalling days when the MER was almost extended to the quayside and could so easily have met up with the MNR harbour extension.

It is, then, nothing short of a miracle, against all the odds of dubious accounting, bankruptcy, perennial lack of financial viability, nationalisation, complete closure and dwindling visitor numbers, that the MER has survived to reach 116 years of operation to the centre of Royal Ramsey in 2015. There surely cannot be a more beautiful tramway or narrow-gauge railway in Britain, or perhaps elsewhere. To quote Blair's Guide series of 1902: There are so many really delightful excursions available to the holidaymaker in this favoured Island that it seems invidious to refer to any particular one as being the best. However, it can fairly be said that the Manx Electric Railway affords some of the grandest trips in the kingdom. The thousands of visitors who have travelled from Douglas to Ramsey by the Electric Railway all testify to the delight of this route and the mode of travel.

Hopefully one day soon increased visitor numbers will be tempted to ride over a route once graced by Royalty, enjoy the sea and mountain breezes and delight in the 'continuous panorama of charming coast, mountain and woodland scenery' that is no less perfect now than in 1898. Those who do love the line, or return to experience it once more, cannot fail to be fascinated by

the pioneering MER we know and love, and marvel at its survival. Long may this great Manx asset continue to delight and, with greater exploitation, reach a wider and appreciative travelling public. Cherish it, for it is truly a Manx treasure, a jewel in Man's crown. Let Blair have the final word:

'If you have experienced it [Douglas - Ramsey] once, you will want to do it again; if you have not, then you have a treat in store. From the beginning to the end, the scenery is pleasing and varied, every inch of the journey, much of which is by the sea, and through a charming country, is full of interest. If the day be fine, one should get aboard an open, in preference to a covered car, in order to have the full benefit of the exhilarating air.'

This is the Manx Electric Railway.

Chris Pulling

Above Regular Ramsey crew, the late Mike Goodwyn and Dave Hodgson, are in good spirits as they close Ramsey Car Shed at the end of another long day. The car set is never shunted until the next day and so Winter Saloon 22 and its trailer have been driven straight into the shed at the end of the day. Freight Car 23 can be glimpsed through the door on the left, making a numerical pairing! As the door closes on the car shed, it also closes on this book. We hope you have enjoyed the journey along the Manx Electric Railway as much as we have. Railroading in the raw on this most beautiful vintage railway... it's highly recommended!
NM

Appendix

Tram Gallery
and
Charts

Tram Gallery

The MER has survived many changes over its history. The aim of the gallery is to show the MER fleet entirely in colour at a fixed time in its history: the end of the 2014 season. If the tram is operable, then it is shown in service, otherwise stored but photographable.

Car 1
Built 1893

Car 2
Built 1893

Car 5
Built 1894

Car 6
Built 1894

Car 7
Built 1894 - Rebuilt 2010

Car 9
Built 1894

Car 14
Built 1898

Car 15
Built 1898

Car 16
Built 1898

Car 17
Built 1898

Car 18
Built 1898

Car 19
Built 1899

Car 20
Built 1899

Car 21
Built 1899

Car 22
Built 1899 - Rebuilt 1992

Loco 23
Built 1900 - Rebuilt 1925

Car 25
Built 1898

Car 26
Built 1898

Car 27
Built 1898

Car 28
Built 1904

Car 29
Built 1904

Car 30
Built 1904

Car 31
Built 1904

Car 32
Built 1906

Car 33
Built 1906

Car 34
Built 1995 - Rebuilt 2003

Car 36
Built 1894

Car 37
Built 1894

Car 40
Built 1930

Car 41
Built 1930

Car 42
Built 1903

Car 43
Built 1903

Car 44
Built 1930

Car 45
Built 1899 - Rebuilt 2004

Car 46
Built 1899

Car 47
Built 1899

Car 48
Built 1899

Car 49
Built 1893

Car 50
Built 1893

Car 51
Built 1893

Car 52
Built 1893 - Rebuilt 1951

Car 53
Built 1893

Car 54
Built 1893

Car 55
Built 1904

Car 56
Built 1904 - Rebuilt 1995

Car 57
Built 1904

Car 58
Built 1904

Car 59
Built 1895

Car 60
Built 1896

Car 61
Built 1906

Car 62
Built 1906

Gallery photographs provided by:

Nick Meskell, Jono Niblock and David Umpleby.

Stopping Places/Poles

Table 1 — Stops 1–35 (Derby Castle → Dhoon Glen)

Stop No.	Stop Name (Bold shows fare stage. Stops in *italics* are not in regular use)	Traction Poles	DISTANCE ex-Douglas	DISTANCE ex-Ramsey	Waiting Shelter	X-over	Substation
1	**DERBY CASTLE**	1-5		17.88	s	XX	S
2	Port Jack	16					
3	**ONCHAN HEAD**	33	0.50	17.38	s	X	
4	Howe Road	46					
5	Majestic	50	0.75	17.13	s		
6	Braeside	59	1.00	16.88	s		
7	Far End	66	1.25	16.63	s		
8	Howstrake	87			s		
9	Groudle Old Road / Village	107			s		
10	**GROUDLE GLEN**	117	2.25	15.63	s	X	S
11	Eskadale	147			s		
12	**HALFWAY HOUSE**	179	3.50	14.38	s		
13	Scaffe's Crossing	193			s	X	
14	Ballameanagh	199	4.00	13.88	s		
15	Baldrine	215	4.25	13.63	s		
16	*Sunnycot(t)*	221			s	X	
17	Garwick Glen	244	4.75	13.13	s		
18	Ballaglawne	257					
19	**BALLABEG**	282	5.25	12.63	s	X	
20	Lamb's Crossing	304	6.00	11.88	s		
21	Fairy Cottage	307			s		
22	Preston's Crossing	312					
23	South Cape	320	6.25	11.63	s		
24	Miller's Crossing	325			s		
25	Laxey Car Sheds	345				S	
26	**LAXEY STATION**	356	7.00	10.88	s		S
27	Dumbell's Row / Mines Rd	372			s	X	
28	Minorca	409	7.25	10.63			
29	Laxey Old Road	424	8.00	9.88			
30	Skinscoe	459	8.75	9.13			
31	Ballamoar (Down)	462					
32	Ballamoar (Up)	465				X	
33	**BALLARAGH**	490	9.50	8.38			
34	Bulgham	508					
35	**DHOON GLEN**	531	10.00	7.88			

Table 2 — Stops 36–70 (Burn's Crossing → Ramsey)

Stop No.	Stop Name (Bold shows fare stage. Stops in *italics* are not in regular use)	Traction Poles	DISTANCE ex-Douglas	DISTANCE ex-Ramsey	Waiting Shelter	X-over	Substation
36	Burn's Crossing	540	10.25	7.63			
37	Dhoon Farm	550					
38	Dhoon Quarry	556	10.75	7.13			
39	Thalloo Mitchell	563					X
40	Brown's Crossing	568	11.25	6.63			
41	Baillelin	579					
42	Ballig	590					
43	Ballasholague	602					
44	Corkhill's/Looney's Crossing	607	11.75	6.13			
45	**GLEN MONA**	611			s	X	
46	The Garey (Dhoon Church)	616					
47	Ballagorry	624	12.25	5.63			
48	Watson's Crossing	636					
49	Dolland	644					
50	**BALLAGLASS GLEN**	654	13.25	4.63	s		
51	Cornaa	688			s		
52	Murray's Road / Crowcreen	699	13.75	4.13			
53	Ballaskeig	718			s		
54	Ballafayle (Corteens)	731	14.00	3.88			
55	Ballaconnell	733-734	14.25	3.63			
56	Ballafayle (Kerruish)	745	14.50	3.38			
57	Rome's Crossing	752	14.75	3.13			
58	**BALLAJORA**	763	15.25	2.63	s		
59	Ballajora Quarry	777			s		
60	Dreemskerry	780	15.75	2.13	s		
61	Crowville	789			s		
62	Dreemskerry Farm	795					
63	**LEWAIGUE**	811	16.50	1.38	s	X	
64	**BELLE VUE**	840			s		S
65	Ballure	869	17.25	0.63	s		
66	Queen's Valley	881					
67	Walpole Drive	885					
68	Queen's Drive	890					
69	Ballastowell	898					
70	**RAMSEY**	903	17.88	0.00		XX	

Notes

1: Certain stops have always been 'WINTER ONLY' such as 'Sunnycot'

2: Certain stops fell into disuse many years ago, such as 'Crowville.' However, crews will observe such stops if requested

3: Certain stops are not regarded as 'official' unless for purposes of private hire or during heritage festival periods

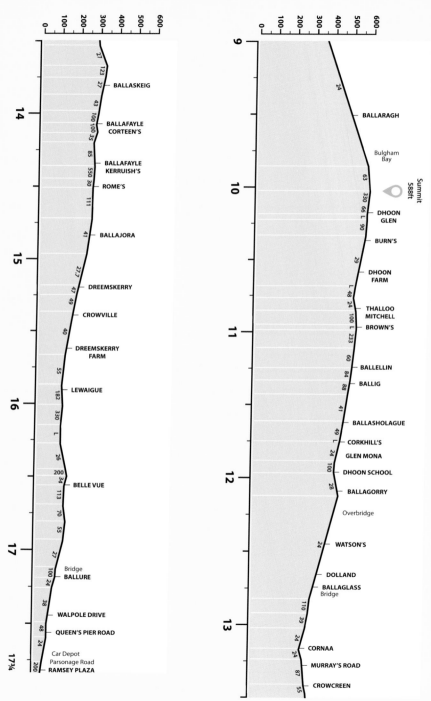

Left profile (top scale 0–600):

27
123
27 BALLASKEIG
43
100 100 35 BALLAFAYLE CORTEEN'S
85 BALLAFAYLE KERRUISH'S
550 30 ROME'S
111
41 BALLAJORA
27.7
47 DREEMSKERRY
49
CROWVILLE
40 DREEMSKERRY FARM
55
182 LEWAIGUE
330
L
26
200
34 BELLE VUE
113
70
55
27
100 24 Bridge BALLURE
38 WALPOLE DRIVE
48 QUEEN'S PIER ROAD
24
Car Depot
Parsonage Road
200 RAMSEY PLAZA

14
15
16
17
17¾

Right profile (top scale 0–600):

9
24
BALLARAGH
Bulgham Bay
Summit 588ft
63
330 66 L DHOON GLEN
90 BURN'S
29 DHOON FARM
L 48 24
100 L THALLOO MITCHELL
233 BROWN'S
60 BALLELLIN
84 88 BALLIG
41 BALLASHOLAGUE
49 L CORKHILL'S
24 GLEN MONA
100 DHOON SCHOOL
28 BALLAGORRY
Overbridge
24 WATSON'S
DOLLAND
BALLAGLASS Bridge
110
39
24 CORNAA
24 MURRAY'S ROAD
87 CROWCREEN
55

10
11
12
13

Gradient Profiles

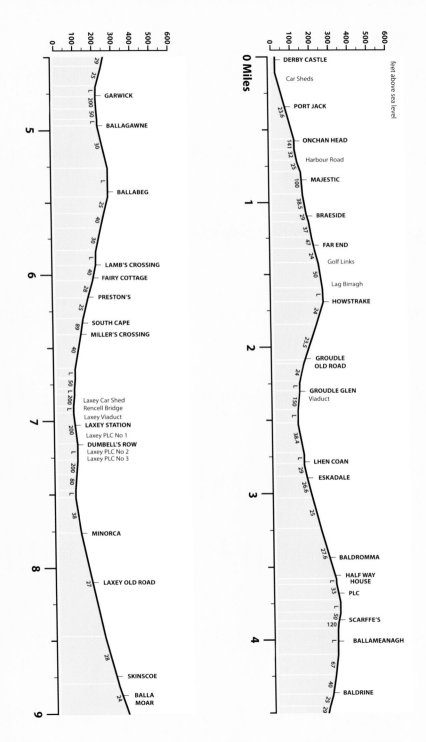

feet above sea level

0 Miles

DERBY CASTLE
Car Sheds
PORT JACK
23.6
ONCHAN HEAD
141 32 25
Harbour Road
100
MAJESTIC
38.5
BRAESIDE
29
37
FAR END
47
24
Golf Links
50
Lag Birragh
HOWSTRAKE
24
23.5
GROUDLE OLD ROAD
24
GROUDLE GLEN
150
Viaduct
38.4
LHEN COAN
29
ESKADALE
26.6
25
BALDROMMA
27.6
HALF WAY HOUSE
PLC
33
SCARFFE'S
50
120
BALLAMEANAGH
BALDRINE
67
40
25 29

29
25
GARWICK
200 50
BALLAGAWNE
30
BALLABEG
25
40
30
LAMB'S CROSSING
40
FAIRY COTTAGE
28
PRESTON'S
25
SOUTH CAPE
89
MILLER'S CROSSING
40
50 200
Laxey Car Shed
Rencell Bridge
Laxey Viaduct
LAXEY STATION
200
Laxey PLC No 1
DUMBELL'S ROW
Laxey PLC No 2
Laxey PLC No 3
200 80
38
MINORCA
27
LAXEY OLD ROAD
28
SKINSCOE
24
BALLA MOAR

291

Manx Electric Railway Fleet List 2015

Trailer	Date	Builder	Type	Seats	Trucks	Motors	Operational Trailers
40	1930	Eng Elec	Crossbench	44	Milnes S.1	N/A	In regular service
41	1930	Eng Elec	Crossbench	44	Milnes S.1	"	In regular service
43	1903	Milnes	Crossbench	44	Milnes S.1	"	In regular service
44	1930	Eng Elec	Crossbench	44	Milnes S.3	"	In regular service
46	1899	Milnes	Crossbench	44	Milnes S.1	"	In regular service
47	1899	Milnes	Crossbench	44	Milnes S.1	"	In regular service
48	1899	Milnes	Crossbench	44	Milnes S.2	"	In service. Painted in IOMT&EPCo, Prussian blue livery (see Motor 7)
51	1893	Milnes	Crossbench	44	Milnes S.1	"	In regular service
56	1904/1995	ER & TCW/MER	Enclosed Saloon	18	Milnes S.1	"	In Service as Disabled Trailer
57	1904	ER & TCW	Unvestibuled Saloon	32	Brill 27CxT	"	In regular service
58	1904	ER & TCW	Unvestibuled Saloon	32	Brill 27CxT	"	In regular service
59	1895	Milnes	Unvestibuled Saloon	18	Milnes S.2	"	In regular service
60	1904	ER & TCW	Crossbench	44	Milnes S.1	"	In regular service, in 'Nationalisation' green livery (see Crossbench Motor 16)

TOTAL: 13

Trailer	Date	Builder	Type	Seats	Trucks	Motors	Works Trailers
45	1899	Milnes	Crossbench	44	Milnes S.2	"	Bogie Flat usually based outside Laxey Car Shed or at Dhoon Quarry
52	1893	Milnes	Crossbench	N/A	Milnes S.3	"	Bogie flat with scissors lift used with Wire Car and based at Laxey Car Shed

TOTAL: 2

Trailer	Date	Builder	Type	Seats	Trucks	Motors	Non-Operational Trailers
36	1894	Milnes	Crossbench	44	Milnes S.2	N/A	Stored at Derby Castle Car Shed. Candidate for refurbishment by volunteers
37	1894	Milnes	Crossbench	44	Milnes S.2	"	Out of Service with axle and wheel problems; replacements now in store
42	1903	Milnes	Crossbench	44	Milnes S.3	"	Out of Service, partially stripped, at Derby Castle
49	1893	Milnes	Crossbench	44	Milnes S.1	"	Out of Service with axle and wheel problems. Stored at Derby Castle
50	1893	Milnes	Crossbench	44	Milnes S.1	"	Stored at Laxey Car Shed
53	1893	Milnes	Crossbench	44	Milnes S.1	"	Stored at Derby Castle Car Shed
54	1893	Milnes	Crossbench	44	Milnes S.1	"	Stored at Derby Castle Car Shed
55	1904	ER & TCW	Crossbench	44	Milnes S.1	"	Body stored on hospital roads at Derby Castle Car Shed. Trucks to be motorised
61	1906	UEC	Crossbench	44	Brill 27CxT	"	Out of Service with axle and wheel problems. Stored at Derby Castle Car Shed
62	1906	UEC	Crossbench	44	Brill 27CxT	"	Out of Service with axle and wheel problems. Stored at Derby Castle Car Shed

TOTAL: 10

Trailer	Date	Builder	Type	Seats	Trucks	Motors	Destroyed Trailers
34	1894	Milnes	Crossbench	44	Milnes S.2	N/A	Destroyed in Laxey Car Shed Fire 1930
35	1894	Milnes	Crossbench	44	Milnes S.2	"	Destroyed in Laxey Car Shed Fire 1930
38	1894	Milnes	Crossbench	44	Milnes S.2	"	Destroyed in Laxey Car Shed Fire 1930
39	1894	Milnes	Crossbench	44	Milnes S.2	"	Destroyed in Laxey Car Shed Fire 1930
40	1903	Milnes	Crossbench	44	Milnes S.3	"	Destroyed in Laxey Car Shed Fire 1930
41	1903	Milnes	Crossbench	44	Milnes S.3	"	Destroyed in Laxey Car Shed Fire 1930
44	1899	Milnes	Crossbench	44	Milnes S.1	"	Destroyed in Laxey Car Shed Fire 1930

TOTAL: 7

ALL TRAILERS: 32

...continued

Motor	Date	Builder	Type	Seats	Trucks	Motors	Power Cars Available for Service
1	1893	Milnes	Unvestibuled Saloon	34	Brush Type D	SEHC 4 x 25 hp	In regular service
2	1893	Milnes	Unvestibuled Saloon	34	Brush Type D	SEHC 4 x 25 hp	In regular service
5	1894	Milnes	Tunnel Car	32	Brush Type D	SEHC 4 x 25 hp	In regular service
6	1894	Milnes	Tunnel Car	36	Brush Type D	SEHC 4 x 25 hp	In regular service
7	1894/2010	Milnes/MER	Tunnel Car	32	Brush Type D	SEHC 4 x 25 hp	In regular service in 'original livery as delivered (see Trailer 48)
9	1894	Milnes	Tunnel Car	36	Brush Type D	SEHC 4 x 25 hp	In regular service
16	1898	Milnes	Crossbench	56	Brush Type D	SEHC 4 x 25 hp	In regular service in 'Nationalisation' green livery (see Trailer 60)
19	1899	Milnes	Winter Saloon	48	Brill 27Cx	SEHC 4 x 25 hp	In regular service
20	1899	Milnes	Winter Saloon	48	Brill 27Cx	SEHC 4 x 25 hp	In regular service
21	1899	Milnes	Winter Saloon	48	Brill 27Cx	SEHC 4 x 25 hp	In regular service
22	1899/1992	Milnes/MER	Winter Saloon	48	Brill 27Cx	SEHC 4 x 25 hp	In regular service
32	1906	UEC	Crossbench	56	Brill 27Cx	GE60 4 x 27.5 hp	Used as Wire Car based at Laxey. Available for passenger service if and when required
33	1906	UEC	Crossbench	56	Brill 27Cx	GE60 4 x 27.5 hp	In regular service

TOTAL: 13

Motor	Date	Builder	Type	Seats	Trucks	Motors	Withdrawn Power Cars
14	1898	Milnes	Crossbench	56	Milnes S.3	ECC 4 x 20 hp	Under refurbishment at Derby Castle
15	1898	Milnes	Crossbench	56	Milnes S.3	ECC 4 x 20 hp	Stored at Derby Castle Car Shed
17	1898	Milnes	Crossbench	56	Milnes S.3	ECC 4 x 20 hp	Stored at Derby Castle Car Shed
18	1898	Milnes	Crossbench	56	Milnes S.3	ECC 4 x 20 hp	Stored at Derby Castle Car Shed
25	1898	Milnes	Crossbench	56	Brush Type D	SEHC 4 x 25 hp	Stored at Laxey Car Shed
26	1898	Milnes	Crossbench	56	Brush Type D	SEHC 4 x 25 hp	Stored at Laxey Car Shed
27	1898	Milnes	Crossbench	56	Brush Type D	SEHC 4 x 25 hp	Stored at Laxey Car Shed
28	1904	ER & TCW	Crossbench	56	Milnes S.3	ECC 4 x 20 hp	Stored at Laxey Car Shed
29	1904	ER & TCW	Crossbench	56	Milnes S.3	ECC 4 x 20 hp	Stored at Derby Castle
30	1904	ER & TCW	Crossbench	56	Milnes S.3	ECC 4 x 20 hp	Stored at Laxey Car Shed
31	1904	ER & TCW	Crossbench	56	Milnes S.3	ECC 4 x 20 hp	Stored at Laxey Car Shed

TOTAL: 11

Motor	Date	Builder	Type	Seats	Trucks	Motors	Works Cars
23	1900/1925	IOMT&EPCo/MER	Locomotive	N/A	N/A	N/A	Borrowed trucks from Cars 17 or 33. Body survives on sleepers at Laxey Car Shed
34	1995/2003	MER	N/A	N/A	Brush Type D	SEHC 4 x 25 hp	Permanent Way Car. At Laxey Car Shed. To have Hughes coupler fitted winter 2014-15

TOTAL: 2

Motor	Date	Builder	Type	Seats	Trucks	Motors	Other Former Power Cars
3	1893	Milnes	Unvestibuled Saloon	34	Brush Type D	SEHC 4 x 25 hp	Destroyed in Laxey Car Shed Fire 1930
4	1894	Milnes	Tunnel Car	36	Milnes S.3	ECC 4 x 25 hp	Destroyed in Laxey Car Shed Fire 1930
8	1894	Milnes	Tunnel Car	36	Brush Type D	ECC 4 x 25 hp	Destroyed in Laxey Car Shed Fire 1930
10	1895	Milnes	Vestibuled Saloon	46	Milnes S.3	M & P 2 x 25 hp	Withdrawn c 1902 converted to Freight Car 26 (body survives at Laxey Car Shed)
11	1895	Milnes	Vestibuled Saloon	46	Milnes S.3	M & P 2 x 25 hp	Withdrawn c 1902 converted to Freight Car 21
12	1895	Milnes	Vestibuled Saloon	46	Milnes S.3	M & P 2 x 25 hp	Withdrawn c 1902 converted to Freight Car 22
13	1895	Milnes	Vestibuled Saloon	46	Milnes S.3	M & P 2 x 25 hp	Withdrawn c 1902 converted to Freight Car 23
24	1898	Milnes	Crossbench	56	Brush Type D	SEHC 4 x 25 hp	Destroyed in Laxey Car Shed Fire 1930

TOTAL: 8

All Power Cars: 34

Wagon Fleet List - 2015

No	Date	Builder	Type	OPERATIONAL & AVAILABLE FOR SERVICE
4	1894	G.F.MILNES	6 ton van	In service. Painted Post Office Red with IOMT&EPCo. Lettering
8	1897/8	G.F.MILNES	6 ton open Wagon	In service. Painted in freight grey livey. Overhauled in 2014/15 by Laxey & Lonan Heritage Trust
10	1897/8	G.F.MILNES	6 ton open Wagon	In service. Painted in freight grey livey. Overhauled in 2009/10 by Laxey & Lonan Heritage Trust from former use as Tower wagon
16	1908	M.E.R.	Large mail Van	In service. Painted in green MER livery. Overhauled in 2014/15 by Laxey & Lonan Heritage Trust
21	1926	M.E.R.	12 ton stone wagon	Bogies used from former no 21 with new underframe and sides to make 'Dreadnought' stone wagon Brush 'D' trucks fitted in 1942. Turned into a flat wagon in 1962. Cranes fitted in 1977. Turned into ballast hopper in 2000 (see page 202). Hoppers were removed in 2008 converting it back into a flat wagon. Based at Dhoon Quarry

No	Date	Builder	Type	WITHDRAWN STORED & LOCATION
2	1894	G.F.MILNES	6 ton open Wagon	Scrapped in 1957
5	1896	G.F.MILNES	6 ton open Wagon	Scrapped in 1970s/80s
6	1897/8	G.F.MILNES	6 ton open Wagon	Scapped in 1950s
7	1897/8	G.F.MILNES	6 ton open Wagon	Scrapped in 1970s/80s
15	1908	M.E.R.	Large mail Van	Scrapped in 1944 following runaway at Ballaglass
17	1912	Milnes/Voss	6 ton open Wagon	Scrapped in 1950s
18	1912	Milnes/Voss	6 ton open Wagon	Scrapped in 1950s
19	1912	M.E.R.	Dreadnought Stone Wagon	Scrapped in 1950s
20	1912	M.E.R.	Dreadnought Stone Wagon	Scrapped in 1950s
21	1904	Milnes/M.E.R.	Stone Wagon	Converted from Motor 11 in 1904 and body scrapped c1926.
22	1903	M.E.R.	Converted Bogie Cattle Car	Converted from Motor 12 in 1903 and scrapped in 1927
23	1918	M.E.R.	Converted Freight Trailer	Converted from Motor 13 in 1918. Changed number to 22 in 1927. Scrapped in 1957
24	1904	M.E.R.	Bogie Flat Car	Built as cattle trailers then converted to Stone Wagons in 1924/6. Scrapped in 1957
25	1904	M.E.R.	Bogie Flat Car	Built as cattle trailers then converted to Stone Wagons in 1924/6. Scrapped in 1954

...continued

No	Date	Builder	Type	WITHDRAWN STORED & LOCATION
1	1894	G.F.MILNES	6 ton open Wagon	Converted to Tower Wagon. Stored at Derby Castle. Last operated in 2013
3	1894	G.F.MILNES	6 ton van	Stored Laxey Blacksmith's siding. Last operated in late 1970s
11	1899	G.F.MILNES	6 ton van	Stored Laxey Blacksmith's siding. Last operated in 1997
12	1899	G.F.MILNES	6 ton van	Stored Laxey Blacksmith's siding. Last operated in 2013. Currently has Tower attached to roof
13	1904	G.F.MILNES	5 ton van	Stored off tracks at Dhoon Quarry. Last operated in 1979
14	1904	G.F.MILNES	5 ton van	Stored off tracks at Dhoon Quarry. Last operated in mid 1980s. Converted to flat wagon in 2002
26	1918	M.E.R.	Bogie Freight Trailer	Converted from Motor 10 in 1918. Withdrawn in 1944. Stored in Laxey Car Shed

MER Last Known Operational Year

Motors	Year last operated
14	1982
15	1973
17	1973
18	2000
23	1993
25	1998
26	2009
27	2003
28	1967
29	1979
30	1970
31	2002

Trailers	Year last operated
36	1973
37	2009
42	2007
49	2008
50	1978
53	1978
54	1973
55	1997
61	2008
62	2008

Trams lost in Laxey Fire on Saturday 5th April 1930

Motors	Year last operated
3	1929*
4	1930
8	1930
24	1929*

Trailers	Year last operated
34	1929*
35	1929*
38	1929*
39	1929*#
40	1929*
41	1929*
44	1929

* It is unlikely that these trams operated in 1930. Therefore it is presumed they last operated in 1929.

39 was seriously damaged in the Lambs Crossing Accident in 1928. Believed to have been rebuilt, it was then lost in the fire.

It is arguable whether in the past trams were technically 'withdrawn' or just simply put away for minor faults to be repaired, but those repairs were never undertaken. This is largely the case with the Ratchet Cars (14-15, 17-18 and 28-31).

Moving to the more recent period, trams have been officially withdrawn, such as Trailer 62 with cracked axles.

There is a degree of confusion about dates for both motors and trailers. Some trams have ceased front-line service, but have been employed on Works Duties (for example, Ratchet 28 back in the late 1960s).

The 'Last Known Operational Year' refers to a year when that tramcar operated under normal circumstances. For example, Trailer 42 operated in 2007, but was moved to Ramsey for storage in 2008, meaning its last known operational year was 2007.

The New Laxey Station

Over the winter of 2013-14 Laxey Station was significantly re-modelled. Changes involved the removal of both crossovers within the station and the severing of the railed link from the Goods Shed to the running line. A distinctive realignment of the tracks was implemented at the same time - the first in the MER's history in Laxey Station. The new layout now incorporates a siding within the station confines on the southbound track, crossovers outside the station and the retention of No.2 siding on Dumbell's Row. Shunt manoeuvres are therefore carried out in a revised location. The dual gauge siding has not been relaid as such, but a second section of track has been put in to create the 'cosmetic' effect of dual gauge. The map below summarises the new situation.

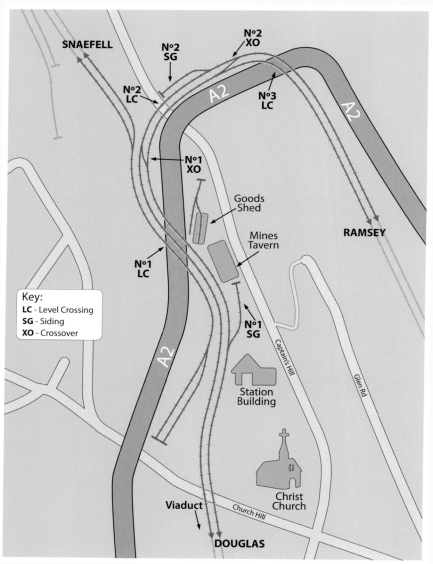

MER Tram Fleet 1893-1906 - Part 1: Motors

YEAR:	1893	1894	1895	1896	1897	1898	1899	1900	1901	1902	1903	1904	1905	1906	CURRENT RUNNERS (2014)
1893	**1**	1	1	1	1	1	1	1	1	1	1	1	1	1	1
1893	**2**	2	2	2	2	2	2	2	2	2	2	2	2	2	2
1893	**3**	3	3	3	3	3	3	3	3	3	3	3	3	3	
1894		**4**	4	4	4	4	4	4	4	4	4	4	4	4	
1894		**5**	5	5	5	5	5	5	5	5	5	5	5	5	5
1894		**6**	6	6	6	6	6	6	6	6	6	6	6	6	6
1894		**7**	7	7	7	7	7	7	7	7	7	7	7	7	7
1894		**8**	8	8	8	8	8	8	8	8	8	8	8	8	
1894		**9**	9	9	9	9	9	9	9	9	9	9	9	9	9
1895			**10**	10	10	10	10	10	10	10	10	10	10		
1895			**11**	11	11	11	11	11	11	11	11	11	11		
1895			**12**	12	12	12	12	12	12	12	12	12	12		
1895			**13**	13	13	13	13	13	13	13	13	13	13		
1898						**14**	14	14	14	14	14	14	14	14	
1898						**15**	15	15	15	15	15	15	15	15	
1898						**16**	16	16	16	16	16	16	16	16	16
1898						**17**	17	17	17	17	17	17	17		
1898						**18**	18	18	18	18	18	18	18		
1899							**19**	19	19	19	19	19	19	19	19
1899							**20**	20	20	20	20	20	20	20	20
1899							**21**	21	21	21	21	21	21	21	21
1899							**22**	22	22	22	22	22	22	22	22
1903											**24**	24	24	24	
1903											**25**	25	25	25	
1903											**26**	26	26	26	
1903											**27**	27	27	27	
1904												**28**	28	28	
1904												**29**	29	29	
1904												**30**	30	30	
1904												**31**	31	31	
1906														**32**	32
1906														**33**	33
TOTALS:	3	9	13	13	13	18	22	22	22	22	26	30	30	32	13

NOTES:

NB. Possible additional 4 places if Ballure was in use (1898-1904)

1: There is a question mark over available capacity at Ramsey. It might have been more than 6 if two depots existed there (one at Ballure, the other at Parsonage Road)

2: A NEGATIVE number IN RED in row below 'Spare Capacity' indicates INSUFFICIENT CAPACITY and that this number of tramcars were stored in the open

Depot Capacity

DEPOT CAPACITY			CUMULATIVE		LOCATION
Derby Castle (DC)					
Shed 1	1893	9	1893	9	DC
Shed 2	1894	8	1894	17	DC
Shed 4	1895	6	1895	23	DC
Shed 3	1896	15	1896	38	DC
Shed 5	1924	2	1898	44	DC and RAMSEY
Shed 6	1924	6	1904	60	DC and LAXEY and RAMSEY
			1924	68	DC and LAXEY and RAMSEY
Laxey	1904	16			
Ramsey	1898/9	6			
TOTAL		68		68	

CUMULATIVE TOTALS

	1893	1894	1895	1896	1897	1898	1899	1900	1901	1902	1903	1904	1905	1906 >> 1924
Capacity	9	17	23	38	38	44	44	44	44	44	44	60	60	60 >> 68
Trams in stock	9	21	26	27	27	36	46	47	47	47	51	58	58	62 >> 62
Spare Capacity	0	-4	-3	11	11	8	-2	-3	-3	-3	-7	2	2	-2 >> 6

MER Tram Fleet 1893-1906
Part 2: Trailers and Loco

YEAR:	1893	1894	1895		1896		1897		1898			1899			1900			1901		
1893	11	11	23	11	23	11	23	11	28	23	11	28	23	11	28	23	11	28	23	11
1893	12	12	24	12	24	12	24	12	29	24	12	29	24	12	29	24	12	29	24	12
1893	13	13	25	13	25	13	25	13	30	25	13	30	25	13	30	25	13	30	25	13
1893	14	14	17	14	17	14	17	14	31	17	14	31	17	14	31	17	14	31	17	14
1893	15	15	18	15	18	15	18	15	32	18	15	32	18	15	32	18	15	32	18	15
1893	16	16	19	16	19	16	19	16	33	19	16	33	19	16	33	19	16	33	19	16
1894		17	20	17	20	17	20	17	34	20	17	34	20	17	34	20	17	34	20	17
1894		18	21	18	21	18	21	18	35	21	18	35	21	18	35	21	18	35	21	18
1894		19	22	19	22	19	22	19	36	22	19	36	22	19	36	22	19	36	22	19
1894		20	23	20	23	20	23	20	37	23	20	37	23	20	37	23	20	37	23	20
1894		21	24	21	24	21	24	21	38	24	21	38	24	21	38	24	21	38	24	21
1894		22	25	22	25	22	25	22	39	25	22	39	25	22	39	25	22	39	25	22
1895			26		26		26		26	26		26	26		26	26		26	26	
1896					27		27		27	27		27	27		27	27		27	27	
1898									40			40			40			40		
1898									41			41			41			41		
1898									42			42			42			42		
1898									43			43			43			43		
1899												44			44			44		
1899												45			45			45		
1899												46			46			46		
1899												47			47			47		
1899												48			48			48		
1903																				
1903																				
1903																				
1903																				
1904																				
1904																				
1904																				
1904																				
1906																				
1906																				
TOTALS	6	12	13		14		14		18			24			24			24		
LOCO	1893	1894	1895		1896		1897		1898			1899			1900			1901		
															23			23		
TOTALS	0	0	0		0		0		0			0			1			1		
FLEET																				
TOTAL:	9	21	26		27		27		36			46			47			47		

...continued

YEAR:	1902			1903				1904				1905				1906					CURRENT RUNNERS (2014)
1893	28	23	11	49	28	23	11	49	28	23	11	49	28	23	11	49	49	28	23	11	
1893	29	24	12	50	29	24	12	50	29	24	12	50	29	24	12	50	50	29	24	12	
1893	30	25	13	51	30	25	13	51	30	25	13	51	30	25	13	51	51	30	25	13	51
1893	31	17	14	52	31	17	14	52	31	17	14	52	31	17	14	52	52	31	17	14	
1893	32	18	15	53	32	18	15	53	32	18	15	53	32	18	15	53	53	32	18	15	
1893	33	19	16	54	33	19	16	54	33	19	16	54	33	19	16	54	54	33	19	16	
1894	34	20	17	34	34	20	17	34	34	20	17	34	34	20	17	34	34	34	20	17	
1894	35	21	18	35	35	21	18	35	35	21	18	35	35	21	18	35	35	35	21	18	
1894	36	22	19	36	36	22	19	36	36	22	19	36	36	22	19	36	36	36	22	19	
1894	37	23	20	37	37	23	20	37	37	23	20	37	37	23	20	37	37	37	23	20	
1894	38	24	21	38	38	24	21	38	38	24	21	38	38	24	21	38	38	38	24	21	
1894	39	25	22	39	39	25	22	39	39	25	22	39	39	25	22	39	39	39	25	22	
1895	26	26		32	26	26		32	26	26		32	26	26		59	32	26	26		59
1896	27	27		60	27	27		60	27	27		60	27	27		60	60	27	27		60
1898	40																				
1898	41																				
1898	42																				
1898	43																				
1899	44			44				44				44				44	*				44
1899	45			45				45				45				45					
1899	46			46				46				46				46					46
1899	47			47				47				47				47					47
1899	48			48				48				48				48					48
1903				40				40				40				40	*				40
1903				41				41				41				41	*				41
1903				42				42				42				42					
1903				43				43				43				43					43
1904								55				55				55					
1904								56				56				56					56
1904								57				57				57					57
1904								58				58				58					58
1906																61					
1906																62					
TOTALS:	24			24				27				27				29					13
LOCO	1902			1903				1904				1905				1906					
	23			23				23				23				23					
TOTALS:	1			1				1				1				1					
FLEET																					
TOTAL:	47			51				58				58				62					26

NOTES:

1: Trailer renumbering is as precise as possible; there are issues because of irregular MER records

2: Colour-coded numbers indicate previously carried numbers; e.g. Trailer 35 formerly carried both numbers 21 and 18

3: Trailer 26 is the assumed number for 'Royal Saloon' 59, though it may never have carried this number

4: 26 may simply have been a 'book number', later becoming 32, which may also have been a 'book number'

5: The first definite carrying of the number 59 took place at some time between 1903 and 1906

6: 27 is the assumed number (and is virtually certain) for Car 60

7: The renumbering of Cars 11-13 to 23-25 in 1895 appears to lack reason but took place (photographic evidence exists)

8: Trailers 40-43 noted from 1898 to 1902 became motors 24-27

9: New 1903 trailers 40-43 have been listed after the last of the 1899 trailers to keep sequential delivery order

10: * indicates the three trailers 40, 41 & 44 destroyed in the Great Laxey Fire of 1930. Current cars 40-41 & 44 are replacements

Bibliography

A Chronicle of the 20th Century, Volumes I & II; Basnett, Stan: Hidden Places of Mann and Mann on Fire; Edwards, B.: The Manx Electric Railway (1998); Goodwyn, A.M.: All About the Manx Electric Railway (1989); Manx Electric (1993); Gray, E.: Manx Railways & Tramways (1998); Hendry, Dr R. Preston & R Powell: Manx Electric Railway Album (1978); Manx Transport Review (various); Pearson, F.K.: Isle of Man Tramways (1970); One Hundred Years of the Manx Electric Railway (1993); Trams Magazine (various); Webber, D.T.: An Illustrated Encyclopedia of the Isle of Man (1987); revised by Cowin, F. and Radcliffe, F.J. (1997); Publications of the Laxey and Lonan Heritage Trust (2004-14).

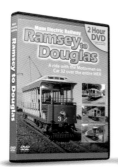